Data Collection in Context
Second Edition

WITHDRAWN

ASPECTS OF MODERN SOCIOLOGY

General Editor: Professor Maurice Craft, Foundation Dean of Humanities and Social Science, Hong Kong University of Science and Technology

SOCIAL RESEARCH

THE LIMITATIONS OF SOCIAL RESEARCH
Marten Shipman

DATA COLLECTION IN CONTEXT
2nd edition
Stephen Ackroyd & John A. Hughes

THE PHILOSOPHY OF SOCIAL RESEARCH
2nd edition
John A. Hughes

READING ETHNOGRAPHIC RESEARCH
Martyn Hammersley

ETHICS IN SOCIAL RESEARCH
Roger Homan

FORTHCOMING:

SOCIAL RESEARCH AND SOCIAL POLICY
Roger Burrows

Data Collection in Context

Second Edition

Stephen Ackroyd
and
John A. Hughes

LONGMAN
London and New York

LONGMAN GROUP UK LIMITED
Longman House, Burnt Mill, Harlow,
Essex CM20 2JE, England
and Associated Companies throughout the world.

*Published in the United States of America
by Longman Inc., New York*

First published 1981
Second edition 1992

British Library Cataloguing in Publication Data
A catalogue record for this book is available from the British Library

Library of Congress Cataloging in Publication Data
Ackroyd, Stephen
    Data collection in context / by Stephen Ackroyd and John A. Hughes.—2nd ed.
        p. cm.— (Aspects of modern sociology. Social research)
    Includes bibliographical references and index.
    ISBN 0-582-05311-0:
        1. Social sciences—Methodology. 2. Social sciences—Research.
I. Hughes, J.A., 1941–   . II. Title. III. Series.
H61.A385 1992
300'.72—dc20

                                                        91-30756
                                                        CIP

Set in 10/12 Times

Printed in Malaysia by PMS

CONTENTS

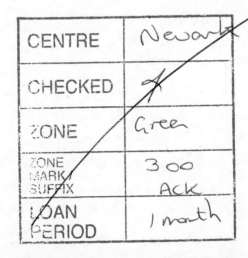

EDITOR'S PREFACE

The first series in Longman's *Aspects of Modern Sociology* library was concerned with the social structure of modern Britain, and was intended for students following professional and other courses in universities, polytechnics, colleges of higher education, and elsewhere in further and higher education, as well as for those members of a wider public wishing to pursue an interest in the nature and structure of British society.

This further series sets out to examine the history, aims, techniques and limitations of social research, and it is hoped that it will be of interest to the same readership. It will seek to offer an informative but not uncritical introduction to some of the methodologies of social science.

Maurice Craft

A C K N O W L E D G E M E N T S

The second edition of this book enters during a period in social research in which the traditional orthodoxies are not held with quite the same confidence. The normal division between quantitative and qualitative methods is undergoing a new lease of life in which not only are qualitative methods no longer regarded as quite so subservient to the quantitative, but also the distinction itself is shining less brightly as a sensible division which reflects the methodological state of affairs in sociology and social research. In a word, matters are messier than they were. The small but growing number of historical studies of the development of sociology and social research have begun to question the orthodox Whiggish view that social research progressed in an almost unbroken evolutionary path toward the quantitative, survey-based research that, until very recently, was regarded as the *sine qua non* of social research. It is now seen that this state of affairs owed as much to the desire to present social research as a professionalised activity as it did to any putative superiority of such methods over others.

The major differences between the first edition and this are a new chapter explicating more fully the logic of variable analysis and measurement, and one discussing some of the recent developments in social research especially within interdisciplinary and applied contexts. Other chapters have been updated and sometimes given a different slant more in keeping with recent thinking on methodological matters. In many respects the focus on *data collection* at the expense of *data analysis* has been so artificially constraining that we have had to make more than just a little reference to the latter issues. The chapter on variable analysis, for example, could not be written purely as a discussion of data collection.

As always there are many people to thank for help and assistance including the colleagues and particularly the students within both our departments for providing a stimulating environment in which to work and teach. For specific help we would like to thank Professor K. Soothill, a long-time colleague, friend and somewhat to the surprise, no doubt, of the members of his department, jokester. To Richard Harper, who has moved to pastures new and elevated at Rank Xerox EuroPARC after some years' service as research colleague and friend.

To Corinne Wattam, who demonstrates to sometimes jaded palettes that data collection and research can still be a joy. To Professor Karen Legge, for her constant support, and Dr. Hugo Letiche, for constant reminders of the parochialism of British research practice. To Maeve and Chris, who are thankful they did not have to type any of this. To Dan Shapiro, who carried other burdens while the authors fell out. And, finally, to Dave Randall, Vernon, Bente, and Henry, for showing some interest in empirical sociology, and to the MA students in Behaviour in Organisations for demands that you back up what you say with intellectual justifications and practical examples.

ABOUT THE AUTHORS:

Mr. Stephen Ackroyd is Lecturer in the Department of Behaviour in Organisations, Lancaster University.
Dr. John A. Hughes, is Professor of Sociological Analysis, Department of Sociology, Lancaster University.

Theory, methods and data

The triumvirate of words that are the title of this chapter summarises the essential pieces out of which sociology, and other disciplines, are built though saying this is one thing, saying how they are so built quite another. Sociology aims at accounting for or understanding features of the social world and does so by means of the theories it develops, the methods of inquiry it uses and the data it collects. Of course, as stated, this says very little concerning the kinds of things this endeavour involves and certainly gives no indication of just what procedures are required in order to go about it. What is offered as theory in sociology is a veritable feast of notions, viewpoints, perspectives, abstractions and ideas which play different roles in sociological inquiry. Methods, too, range from the highly formal, the thoroughly quantitative to the thoroughly qualitative, the impressionistic and even the journalistic. And about the relationship between theory and method there is considerable debate within the discipline. As a result, what counts as data is also highly varied ranging from the regression coefficients and equations of causal modelling to the transcriptions of talk and the vignettes of life presented by ethnographers. To a large degree this variation in data reflects the variations in sociology itself. Lepenies, for example, in his history of sociology describes the discipline as oscillating between the more literary and the more scientific styles: a choice not constrained entirely by the nature of the problems but by wider social influences.[1] So, the relationship between theory, methods and data is a contested one – and properly so – and a contest which very often reaches beyond the narrowly academic.

Our major preoccupation in this book is with the methods component of the triumvirate, though this has to be a matter of emphasis since it cannot be considered independently of the others. Methods are ways of getting investigations done; one reason, perhaps, why some social scientists tend to view them as merely practical activities of no great importance in the intellectual scheme of things, and secondary to theoretical work.[2] That methods are necessary is a commonly held view, but not really very exciting and, further, probably best left to experts in the research technologies involved, such as friendly statisticians or computer programmers, who generously give their time and skills to resolving problems that ought to have been thought about long before.

This tendency is reinforced, of course, by the tremendous innovations in machines for data processing which, rightly or wrongly, seem to be less 'user-friendly' even than the 'stone age' card sorter which is, incidentally, an unsung innovation which made the analysis of large-scale data sets possible.[3] The vehicle of this is the computer, a machine capable of processing prodigious amounts of information extremely quickly. Business people, market researchers, social workers, police forces, governments, as well as academic researchers, and more, are eager, for various reasons, to use this capacity of the computer to process ever larger and larger amounts of information exceedingly quickly. Yet, while the technology and the statistical operations it performs are complicated beyond the imagining of ordinary mortals, none of these adds up to good reasons for regarding research methods as solely technical matters, as the province of people expert in programming or in statistical analysis. For one obvious point, a computer, unlike the research methods it sometimes serves, is only a machine usable in social research to the extent, *and only to this extent*, that it is capable of serving research goals; that is, producing material relevant to the questions the research asks. Simply because such a technology is available is no reason for presuming that all social research requires the assistance of a computer. One of the irritations of our age is the justification offered by, for example, news reporters that the results of some study showing, say, that vandalism had increased in X town were analysed by computer, as if this alone guaranteed or validated the results of the study. Moreover, even if a computer is useful for *some* social research, the results it produces can be only as good as the initial data it is given, the operations it is asked to perform, and the interpretations made on those data. Even so, and assuming that the data are of the best that can be achieved, and that a researcher is using the appropriate operations on those data, the results still have to be made relevant to the problem that provoked the research in the first place, and this is not a matter for any machine, no matter how sophisticated. Indeed, it can be argued, and not implausibly, that in some respects the availability of relatively cheap computer processing has hindered social research as much as it has benefited it, if only for the reason that it has encouraged larger and larger data sets as a substitute for thinking about whether the sociological problems require such.

Be this as it may, our concern in this book is with the methods and techniques of data collection as used in the social sciences, especially sociology. However, although our own particular experience is derived from this discipline the methods and the techniques we discuss are by no means restricted to sociology but are used by a variety of other specialised social sciences as well as government and commercial agencies. Indeed, and again as we shall see, many of them were invented and developed in commercial fields such as market research and policy research. None the less, the point we want to make early on is that whatever differences and similarities there might be between the disciplinary and organisational contexts of the various methods, the aim of methods of research is to effect a link between the empirical world, to call it that, and theoretical conceptions of it. By examining the world in a systematic way we can assess the adequacy, plausibility, accuracy, fruitfulness, truth even, of theories about the world.

Although we have used the term 'theory' here, we do not mean anything especially wonderful about this, least of all imply that what is offered as theory in the social sciences is close to the kinds of offerings one might receive in physics or chemistry. The term 'theory' as used in the social sciences covers a wide range of constructions including, for example, general perspectives such as Marxism, symbolic interactionism, general systems theory, feminism, as well as less all-embracing, more specific theories of what Merton many years ago called 'the middle range'.[4] It also includes many theories whose status as serious scientific theories is highly arguable. However, for now all we wish to do is note this and make any further distinctions as necessary and also take the opportunity to remind ourselves that although theories are vitally important for any science, a great deal of research is not always explicitly about theories, hypothesis testing or developing theoretical explanations but more aptly characterised as 'just describing things'.

From our point of view data are very much the outcome, the creation even, of procedures of empirical research. Data, of whatever form, do not just appear or lie around waiting to be casually picked up by some passing social researcher but have to be given form and shape in order to qualify as data; made relevant, in a word, to a research problem. The artifacts of archaeology, for example, though the detritus of time, are relevant for archaeology only when constituted as data indicative of matters of concern for archeologists. Pottery shards can reveal a great deal about a past society and its culture, its technology, its sources and patterns of trade, the possible structure of its economy, and so on. The various happenings, objects and people of the world are not data until made relevant within a framework which constitutes them as evidential materials for some purpose. To be involved with data is to be involved within an inferential process whereby the data, whatever their form and content, can be treated as 'standing on behalf of' something else, namely some phenomenon of interest to a researcher. Thus, and to use the archaeological example once again, the pottery shards can be taken as indicative of a whole set of features of the society that produced them; features that are inferred, sometime reliably, sometimes by little more than good guess-work, from the detailed knowledge of the shards themselves, their style, their material composition, location, technology involved in their production, and so on, once the inferential structures are in place. More close to home, the responses to questionnaire items, for example, are treated as indications of phenomena specified as 'attitudes', 'levels of income', 'levels of education', or whatever the item is intended to measure, once we have in place the relevant interpretative framework. In just the same way, the vignettes presented by a participant observer are indicative and illuminating about the way of life of a group.

We can formulate the point we have made here in terms of a distinction between the universe of potentially observable phenomena, the subset of these that come to be constructed as 'data', and the process of transforming data into potentially useful or interesting information. What the distinction draws attention to in a helpful way is the active processes of construction that occur in the production of knowledge out of the complex world of events and things.

In sociological methods these inferential procedures are variously codified, structured and formalised as explicit methods. As far as quantitative methods are concerned, the structure of statistical inference, on which much of them depend, is highly formalised precisely as a tight mathematical-cum-logical chain of inference. More qualitative methods rely upon an inferential apparatus that is more interpretative, less formal in character. However, it is important to stress (as we shall argue more fully later) that there is no especial general virtue in the formality of the inferential structure used; any virtue there might be resides in the purposes for which the inferential apparatus is intended to serve, the questions it is being used to answer. Further, as should be clear from the archaeological example, an essential part of making inferences from the data to some conclusion, has to do with the properties of the data material itself. There are no guarantees, it is important to note, that the inferences we make on the basis of some data are the correct ones. Even when using statistical inference, interpretative work is essential and without which the mathematical procedures, even though they may be correctly applied, may well fail to provide the right answers to our problem, especially if we deploy an inappropriate model of what the problem is. But getting to know this is itself, more often than not, a matter of working through what can turn out to be wrong answers.[5] Items on a questionnaire, for brief example, may be deemed to indicate attitudes, but they may well be taken as indicating something else such as a respondent's desire to appear to give 'socially desirable' answers that he or she thinks the interviewer wants to hear. More seriously, by referring to a very different conception of attitudes, a different interpretative framework, the whole enterprise of 'tapping' attitudes in this way becomes highly contentious, raising the issue that what are normally regarded as 'attitudes' may not, in fact, display the properties they are assumed to display for the purposes of social measurement.

The process of creating data, and the word 'creating' here is deliberate, entails treating what we might call the things of the everyday world rather differently from the ways that they are likely to be treated in ordinary life. Natural science, for one, has warned us how complex and different is the ordinary world around us when looked at 'scientifically'. One has only to think of the way in which a chemist might describe the molecular structure of the paper on which this book is printed to appreciate this point. However, it is vital to realise that such a description would not exhaust all that it is possible to say about the paper. Indeed, depending on the point of view of the observer, and the reason for any description, the paper can be described in any number of ways. A printer's concern with, say, the quality of the paper might well have much to do with the chemistry of the paper, but need not necessarily invoke the kind of features a chemical description would need to note. The point is that what things are, how they are to be described, is rarely, if ever, a matter of finding the one true description that fits every eventuality and purpose, but of finding a description from a point of view. Data are always the result of a selection from what can possibly be said about some phenomenon. This is as true of the natural sciences as it is of the social sciences. Creating data is a selective exercise – though this is often forgotten or ignored – and, for this reason, is specific to points of view, whether these be theories or theoretical frameworks, or simply 'fact finding'. Both these endeavours, which we have glossed for now as theory or fact-finding, still involve a selectivity in the creation of data. What are to count as facts about the census population, for example, require that decisions be made about what events, features and properties of the individual members of the UK population are to be counted, and this is not a straightforward matter, and neither is what the 'facts' are presumed to be, what they indicate, independent of *any* framework.

THEORY AND METHODS OF RESEARCH

One of the dominating images of research in the social sciences takes its tone, and much else besides, from what is commonly regarded as the practice of natural science. Research is carried out to test hypotheses which are derived from theories intended to explain some feature of the world. But it would be misleading to regard this as the model for all research, even in the context of 'pure' science. Another common object of research is, to put it colloquially but not inaccurately, to 'find things out' about the world. The search for new sub-atomic particles would be a case of this, as would finding out how many people possess a car or a microwave oven. The archaeologist digging beneath the foundations of some new office development is trying to discover some object or relic, some variation in soil composition, etc., which will tell him or her something about a long defunct and little-known society. An anatomist examining the physiological structure of some specimen is trying to find out how it works. And so on, in all the variety of ways in which researchers can make inquiries. Not all of these are motivated by the need to test hypotheses, though this is not to say that theories, or even hypotheses, are uninvolved. Facts need frameworks for their significance and theories are one of the ways in which this is achieved.

But, whatever the objectives of the research, what is clear is that the research process involving the collection of relevant materials for the research cannot be haphazard. Thus, the physicist uses a vast armoury of instrumentation to record data; instruments ranging from the simple ruler or thermometer to the incomprehensibles of the electron microscope and the 'atom smasher'. Similarly, the social scientist has at his or her disposal such techniques or instruments as questionnaires, attitudes scales, tape and video-recorders, methods of observation, statistical formulae, and so forth. By and large, natural scientists and social scientists do not make use of the same instruments. The reason for this is obvious but still worth stating: they deal with different subject matters and, hence, have needed to develop instruments of research suited to their respective subject matters.

This last observation points toward an issue which has been a recurrent one in social thought for a long time, namely the consequences of the distinction between the human and the non-human world. It is the latter which is largely seen as the province of the natural sciences, and the former that of the social or human sciences. Although largely a distinction which, in much of its form, is a contingent feature of European intellectual development, it is one which has major implications for the conception of the nature of the social sciences. What the distinction recognises, at a minimum, is that human beings possess unique properties. Above all else they have culture and language which makes possible the development of societies which can change and adapt, though not always in foreseen ways, as a response to human will. Although the natural sciences study human beings, they do not study human beings as social and cultural creatures. For some social thinkers, this puts humanity beyond the scope of scientific inquiry, at least beyond a model presupposed in the manner and form of the natural sciences. Human action, it is claimed, cannot be studied in the same way as inanimate nature.[6] The knowledge that we require, indeed can have, of human social life is of a different order to that knowledge produced by natural science. Others, however, have not taken this dichotomy quite so radically, arguing instead that although the human and the physical world are different in a number of respects they can, nevertheless, be studied using the same logic of scientific inquiry, if not precisely the same methods.

Whatever one's stand on this issue, the point is that research instruments or techniques used for collecting and creating data have to be sensitive to the nature of the phenomena that are the subject matter of the discipline. And, it should be noted here for later discussion, that this is not straightforwardly achieved, especially when, as in the social sciences, the nature of the phenomenon being investigated is imperfectly known. But an essential part of the inferential process in which data are involved are the characterisations and properties of the data themselves: the link between the data and what they 'stand for', what they indicate, is established through 'instrumental presuppositions'. That is, ideas and claims which entitle a particular instrument as a method which will do the job for which it is used. At its simplest, this notion refers to the conceptions a scientific community holds about what it is that enables a particular instrument or technique to do its intended work; in other words, theories about the kinds of data an instrument, whatever it might be, generates. In physics, for example, temperature can be measured using an ordinary mercury thermometer or by electronic means. Distance can be measured by using an ordinary tape measure or by the time it takes light to travel between two points. In each case the instrument is seen to work because it embodies various relevant theories in its construction as an instrument. The same, to a degree, is true of social research instruments. Questionnaires derive their status as research instruments from conceptions held by their users of the relationship between the spoken word and social behaviour. So, both natural and social scientists are committed to various sorts of instrumental presuppositions that underpin their research methods and instruments. They are relevant to how it is that a research instrument is seen as doing a particular kind of job in the research process. We shall, of course, discuss many of these instrumental presuppositions in the course of this book.

Instrumental presuppositions are, of course, closely related to the substantive theories belonging to particular disciplines. These, too, contain implications for research methodology. It is no accident that styles of sociological research, for example, are often closely associated with theoretical perspectives. The social survey grew out of a tradition which, among other things, claimed that the proper application of the scientific method to the study of society could result in the rational reconstruction of society for the benefit of all.[7] The major advantages of the survey, its ability to reach many thousands of widely distributed people, the statistical analyses that can be performed on its data, the use of experimental designs, and so on, places it very clearly in the tradition, though whether it successfully incorporates science is another debatable matter, which sees social science as following the path already trodden so firmly by the natural sciences. The social survey also takes seriously the idea of a social collectivity that can be studied by means of randomly selected informants, so that the analyst can move between individual characteristics and those of the larger collectivity. The survey, along with other methods of social research, embodies conceptions of society, the individual and the relationship between them as essential instrumental presuppositions of its own status as a method of research.

The connection between theories and data is not simply a matter that data must be relevant to the theory, so that if we are interested in examining theories of conflict then our data must be, at a minimum, about conflicts. More deeply, the concepts in the theory will have to make specifications about what in the world are to count as conflicts. Are we, say, to be concerned only with political conflicts or do we include such things as strikes, divorces, elections, and so on? Again, there are no answers in advance to questions such as these but they are matters that must concern the researcher and the theoretical perspective being deployed. This is just as true if the research is of the 'fact-finding' type. Facts are not self-evidently lying around just to be discovered and counted. To use a prosaic example, finding out how many outside toilets there are in town X will require the researcher to make decisions about what is to count as an 'outside toilet'. Is it one which is standing and usable but as a matter of fact just used as a store room? Or, to count as an 'outside toilet' must it still be in use for that, and only that, purpose? Similarly, surveys of ethnic origins have to make decisions about those born of, say, West Indian grandparents but who have lived in this country since their birth. Such decisions are, of course, fateful for the kinds of conclusions to be drawn from the study. All sociological theories imply a conception of the individual and society and the relationship between the two: they could not do otherwise. And this, too, has a profound effect on the shape of the investigation and the data it needs. If, for example, one is committed to a sociological perspective such as symbolic interactionism, which sees social action as a formative process in which the members of society are continually engaged in 'directing, checking, bending, and transforming their lines of action in light of what they encounter in the actions of others', then the research methods, the data gathered and the conclusions reached will need to take this conception seriously.[8] The style and the methods of the research will need to capture this image of the actor; something the survey, for example, is not likely to do.

Social theory is not, of course, the central concern of this book, which intends to deal with methods of data collection in social research, but it is of primary importance to its subject. Methods are normally taken as covering what we might refer to as the technical aspects of research and dealing with such matters as how to construct a questionnaire, conduct an interview, draw up a random sample, and so on. To this extent, research methods and the techniques of data collection designate the business end of a much more complicated piece of machinery. The remainder of the machine, and essential to its working, are the instrumental and theoretical presuppositions we have just been discussing. No method or technique can be atheoretical, but involves the user in a nest of theoretical commitments, many of them implicit, which reach up to the most fundamental questions and postulations of the discipline.

Although we have just been stressing the importance of the theoretical ideas which underpin research methods, in recent decades there has been a growing tendency for methods to be treated as if they are independent of theory; as if methods were simply tools waiting to be used for the relevant task. This is apparent in the way in which theory and methods courses are taught independently of each other. Though there are often good practical reasons for this, it does, we feel, also represent not only a difference in professional aptitudes and interests, but also a difference in the relative status of theory over methods. Indeed, if one looks at the history of research methods, one can see a gradual but definite process of specialisation and self-consciousness about methodological distinctiveness. As Bulmer shows in his study of the pioneering group of empirically oriented sociologists at the University of Chicago in the first quarter of the twentieth century, under scholars such as Thomas, Park and, later, Burgess, a group traditionally identified with the development of qualitative methods, was, in fact, much more eclectic in their use of methods, both qualitative and quantitative. Such a sharp distinction was not drawn as they began innovative work in statistical analysis, random sampling, surveys and questionnaires as a complement to their earlier, more qualitative inquiries.[9] However, through the greater 'refinement' of quantitative methods, at Columbia under Lazarsfeld, for example, there is not only a greater divide in sociology between styles of research, and their associated theories, but also much less conversation between them.

One consequence of this has been for a minority of social scientists to concentrate their energies on becoming experts in methods which have been associated with what is from some points of view an impressive refinement in methods of data analysis, research design, and in statistical modelling. Such is the degree of this development that it has become exceedingly difficult for any one person to master thoroughly all the available techniques, let alone gain expertise in more substantive areas of disciplines: a reason for many to leave methods and data analysis to statisticians and/or computer programmers.[10] However, it should not be forgotten that methods, as the generic name should imply but often fails to do so in practice, are a means to an end, namely, better-grounded, social scientific knowledge. Quite what this 'better grounded knowledge' ought to look like is an issue beyond method *per se* but still of vital importance.

Relevant to this are the patterns of change which can sometimes be discerned in the use of methods in social research. Periodically, some methods assume a greater importance and salience than others. Over the last few years analytic survey research has been the predominant method used in social research, not just in sociology but also in the fields of education, market research, social policy and political science. No doubt some of the reasons for this have to do with the kinds of research problems that are of interest. But there can also be discerned a particular preference for research which produces quantitative results, one of the major features of the survey. There is also a widespread belief, as we noted earlier in connection with some remarks about computers, that the bigger the data set, the more data produced, the better. Modern methods of machine processing mean that larger and larger samples can be analysed, more and more variables deployed and analysed. The tendency is, accordingly, to see these methods of social research as having paragon status and that other methods can only be but poor relations. This, we want to say, is quite wrong. As the notion of instrumental presuppositions discussed earlier should alert us, the arguments about the interconnections between theory, method and data mean that methods of social research are deeply debatable within sociology. There are vital and reasoned differences of view about the nature and role of method within the discipline. Further, it is not clear that any one method has any intrinsic and canonical superiority over any other. All have their problems and are in the same boat as far as their worth and merits are concerned.[11] There is every reason to recognise and accept that there is no one method, no one key approach, to sociological problems, but a variety of them that have to be understood, worried about, and, importantly, thought about not simply as difficulties of method, but as problems to do with making sociological investigations work out as best they can be.

All social research, no matter how it might appear in published form, is a compromise between ideas, resources and, as important, solutions to the practical problems faced during the research itself; solutions which rarely conform at all strictly to the canons of inquiry.[12] Indeed, it can be argued that the solutions to the practical problems and exigencies that arise in the course of research are necessary *because* of the difficulties of sticking to the canons of inquiry. A questionnaire item is not providing quite the kinds of answers looked for, selected respondents are not available, an intended interviewee refuses to co-operate, a valued research officer gets another job midway through the research, the hoped for high correlation between variables turns out to be not so high, the coding takes longer and is more costly than expected, and so on: all these, and many more, have to be dealt with in order to do the research. The point is, and though it is an obvious one is still worth saying, that no research can ever be perfectly implemented. It can be more or less effective, and more or less valuable despite being less than perfect.

Making studies work out, even at a modest level of success, is difficult and some achievement when they do. Accordingly, we should not think of the mastery of the methods of social research as a guarantee that first-rate studies will always be produced or that investigations will work out in the way hoped for. If such a guarantee could be had research would not be so hard to do. None the less, one important function that methods can serve is to provide sufficient discipline to make sure that the researcher 'makes do' rather than 'makes up'.[13]

In Chapter 2 we shall discuss in more detail some of the ideas flagged in this. Later chapters deal with the main, currently used, methods of social research: the survey, the interview, and observational methods and the fast growing area of applied social research. In each chapter we shall try to give some of the historical context of each method as well as engage in more theoretical and analytic arguments. After all, the early social researchers, like the early social theorists, were serious scholars trying to deal with difficult problems and their efforts can still have a bearing upon current ones.

NOTES

1. W. Lepenies. *Between Literature and Science*, London, Cambridge University Press, 1988.
2. One sign of this, perhaps, is the fact that whenever the great theorists, such as Marx, Weber, Durkheim, Parsons, and so on, are justly celebrated within sociology, there are few plaudits given to P.F. Lazarsfeld who, with numerous colleagues, was largely responsible for creating much of the character of contemporary social research. Also, and interestingly, empirical studies do not wear well. There are one or two remembered, and taught, as exemplary studies, such as Whyte's *Street Corner Society* or Durkheim's *Suicide*, but, by and large, the thousands of empirical studies normally end up as footnotes, if that. However, this is not to say that this is useless. A similar observation could be made of all disciplines, including those of natural science. Nevertheless, the empirical corpus constitutes a resource for the development of knowledge.
3. The origins of the card sorter as the predecessor of the computerised analysis of large data sets lie in the Jaquard loom which was 'programmed' by a punched card to weave selected patterns. This was picked up by Hollerith in the United States, and used to analyse the census data, and in the 1920s in research done in Chicago.
4. See R.K. Merton, *Social Theory and Social Structure*, 3rd edn, New York, Free Press, 1968. Merton was contrasting the highly abstracted theories of Parsonian structural-functionalism with the

very empiricist tone of much of social research, arguing for a bridge between the two using less general theories tied to more specific domains. His own elaborations of anomie theory in deviance would be a case in point.

5. This should not be taken as a deterrent since, if one thinks about it, many of the theories of natural science often turn out to be wrong theories. In science as in so much else, making progress is often about finding out which are the wrong turnings: lines of inquiry which might look promising but which turn out not to be.

6. For a discussion of these themes, see J. A. Hughes, *The Philosophy of Social Research*, 2nd and rev. edn, London, Longman, 1990.

7. G. Easthope, *A History of Social Research Methods*, London, Longman, 1974, ch. 3. Of course, procedures similar to the modern survey have been used since ancient times. What makes the modern social survey different from its older predecessors are the instrumental theories which underwrite its use.

8. See, for example, H. Blumer, *Symbolic Interactionism*, Englewood Cliffs, NJ, Prentice-Hall, 1969. Also P. Rock, *The Making of Symbolic Interactionism*, London, Macmillan, 1979.

9. M. Bulmer, *The Chicago School of Sociology: Institutionalisation, Diversity and the Rise of Social Research*, Chicago, University of Chicago Press, 1984.

10. During the 1980s suites of generic data analysis programmes, such as SPSS-X, have become widely available. More recently a growing number of packages for the analysis of qualitative data, usually text, have also become available. As always, this availability does not, by itself, mean that they are essential or effective in research.

11. See R.J. Anderson, J.A. Hughes and W.W. Sharrock, *The Sociology Game: An Introduction to Sociological Reasoning*, London, Longman, 1985.

12. A few years ago there was a burst of literature in which researchers told the 'real' stories of their research, focusing particularly on how it rarely conforms to the strictures of methods. See, for example, C. Bell and H. Newby (eds) *Doing Sociological Research*, London, Allen & Unwin, 1977. C. Bell and S. Encel, *Inside the Whale*, Sydney, Pergamon, 1978; C. Bell and H. Roberts (eds) *Social Researching: Politics, Problems and Practice*, London, Routledge, 1984; A. Bryman (ed.) *Doing Research in Organisations*, London, Routledge, 1988.

13. There are interesting layers of meaning involved in the idea of 'making up'. 'Making up' as cosmetic, as an 'adding to', as well as 'inventing', all of which have their place, no doubt, in social research.

CHAPTER 2

Research practice, theory, methods and data

Chapter 1 offered some introductory remarks on the nature of social research and the role of theory, methods and data in the research process. It is now time to flesh these remarks out a little more and begin to orient the discussion toward some of the themes we shall be discussing in succeeding chapters. We shall also take the opportunity to make some ground-clearing observations of a rather wider methodological import in order to provide an appropriate context for much of what follows.

THE POINT OF RESEARCH

We want to begin by posing the question: what is the point of research? We ask this not as a government minister might, faced with the seemingly interminable demands of research scientists for more and more funds, but to try to see what relationship research bears to knowledge. In Umberto Eco's novel, *The Name of the Rose*, the story of the conflict between a theological and a rational-scientific explanation of a series of murders in a monastery in the fourteenth century, Father Jorge, the self-appointed censor of heretical literature, preached that knowledge is not something to be furthered, only refined.[1] Such a view could not be sustained today. The advent of scientific thinking has institutionalised the idea that knowledge has to progress and can do so only through research. None the less, the question we have posed is an important one even if it has no ready answer; important because it directs our attention to the ways in which disciplines acquire, develop and, not to be forgotten, discard knowledge.

We remarked in Chapter 1 that research is about 'finding things out', and there are many activities consistent with this description. Looking up a reference in a library on some topic, a firm doing market research for a new product, an opinion poll prior to an election, physicists building particle colliders to find an elusive sub-atomic particle, the search for a cure for AIDs, and many, many more would all qualify as research in this sense. 'Finding things out' is not an inappropriate rendering of what research is about. However, as it stands this is far too simple. It says little about the 'why' of 'finding things out'. Of course, one kind of answer to the why has to do with the particularities of each and every research project. More generally, the 'why's' have to do with providing answers to problems or questions: what has been written about this topic? What are the likely market trends? Which party is likely to win the election? Does the Z particle exist? And so on.

Of course, any piece of research will involve more than one question. But our main point is that the problems that research is designed to solve, throw light upon or shape up, do not stand alone but are part of a wider context. Even so-called 'fact-finding' research is rarely, if ever, just that but is normally part of a wider enterprise into which the 'facts' discovered in the research are fitted. In the course of ordinary life many of the kinds of activities that could fairly be described as research are an aid to practical decisions and conclusions, answer practical problems. But even when practical concerns are uppermost there is still a framework, a wider context, into which the research and the questions to which it is directed have to fit. In science, and we include the social sciences in this despite the arguments both about the nature of science and whether or not the social sciences can be counted as such, an important, indeed essential, element of the context of research problems is theory. As we pointed out in Chapter 1, the importance of theories in the pursuit of and in the constitution of 'facts' is hard to underestimate.

Having said this, however, the notion of theory is a troublesome one. In sociology, for example, it embraces the broad perspectives or approaches, such as Marxism, symbolic interactionism, structuralism, to mention but a few, to more specific explanations of, say, social mobility or suicide, to the highly particularistic hypotheses specific to a research project. Some theories are more formal than others. Some have a much more general scope than others. Some are little more than loose collections of concepts, while others try to achieve a higher level of integration among their concepts. Some, and one can use Goffman's 'dramaturgical approach' as an example, constitute methodological metaphors, and yet others are simply empirical generalisations. There is, to put it briefly, a plethora of offerings to which the term theory has been applied in sociology. Not only are there different kinds of theories but also there are different priorities awarded to theories *vis-à-vis* methods. Sometimes theories are all important and drive the research and the use of data. In some extreme cases, theorising obliterates any need for empirical method. Thus, much of sociological theorising consists of commentaries upon commentaries on other theories rather than trying to bring data systematically to bear upon theoretical problems.² Sometimes the methodological apparatus dictates or shapes the theorising. For example, the experimental style of psychology is very often treated as a precondition of effective theorising. Similarly, some ways in which the survey is regarded define the scope of social science for its exponents.

A basic starting point for us is, then, that concepts and theories give meaning to potentially observable things and events, and in this sociology is like other sciences. These potentially observable things may, with or without the help of more precise concepts and ideas, be used to construct data. Data is valuable because, in conjunction with theories it illustrates, discovers and explains. All this will be elaborated more fully in the course of this chapter. However, before proceeding, it is important to note the way in which diverse and sometimes contradictory theories – together with their associated methods – find a place in a broader entity. This is the academic discipline which is the intellectual concept of both theories and methods.

There are a number of implications to be drawn from this observation which have relevance for the context of data. The ordinary world as known to common sense is full of things, events, people and happenings; full of, for brief illustration, tables, chairs, friends, enemies, measles, drugs, books, cats, dogs, Golden Virginia, deceit, honesty, teachers, poor essay marks, good luck, all the infinitude of things that we, in our ordinary experience know about, talk about, ignore, are aware of, are not aware of, and so forth. However, a discipline's interest in this world, and any discipline will do as an example here, is not like the interest that any of us show in that world as a world in which we have to do, and know about, the quite ordinary and mundane things that we do. As everyday creatures our interest in the ordinary world is very much a practical rather than a theoretic one. We have no need to theorise about bus timetables in order to catch a bus into town. We have no need to theorise about this world as a condition for acting in it. There is much in the ordinary world that we do, and have to do in order to act within it, take for granted.[3] Disciplines can choose to doubt matters that we in our everyday lives take for granted. For one thing, a discipline's interest in the ordinary world is highly selective. No discipline is, or could be, interested in everything about the common-sense world but in those things, those aspects, those properties, those attributes, conceived in terms of its conceptual apparatus and its theories. A discipline, if you like, abstracts and selects from the totality of the world those features that are its own special province. The human sciences differ on how human behaviour should be conceived. Economists, for example, often work with theories which stipulate that human economic behaviour is motivated by rationality, more or less conceived as the maximisation of means to ends. Psychologists tend to focus on behaviour as the expression of certain psychological propensities while sociologists tend to see human behaviour as shaped in its course by the social context of human life. Such pithy pronouncements on what a discipline is about can be only of heuristic guidance. They cannot tell us in any detail what kinds of investigations might be prompted by such conceptions, or how they may be carried out, what concepts and theories are relevant, and so on. Even within disciplines there are differences as to how, in sociology for example, the 'social' itself should be conceptualised. Some propose that social behaviour is caused by external social forces while others, such as the symbolic interactionists or the ethnomethodologists, want to see social behaviour as actions mutually created and sustained by parties to social arrangements. Such differences (and we have sketched them only very briefly here), are entirely right and proper within and between disciplines which are alive with debate and curiosity about the aspects of the world they have as this domain of inquiry.

In important respects, this is the point. The domain assumptions of a discipline provide a context for research but are themselves relatively unresponsive to the conclusions of the research. To put it simply, the economist's assumptions about the maximising propensities of human beings are precisely that, namely assumptions; they are a place to start. Economists know that real flesh and blood human beings are not like that at all; sometimes they are, but sometimes human beings do things which are manifestly not in their best economic interests.[4] Part of being selective is that it is also necessary to simplify the world in order to try to see more clearly just what a discipline can say about aspects of the world.

Differences between disciplines are not, of course, hard and fast even though, at times, they can become crucial. Disciplines, or more accurately, theories belonging to disciplines, constitute their phenomena as selected aspects of the totality of the world. Some years ago a number of philosophers of science and some scientists had the vision of a unified science in which all the separate disciplines would be integrated within a set of all-embracing, mutually coherent theories. Such a dream, if it is realisable at all, is certainly one for the far future. There are, it is true, many points of contact between disciplines, for example, between biology and chemistry, physics and medicine, psychology and sociology, but these are local rather than overall points of contact. Many current points of contact are likely to change as our knowledge changes, as our ideas develop and change. Disciplines take a special interest in the world as shaped and reflected in the theories they produce; theories which constitute their respective phenomena of interest. Physics abstracts and selects those properties in the world that it is interested in not billiard balls, tables, chairs, but objects in motion, angles of momentum, and so on. Thus, though one might for some purposes characterise the human sciences as concerned with human behaviour in all its fullness this is to misrepresent what turn out to be very different ways of looking at or being interested in the world of human beings. Economists make very different specifications about the nature of human behaviour than do sociologists or psychologists. The economist's rationale for selectivity is human *economic* life and other features of human life are subordinated to this. Though typically economists look at the way in which human beings create and distribute goods and services, often with an eye on issues to do with efficiency according to some rational criteria, this does not prevent them using economic theories to examine, for example, educational provision, the supply of blood donors, voting choice, to name but a few. The point is that they examine such areas with very different specifications in mind to, say, the sociologist, the historian or the political scientist. This is not to imply that they are exceeding their disciplinary mandate in examining topics which might be said to belong to some other discipline; simply that their interests in doing so are different. Indeed, one might say, though a little misleadingly, that it is not so much the substantive topics which distinguish disciplines, but their theoretical interests. Accordingly, the differences of disciplinary interests mean that one needs to be very careful about the kinds of problems that are being addressed. Sociological problems are not those of economics, or of political science, or of psychology.

However, there are one or two qualifications which must be made at this point with respect to the human sciences. The first is that there is a widespread notion that a full explanation and understanding of human behaviour needs the contribution of all the various disciplines. Institutionally this is reflected in the growing fields of educational research, management sciences, organisation studies and communication studies where the contributions from relevant human science disciplines are directed to understanding one area of human life. There is no doubt that this kind of focus is likely to become more common and likely to make major changes in the contributory disciplines themselves. A second qualification, and really one to stress a point made earlier, is that no discipline is a static enterprise but is continually shifting and changing in both its knowledge and its interests. A final qualification is that the issues we are pointing to here are thoroughly debatable. What we are stressing is that the disciplinary context is important to understanding what kind of contribution is on offer, and this includes understanding the special limited concern a discipline has toward the world, and is an essential consideration in evaluating its research and the data it produces. We shall have more to say on such matters throughout the chapters to follow.

We have stressed the importance of theories in constituting the phenomena of a discipline and also recognised that within disciplines there are right and proper arguments about just what these phenomena might be.[5] No more so than in sociology. To some this might seem puzzling: surely a discipline knows what it is about, what aspects of the world it is interested in? Why are there arguments about this? Sociologists are interested in human society, so what is the problem?

The problem is that saying this, or offering any simple definition for other than heuristic purposes, is the beginning not the end of inquiry. Durkheim and Weber, two immensely influential figures, spent a great deal of time not merely defining sociology's subject matter, but arguing for and demonstrating what the consequences of each of their different conceptions might amount to as a disciplined inquiry. In significant respects both differed on what a study of human society might look like, and both made strenuous and hard-won efforts to carry through their respective conceptions through argument and research into the phenomena they tried to identify as sociology's subject matter. Clearly, what a study of society might look like is closely, one might say intimately, related to not only the phenomena but also the data relevant to those phenomena. For Durkheim, the phenomena of sociology were 'social facts', those products of human collectivities that displayed 'thing-like' qualities of externality, constraint and generality. For him, though rather ambiguously, the subjective perceptions of social actors were subsidiary to 'social facts' which were the reality with which sociology dealt as its special province. Subjective meanings, however, for Weber were the very constituent of actions that made them social and, hence, the subject matter of sociology.[6]

So, although 'finding things out' is not an inaccurate rendering of what research is directed toward, often this is finding out whether a particular conception of the discipline, in sociological terms a perspective or an approach, *can* be deployed in research inquiry rather than trying to find out whether a particular theory is true or false. Much of sociological research is, we might say following Garfinkel, trying to 'find the animal in the foliage' or, to extend the implication of the metaphor, trying to see if an idea can be made to say something of sociological interest. Fielding, for example, describes his research strategy for studying the National Front as follows:

> to understand why NF members believe what they do, and to examine the link between their ideology and their actions. . . . The ideology's appeal was seen in terms of its ability to solve problems of the individual's experience. Commitment to a particular ideology was seen as a rational choice originating in the individual's assessment of the situation. . . . Political deviance was the rational, constructive activity of those with a claim to political self-awareness.[7]

This is a statement not of something that the research is going to conclude, is going to find out, but a statement of how the inquiry is to be directed, what it is going to investigate, look at, examine, and so on. This does not mean that its findings will be biased because of this; it is simply setting out the parameters and the objectives of the research and the kinds of ideas that will inform it. Similarly, and to refer to a figure mentioned earlier, Goffman's 'dramaturgical approach' is not a theory of social behaviour but a metaphor, a way of seeing, pointing up, features of the system of interpersonal communication in public places. The data he used, which were highly variable including field observations, quotations from etiquette books and extracts from novels, illustrate rather than prove or disprove hypotheses.[8] So, much of the context of research has to do with trying to see if a particular approach, a particular theoretical conception can be made to yield matters of sociological interest. Finding this out is not a matter of one or two studies but can take many years. Approaches and perspectives are more or less fruitful in encouraging promising lines in inquiry, rather than being true or false or responsive to empirical test. They constitute agendas for research rather than a collection of findings and substantiated theories of social life. And this makes a difference to the role of data. Thus, Goffman's material is intended to illustrate, illuminate, try out and display his perspective. In other cases, evidence has to be weighed and balanced, whereas in so much of quantitative research the aim is explicitly to test hypotheses.

So one of the purposes of research is to find things out by seeing if the world can be investigated using a particular set of assumptions, a particular perspective or a particular approach, trying to see if they yield promising and interesting findings, answer problems that preoccupy researchers, and so on. Looking at this as one of the points of research avoids some of the narrowness of the kind of conception that has tended to dominate thinking about social research, namely that it is about testing theoretical explanations of the facts. This emphasis is misleading in a number of ways. For one, much of scientific activity is not concerned with explanation as normally understood but with, 'just finding out how things are', 'how things work', 'what things look like'. Much of biology and botany, for example, is concerned with taxonomy or classification rather than with explanation. Although to be effective taxonomy needs to be informed by theoretical and research requirements, it is not explanatory in the sense that theories are expected to be.[9] Much of science is concerned with describing things rather than with explanation. Although there is perhaps a sense in which both taxonomy and description are related to explanatory purposes, this is not in any straightforward or enlightening fashion. Thus, in social science much research activity is directed at simply describing how things work, how conversations are organised, how slaughtermen do their work, how managers manage, what police-officers do on the beat, and so on; activities which are not especially motivated by explanation as the point of inquiry. This is not to say that at some point such studies may not eventually facilitate or enter into explanations of a traditional theoretical kind, but this is not their point. Further, and although this will not be our major preoccupation, 'finding out' new theories, new perspectives and new approaches, looking to see how well they work and what problems they can deal with, is as much part of research as 'finding out' new facts. A new theoretical formulation or a new analogy can be immensely important in furthering knowledge; certainly just as much as can finding out a new fact. Indeed, one could say that the latter without the former is more use to the game of Trivial Pursuit than it is to science. Darwin's great innovation, for example, was not so much in finding out new flora and fauna during his voyage in the *Beagle*, but in thinking about them in a new and interesting fashion; one of major consequence for our understanding of the nature of life on this planet and driving much of biological research explicating and developing the programme that Darwin's theory initiated.[10] Similarly, a great many of the data Marx used in his theory of capitalist society were taken from 'fact-finding' Royal Commissions established during the nineteenth century.[11]

There is one additional point we want to make about research which has to do with its collective and temporal character. By these we do not just mean that lots of people do research and take time over it. It is to stress than no piece of research, no matter how expensive or extensive, stands alone but becomes part of a corpus that is argued over, debated, used, criticised, ignored, reviewed, assessed, discarded, used as the basis for further research, and more.[12] There is a strong sense in which the audience for research is other researchers. The significance of any research can never be merely an internal matter but is very much one determined by the response and judgements of fellow researchers and a fact of research life.

THE ROLE OF PHILOSOPHY IN SOCIAL RESEARCH

Perhaps one of the more puzzling contexts of social research is philosophy. Earlier we spoke of the selective interests that disciplines take in the world. For most this is a consequence of them being, or aspiring to be, objective sciences incorporating, well or badly, the scientific method. Physics is interested only in those abstracted features of the world which its theories specify: one way of describing what physics does is 'go beneath' how the world appears to us to uncover the 'real' physical principles and processes which produce the ordered universe. In hindsight it is, in some respects, a pity that the social sciences, and sociology in particular, have taken physics as the exemplar of science; the science that it is the aspiration of all sciences, including the newer ones, to emulate. It is a pity not because sociology cannot become like physics or, indeed, become a science – it is far too early for us to decide about either of these and related questions – but because sociology looked outside itself in order to discover the appropriate model of science to follow and, as it happened, it looked toward philosophical versions of science rather than to the practices of the sciences themselves. In one sense this was a reasonable step to take. If physics is to be taken as the acme of scientific knowledge, then it would make sense to try to emulate the methods that physics uses to gain its knowledge, and where else could one go for this by way of a shortcut but to philosophy, the discipline that has been endlessly preoccupied with the foundations of human knowledge. If there is a scientific method, then philosophy is likely to be the place to find it set out.

Unfortunately, philosophy has proved to be a poor guide in this respect. Not because of any failure on its part, but because of its own nature as an argument subject. Philosophy's business is with argument, and its theses, assuming that this is its endeavour (which is arguable), generate yet more argument, such that issues are never finally settled, and this is just as true for its ideas about the scientific method.[13] None the less, given that sociology did award philosophy a juridical role in determining how sociology should conduct its business, the effect has been to make social research methods extremely sensitive to judgements about whether or not they conform to the appropriate methodological criteria. Methodological criteria, in fact, derived from philosophical versions of the so-called scientific method. For our part, we wish to step back from philosophical issues, not because they are totally irrelevant but because we believe that it is not necessary, from a sociological research point of view, to take them up. The problems of social research are themselves difficult enough and ought to be approached in the spirit of treating them as sociological and methodological problems rather than philosophical problems. Nevertheless, some general, if brief, discussion of some of the more directly relevant philosophical issues may help clarify matters.[14]

It is possible to distinguish, albeit rather grossly, between two contrasting philosophical positions regarding the relationship between theory and data. Both agree that it is theories which do the job of explanation, but disagree on precisely how it achieves this and, as a result, on the nature of theory itself. The first view we can call the 'empiricist', and derives from a philosophical tradition which reaches back as far as Aristotle and runs through more historically recent figures such as Bacon, Locke, Hume, J.S. Mill, and, in the twentieth century, the logical positivists and, latterly, the neo-realists. The second view owes more to the rationalist philosophical tradition usually associated with continental philosophers such as Descartes, Kant, Leibnitz and, much more recently, structuralist philosophers.

Briefly, the difference between these traditions is not their objective of seeking the basis of human knowledge, but the place where they saw it located. The 'empiricist' view sought the foundation of human knowledge in indubitable experience of the external world. The task of science was to formulate procedures whereby this external world could be described, measured, and otherwise charted with certitude. Pride of place in this endeavour was given to systematic and properly grounded empirical investigation. What is important, for our immediate purposes, about this view is its stress on publicly verifiable, observable sensory data, systematically collected and collated, as the route to knowledge. The theoretical task, and in a significant sense secondary to the activity of producing 'facts', was to link observations together within some causal scheme. J.S. Mill, for example, proposed certain 'canons', or principles, by which causal relations could be determined. One of these was the 'method of agreement' which stated that if two or more instances of a phenomenon have only one element in common, then this is the cause (or the effect) of the phenomenon in question. Similarly, his principle of 'concomitant variation' proposed that whatever phenomenon varies whenever another phenomenon varies, is either the cause or the effect of that phenomenon – a principle more familiarly known as correlation. By using these and other principles, which are embodied in the logic of experimental design, causal patterns could be determined empirically and theories built upon these.

For immediate purposes what is important about this and similar procedures is that the theoretical generalisation is induced from systematically gathered data. Theory is subsequent to the collection of data or facts about the world, even when the data are being used to test theoretically derived hypotheses. We shall see in later chapters how this conception shaped many of the uses of the social survey, to mention but one example. Such researchers saw their task as collecting facts about a population. For them, the survey embodied the scientific method because it sought to make basic observations of the phenomena of interest and out of this formulate generalisations. Such surveys routinely now make use of various inductive statistics to secure the generalisation from sample to population. To some extent, though less so than with survey researchers, the same spirit informed the early exponents of participant observation. They argued, and some still do, that in order to grasp fully how social situations are created and sustained by social actors, social investigators need to immerse themselves in the social world under study. Only then could theoretical speculation take place. Although they differed markedly in the kinds of data it was thought necessary to collect, they held to a similar conception of the relationship between theory and data.

However, the conception we have just been briefly outlining came up against a number of philosophical difficulties. One of the more crucial ones concerned the empirical interpretation of scientific generalisations and theory. Laws in science, so it was argued, were of the logical form 'All As are Bs', (for example all swans are white) yet it is impossible to investigate empirically all As. Empirical investigation always deals with a sample of a phenomenon, never a fully enumerated population. Even natural scientists experiment upon particular elements, chemical compounds, organisms, or whatever; never with all the instances of these that have, do, and will exist. We cannot examine all water to see if, when an electric current is passed through it, at one electrode hydrogen is given off, at another oxygen. We cannot examine all gas to see if Boyle's law, to the effect that volume is proportionate to temperature, operates universally. Accordingly, it appeared that all law-like generalisations were always derived inductively whereby the instances investigated stood as proxy for some total population. Unfortunately, this inductive procedure could not, logically, underpin universal and determinate laws since no finite number of events can ever guarantee the truth of a universal statement. It was this kind of objection which led to the influential doctrine of falsification and the conception of the hypothetico-deductive model of explanation which is sketched below.[15]

The second of the views we have noted derives from a claim that the route to indubitable knowledge is not through empirical experience of the external world, but through logical, that is rational, principles which are beyond doubt. Whereas, for the empiricists the criteria of knowledge were to be found in the practices of empirical science, for the rationalists the appropriate models were those of logic and mathematics. Here the logical principle is deduction. On this view, theories are deductive systems of thought in which 'facts' are deduced from higher order principles, much like geometricians effect a proof by showing how the conclusion logically follows from one or two general premises or postulates. Theories, on this view, are of much greater importance than on the empiricist tradition.

The orthodox account of scientific practice represents a marriage between the two traditions just outlined. The empiricist account of theories as empirical generalisations has largely been discredited, but not the stress laid upon systematic methods of investigation. The principle of deduction is incorporated by seeing empirical investigation as primarily a procedure for testing theories through hypotheses deduced from the theory itself. This model, known as the 'hypothetico-deductive model', uses the general statements of the theory as premises in a deductive argument, along with statements describing the conditions under which the test is carried out, a testable conclusion, or prediction, can be deduced and compared with empirical evidence. If the conclusion and the evidence do not match then the theory is falsified; if they do match, then this is some evidential support for the theory and its explanation. Subsequent research will then be devoted to determining its range of applicability and subjecting it to still further tests. We shall see something of this in connection with developments in survey design.

More recently, developments both in the sociology and history of science and in the philosophy of science have begun to question this orthodox model.[16] They point out that in the history of science it is clear that social and political factors play a great part in determining which theories are held on to and which are rejected; certainly they play at least as great a part as the degree to which a theory is seen as having evidential support. This is also consistent with some of the claims of the newer philosophies of science which recognise that theories are under-determined by the nature of the world.[17] That is, it is possible to hold as true a number of theories about the world, it being impossible to choose between them on strictly evidential grounds. Moreover, we can have no theory-independent way of describing the world. It is theories which tell us what the world is like and we cannot make the recourse that empiricist accounts of theory wish to do, to check our theories against a world conceived independently of theories.

Such philosophical arguments can go on endlessly as is the nature of philosophy. Despite many protestations to the contrary, its arguments fail to offer solutions to the problems of empirical research. Because of the status philosophy has been awarded in sociology, the conception of the scientific method derived from philosophical ruminations has proved inhibiting to social research in a number of ways. For one, the hypothetico-deductive method has too often been accorded paragon status as the form which all social research should seek to adopt. Anything less than this is a measure of the extent to which the research falls short of scientific standards. But (as we said before in another connection) even much of natural scientific activity does not conform to this model, is not so much concerned with explanation but with taxonomy, for example, or with finding out how things work, looking for things, and so on. It is not that testing rigorously formulated theories from deduced hypotheses is never done, only that it is *not the standard* of scientificity. It is even less so in the social sciences where there is a dearth of sufficiently well-worked-out theories to test in this way. But testing is not the only point of theories.

Given philosophy's interest in the foundations of human knowledge it is not surprising that it should spend a considerable amount of its concern with science, the form of human knowledge which has achieved so much. Philosophy has its own way of being interested in the world, its own problems to solve by its own lights, and these are not those of empirical sociology.[18] Philosophical guidance can never resolve the particular problems of social research.

THE PLACE OF METHODS

It is now time to review the place of methods in sociology. Methodological approaches in social science emerge, develop and, sometimes, fade away. In this respect, two factors are important to note. First, an approach within a discipline emerges in a particular social context marked, among other things, by influential social groups and authoritative doctrines. Both of these will invariably influence the character of research.[19] Second, an approach is developed by a social group. The perceptions a research community develops will be influenced by a whole set of factors, none more potent than the ideas and practices that have been used previously, as well as those which are seen to yield further advances in understanding. There is an important social dimension necessary to the understanding of both the development of, in this case, methods and methodological thinking, and the kinds of presuppositions on which they are based.[20]

There is one curious feature of sociology that is worth mentioning, namely that methods these days are largely seen as a distinctive branch of the discipline. This is reflected both in teaching and in the fact that, by and large, textbooks are written separately to deal with methods. This state of affairs is, if not unique, certainly unusual among disciplines. It would be strange, for example, to see separate courses on methods for natural scientists. Natural scientists are normally expected to acquire the skills and aptitudes necessary for research through learning the subject itself. Research, theory and method are virtually inseparable activities within the natural sciences. Much the same is true of history, literary criticism, law, accountancy, for further examples. There are, no doubt, many reasons, historical and intellectual, for this distinctive disjointedness between methods and what is regarded as the substance of sociology itself. One consequence, however, is a prevalence of the view that sees methods as more or less atheoretical tools. Research methods are to be treated as a collection of tools designed and thereby suited for particular jobs. Research is simply a matter of defining one's problem and selecting the appropriate tool or method for that problem. This implies, of course, that each method has only a limited potentiality and, to this extent, particular methods can be used only for certain kinds of research objectives.

There is more than just an element of truth in this conception. Our quarrel is with the notion that underpins it, namely that methods are atheoretical which makes it seem that the choice of a research method is governed by technical criteria. While it is often the case that methods are treated as if they were tools in a tool box ready and waiting to be used for their appropriate task, it is vitally important that any aspiring methodologist does not take this too seriously but tries, instead, to understand the presumptions which underpin methods. What we want to emphasise is the theoretical context of method and how this is integral to sociological investigation, not simply as a technique but as something which has profound significance for the possibility of sociology itself. After all, since much of social research requires a direct encounter with the everyday social world, the act of research can be immensely revealing about the nature of social life.

Though here we do not intend this as anything more than a thought-provoking remark we shall see, in connection with the interview method particularly, how much of the technical apparatus of methods requires conceptions about the nature of social encounters.

One upshot of the tool box view is that it invites us to use data generically with little regard for the theoretical auspices of the method. This sits easily with the view summarised earlier that there are 'facts' in the world, recorded in various ways, and the task of research is to gather the appropriate ones in light of the resources and circumstances affecting the particular research project. It matters little whether the 'facts' have been produced by questionnaires, found by searching through records, or are the result of a period of participant observation. There may be problems of a technical nature, but these are of little substantive consequence for sociological theory which is capable of being sustained, or not, by data culled from a variety of sources using a variety of methods.

However, some research methods, along with the data produced by them, are approach- or theory-specific in that they developed within, or have come to represent, a particular theoretical tradition or perspective. Participant observation, for example, although it developed more or less outside of any strong theoretical tradition but simply as a way of getting research of a particularly descriptive kind done, in sociology has come to be closely associated with the symbolic interactionist tradition. By contrast, the social survey was developed as a more generic method. Although the line between the theory-specific and the more generic surveys is a difficult one to draw, it is important as a reminder of the very important point that methods do have theoretical implications of a profound kind, even if these are not always easy to determine.

We have come a long way in this preliminary discussion without saying anything about what actually counts as data in the social sciences. It has to be admitted that there are problems with trying to state what data are without appearing to stipulate their character in advance. Just as different theoretical schools within each of the social sciences, as well as the disciplines themselves, have various views about the nature of human behaviour, how it is conceptualised and conceived, the way in which this should be investigated, then they will also have different ideas about what sorts of things are to count as data. Some would even say that the very term 'data' limits the possible options in this respect by implying that there are special kinds or orders of phenomena which qualify as data. Behaviourists, for example, want only to treat of overt behaviour as the data for psychological research and this is as much a theoretical specification of what, for them, is to count as data as experience and meaning are for non-behaviourists. Durkheim sought to establish the scientific credentials of sociology by arguing that it should be concerned only with its own special order of 'social facts'; that is, those events and processes which possessed the qualities of externality, constraint and generality. Examples of such 'social facts' included language, law, custom, economic and political organisation, and so on. In both of these examples, and there are others, only certain phenomena could qualify as data.

In the human sciences data can encompass narrowly conceived bodily movements, complex packages of statements about motives and attitudes, quantitative descriptions of whole aggregates of people, including whole societies, and highly detailed qualitative descriptions of the life of a group or community. That these, and other materials, are taken as data in research projects is determined not only, or even mainly, by the subject matter of the research, but also by the theoretical presuppositions informing the study. In the end, of course, what is to count as data is whatever materials are grist to the researcher's mill; whatever it is that he or she wants to work with. The historian Lawrence Stone, for example, in an extensive study of the transformation of the family and marriage in England from 1500 to 1800 made use of personal documents, diaries, autobiographies, memoirs, domestic correspondence, handbooks, newspapers, reports of foreign visitors, imaginative literature, art, housing plans, modes of address between husbands and wives, folk customs, legal documents, and demographic statistics.[21] Although this is both extensive and varied by the standards of most of the human sciences, though perhaps not of history, what it illustrates is the difficulty of specifying what is to count as data beyond saying that it is whatever material that researchers need to work with in order to pursue their inquiries.

None the less, it is necessary to point out that there have been a number of attempts to develop what might be called, 'theories of data', that is to specify what can count as suitable data for scientific disciplines: some of these we shall be looking at in this book. One such influential doctrine of this order which, though now discredited in its strong form, still influences methodological thinking is the notion of 'operational definitions'.[22] This, in brief, stated that the meaning of a concept is whatever can define that concept in terms of 'operations', or measures, of observable features of the world. Thus the definition of IQ, under this doctrine, would be whatever an IQ test measures. A more extended example can be provided by the notion of alienation. One tradition argues that this concept refers to a 'state of mind', one that expresses withdrawal from or disenchantment with the life that one leads. Less broadly than this, it can be used to refer to a disenchantment from more specific areas of a person's life, such as his/her work, or from politics, or from religion, and so on. In which case a researcher's task is to translate this rather abstract and vague notion into some operational form. On this rendering of alienation as a state of mind the most usual form of this would be as an attitude scale consisting of a series of statements judged to express alienative feelings, and to which subjects have to respond in terms of their agreement or disagreement. An example of such a statement might be, 'For me life simply has no meaning', or, 'Even when I am enjoying myself I often feel that I don't belong'. A scale of this kind would normally consist of a number of such statements. But the point is that the scale constitutes an 'operational measure' for the theoretical concept of alienation. It effects a translation between the theoretical language and the empirical world by, in this case, constructing a putatively quantitative description of a concept in the language of social research.

However we do not want to engage in the quantitative issue for the moment, but stay with the relationship between the theoretical concept and its operational definition. Theoretical concepts are, by their nature, much wider in their meaning than operational definitions. To refer back to the above example, the statements selected could not exhaust all the possible statements that could have been used. Further, researchers have to take practicalities into account. It may be, for example, that an attitude scale, for whatever reason, could not be used as an 'operational measure'. An observational study of a production line, say, although it might want to talk a great deal about the alienative effects of such work, could not make use of an attitude scale in the way that a questionnaire study might. In this case, then, what is the relationship between one measure and any others than might be used?

The answer to this is as much a theoretical matter as it is a methodological one. The doctrine of operationalism took a particularly extreme view on this issue by stipulating that the meaning of a concept consisted in the operations required to measure it. Thus, strictly interpreted, the meaning of the concept 'alienation' is the attitude scale used to measure it. Of course, the implication of this is that a different measure is also a different concept. This is hardly a satisfactory conclusion and not one seriously intended by the doctrine itself. Instead, the orthodox presumption is that the same concept can be measured in different ways using different indices. Different indices represent the ingenuity with which the theoretical constructs can be made to produce satisfactory elaborations that result in different indices and, equally important, the extent to which different indices can, plausibly, be said to measure the same concept. As we shall see in Chapter 3, this conception of measurement, although originally proposed as an account of scientific measurement in general, bears only a superficial relationship to much of measurement in science which is an activity much more integral to substantive theories than it is in most social research.

What we referred to as 'theories of data', though originally concerned with the mathematical structure of quantitative data in the social and the cognitive sciences, is a notion that can be usefully extended to encompass the relationship between theory and data more generally. It would, of course, under this wider conception also include 'instrumental presuppositions' as well as the more abstracted philosophical discussions already mentioned. What the notion is intended to emphasise are those issues to do with the how and the why of sociology's empirical reference.

We take it that the point of theories, and from this the point of research, is to offer adequate accounts of the empirical world as conceived as the domain of the discipline to which the theory belongs. There are a number of philosophical accounts of how, in science, this is achieved. Its more practical aspects have to do with what we referred to in Chapter 1 as the 'inferential structure of data': that is, how to effect a connection between the empirical materials, whatever their character, and our theoretical knowledge.

The chapters which follow will deal in more detail with the various theories of data involved in the use of social research methods: there are a variety of these, often connected to the same method, just as there are a variety of perspectives in sociology. There is no one solution to sociology's empirical reference, no clear idea as to whether there ever could be, no one canonical method for all sociological research, and no one conception of data: data are whatever a researcher can make useful for meeting his/her research objectives, aims or problems, which is not to say that just any old thing will do. Material has to be made into data and this involves a structure of inference that directs the material to research problems.

One common division in social research that needs to be addressed is that between allegedly different kinds of inferential structure encapsulated in the dichotomy between qualitative and quantitative social research.

QUALITATIVE VERSUS QUANTITATIVE RESEARCH

This is another of those methodological issues which can quickly rise to the point at which it becomes a major issue of principle, and usually a matter of philosophical principle at that. Thus, the issue can be joined as human beings are not like the objects of physical science and therefore cannot be quantified, that human action is concerned with meaning, reasons, intentions and understandings and this, therefore, is an interpretative matter rather than a phenomenon subject to causal explanation, that qualitative studies are not really scientific, and so on. The upshot is that it looks as if major and fundamental matters are at stake about the very nature of sociology itself and that, accordingly, a choice has to be made, and made soon.

Further, it is a debate which displays all the symptoms of degeneration in argument that sociology is too often heir to, namely thinking about issues in dualistic terms; that, in this case, the choice is between two sides, the quantitative and the qualitative and that one cannot have both.[23] This not only serves to give the issues all the appearance of being fundamental and crucial, but also conceals the fact that matters are not so simple as to be accurately captured by such a dualistic portrayal. Thus, we have a collection of antimonies which pretend to describe the two sets of methods: hard versus soft, explanatory versus exploratory, objective versus subjective, causal versus interpretative, generalising versus particularising, rigorous versus unrigorous, and so on. Such labels, of course, not only represent an attitude toward particular styles of social research, differences in theories and philosophies, but also point to significant methodological issues. However, it is important that the latter are seen as methodological issues to be faced rather than as postures to be taken in advance of looking closely at them.

Though we shall have much more to say on the issues that allegedly divide quantitative and qualitative methods in later chapters, the kind of choice just alluded to is neither urgent nor necessary. It is the nature of the research problem that should dictate the appropriate research method; sometimes quantification is required, sometimes not. There is no intrinsic virtue to either style of method. What we are being asked to choose between are promissory notes, not achievements. There is a great deal wrong with quantitative methods just as there is a great deal wrong with qualitative ones. Both kinds are, as it were, in much the same boat. Both have much to do to achieve the aspirations they set themselves: we cannot choose between them in terms of which of them is going to take social research forward. We simply do not know. This is not to say that a preference for one style or the other is inappropriate; it is to recognise that both are still in their infancy and *neither one markedly superior to the other in all respects.*

Of course, none of this is intended to imply that there are no important differences between the two styles of social research, for clearly there are. But the structures of inference involved are not so easily captured by the dualistic thinking spoken of earlier. For example, there is a considerable amount of interpretative work involved in quantification to secure the link between the raw data material and the number systems employed. Further, many qualitative-type studies would make claims to generality and rigour. Similarly, questionnaire designers are keenly sensitive to questions about meaning as a prerequisite for framing their questions appropriately, constructing attitude scales, as well as interpreting the results. They may not, it is true, hold to the conception of meaning which, for example, many interactionists would, but this is, again, a matter for serious analysis and argument rather than sloganeering and posturing. It is not, accordingly, that there are no debates or issues here; on the contrary. But what their character is not is adequately portrayed by the gross distinction between quantitative versus qualitative.

One has only to think of the variety of positions that can be taken with respect to qualitative and quantitative research. Durkheim, as an ardent positivist, urged and pioneered a way of thinking sociologically that lent quantitative data to the testing of theoretically derived hypotheses. Weber, in stressing the meaningful and subjective character of social action, emphasised the importance of interpretative understanding as a method for securing causally adequate explanations of social phenomena. Some symbolic interactionists inveighed against the 'quantomania' of variable analysis and argued in favour of a more interpretative approach to the study of social life which, for some, was more scientific than variable analysis. More recently, there have been critiques from ethnomethodology concerning the categorising procedures of variable analysis which, they argue, owe more to the needs of quantification as proposed by variable analysis than to the properties of social activities themselves. Yet, this is not an argument against quantification *per se*, only against its premature use in advance of knowing what the mathematical properties of the phenomena of social life might be. The issues are complex, varied, resistant to easy resolution and, of course, immensely important: far too important to be encapsulated in a simple dichotomy between quantitative versus qualitative research.

THE SOCIAL SOURCES OF DATA

A further reason why such dichotomies as are embodied in the quantitative–qualitative distinction should not be allowed to dominate our thinking is that they tend to obscure the sheer and sometimes bewildering variety of materials that can qualify as data. The example of Stone's materials cited earlier is an exemplary case of this in one study, but as a feature of social research more generally it is not excessively so. Sociologists have made use of, and again only for brief example, fragments of conversations, records of various kinds, photographs, letters, paintings, attitude scales, film and video, not to mention the materials produced by the more orthodox of research methods such as the questionnaire and the interview.

However, in light of what has been said earlier, it should not be thought that data materials, to call them that, are always restricted to one study, or that the study which originally produced them is their only home. Attention to the instrumental theories underpinning data should point toward the fact that materials are often open to varying interpretations; another way of expressing the idea that theories are under-determined by data. By this we do not mean to imply that any old interpretation will do because, clearly, there are standards involved in any inference from the data materials to the theory, be this a substantive sociological theory or what we have referred to as an instrumental theory.

An example of this process is the secondary analysis of data. We have already remarked that data collection is increasingly prevalent in all kinds of organisation, much of it intended to monitor the performance of the organisation itself. In this respect the various branches of the state are important, economic statistics being simply the most well known. Further, given the cost of large-scale social research, it is tempting to tap these rich resources of data, often for purposes other than those originally intended. The use of official statistics, for example, has a long history in many of the social sciences.

Once again there are different ways in which such data are used, but all share the object of analysing the data anew, using them for different purposes than originally intended. A prevalent use involves showing that the conclusions originally drawn are unwarranted, even incorrect. However, a rather more theoretically informed use of secondary data is exemplified in the work of, again, Durkheim who made use of official statistics in his study of suicides in Europe, particularly France, to demonstrate the validity of his theories of the social causation of suicidal behaviour; an objective for which the original statistics were not intended.[24]

Whether or not Durkheim was justified in using such data as he did has proved to be an enduring and important debate ever since the study was published. What Durkheim did was transform or recontextualise the official statistics, which he well knew were less than satisfactory in many respects, produced by officials for administrative purposes, and relate them to his theoretical concerns. Others have challenged the assumptions and interpretations offered by Durkheim and, in so doing, made important elaborations in sociological theory; elaborations which have profound methodological consequences.[25] (See Table 2.1.)

For our purposes what is important here is the way in which the data materials were transformed by deploying a different theoretical perspective. With reference to the official statistics, Durkheim did this first of all by regarding the rates compiled by officials in the pursuance of their routine duties as not so much a simple factual registration of certain types of death, but as indicators of a 'suicidogenic' current caused by various states of society itself. Much later in the debate, and in time, the same 'raw data' were transformed yet again, this time seen as the negotiated outcomes of actors' methods, particularly the police and coroners, for making sense of and constructing their courses of action which are only imperfectly, if at all, reflected in the figures.[26] This, once again, illustrates how data are intimately responsive for their sense and their meaning to the theoretical context in which they are placed.

Table 2.1 Suicide as a social phenomenon[27]

Perspective	Sociology (Durkheim)	Social psychology (Douglas)	Sociology (Atkinson)
Character of Suicide	Social fact, defined by society	Psychological, defined by individuals	Social fact, defined by social practices
Nature of official statistics	Social fact, because accurate	Inaccurate	Social fact, not questionable through 'more accurate' information
Area of research	Correlations between rates and states of social integration	Meaning of events to participants	Construction of suicide in coroners' proceedings

To refer to a method we shall be discussing more fully in Chapter 3, we can see much the same sort of development with respect to the survey. Used originally to discover demographic facts about a population, this was later widened into seeking from respondents facts of other sorts, such as marital status, housing conditions, levels of education, leisure use, and even attitudinal materials. Thus, the accounts offered by respondents of their experience, their conditions of life, etc. were taken as indicative of a fairly static fabric called the 'social structure'.

The theory, if such it can be called, which underwrote this use of the survey, was a 'naive empiricist structuralism' according to which social structural facts about a society were susceptible to factual observation and description using the survey method. Finding out the 'facts' characteristic of a people who constitute the population of some society, usually a nation, is seen as the essence of social scientific investigation. Significantly, the use of interviews and questionnaires in mass surveys depended upon the notion that the responses offered by respondents about their conditions and experiences were almost as good as the direct observation of the respondents and their lives; a far greater coverage of the population could be achieved than by using observational methods. This is, perhaps, the closest that social science has come to pure 'empiricism' or, as it is sometimes referred to, 'vulgar fact gathering'. Yet, it is important to note that theoretical interpretation, even if unacknowledged, was involved. For example, taking the answer given by a respondent to a question as equivalent to direct observation of the event to which it refers, was an assumption upon which the method rested. It is an assumption which amounts to an instrumental theory about the relationship of types of questions to types of answers and both of these to the context in which answers are elicited. It also commits the user to more typical theoretical questions to do with the nature of the social structure, its facticity, and so on: many of these instrumental and other theoretical conceptions have proved less than durable.

Certainly, more modern uses of the survey method have disregarded some of the rather naive methodological assumptions of the early surveys. In the 1940s and 1950s, especially in the United States, data produced by the survey were differently deployed. It was argued that social acts were essentially motivated behaviour and could be properly understood and explained only in terms of these underlying dispositions. So, data generated from surveys were used to infer the 'latent structure' of respondent attitudes and motivations.[28] Rather than seeing responses to questions as simple indicators of factual properties, these theorists saw them as data from which it was possible to make inferences about the dispositional and motivational character of social actors' behaviours. These, in their turn, were seen as indispensable for the explanation of actual behaviour. In a very real sense, although answers to questions are being elicited in both approaches, the data that result are fundamentally different. Not only do the questions differ, the one asking about 'factual' information, the other about attitude or belief, but also the answers are used in different ways. For the early empiricists the answers taken in conjunction with other facts about the social structure add up to a description of a particular society. For the latent structure analysts, however, the answers index deeper motivational and disposition characteristics of social actors and, when appropriately processed, reveal a respondent's psychosocial orientation which can then be used to explain social conduct and behaviour.

The kind of theory invoked by latent structure analysis was basically socio-psychological and cultural. The argument was that different components of personality are built up in particular individuals as a consequence of cultural conditioning. Hence, the aim of the analysis of attitudes was to reveal the hidden patterns typically sedimented in particular social and cultural contexts. Having a distinctive view about the origin of personality, as well as the structures they might find, these survey users were not nearly so preoccupied with representative samples, but rather with analyses showing intercorrelations between sets of attitudes and other social behaviour.

The importance of these examples is not simply to reinforce the general point that data materials, whatever else they may consist in, have to be 'read' through, in terms of, a theoretical framework to exist as data, but that the theoretical significance of such materials can change. Often, too often perhaps, the impression is conveyed that data are separate from the purposes for which they have been gathered, that data can exist, as it were, on their own. Data are always contextualised even though very often the context is vague, indeterminate and, as these examples illustrate, open to change. The inferences that may be placed in data materials can and do change as theoretical frameworks change and shift. Not in a haphazard or whimsical fashion, but as knowledge itself changes.

It could be said that from the point of view of social research, the world only exists as data and data can exist only through the interpretations placed on materials gathered from the world. In which case, how is it that theories are tested by data? If, as we have been suggesting, the nature of data has much to do with the theoretical presuppositions which underlie their production, how can it be said that theories are tested by means of exposure to data? Theory looks to be testing theory.

Moreover, if we examine social scientific practice at all closely we can often see how substantially the same data can be used to support or discredit very different, sometimes contrary, theories: the generic use of data and methods should not make this too surprising an observation. Indeed, social science theories are under-determined by facts. There are a number of reasons for this, many of them constituting significant areas of debate within social science methodology. One has to do with the fact that many theories in social science are not so much theories susceptible to straightforward empirical confirmation or refutation, but are more like points of view. Marxism, functionalism, symbolic interactionism, marginalist theory in economics, and so on, would be examples of this. Such theories, or perspectives, are really agendas for research programmes. It is not that such agendas are unresponsive to data but they are not responsive by way of direct testing. Their main role is providing ideas and means by which the world can be investigated sociologically; in Lakato's words, they represent a discipline's 'research programmes'.[29]

Another reason has to do with the relative imprecision with which those theories that, arguably, are more susceptible to direct testing are couched. Very often they do not, unlike many natural scientific theories, suggest direct ways of measuring the concepts employed, and, because of this, it is difficult to determine what the limits of a theory might be. A third reason has to do with the non-experimental character of most social research. This means that it becomes difficult, some would say impossible, to specify the *ceteris paribus* conditions of a theory. Newton's law of falling bodies postulates a uniform rate of fall for all bodies in a vacuum *other things being equal*; a condition which enables the theory to assume a very precise quantitative expression to the theory itself. So, the paradox noted earlier is a paradox only if we adopt a particular and constrained view of what theories in social science are about, what role they play in the process of acquiring knowledge. As things currently stand, and there are no compelling reasons to think that matters will suddenly change, there are few theories which could meet the standard of being directly testable, though there are more subsidiary theories within larger frameworks which do gain, or lose, plausibility in light of empirical evidence. An example of this might be the 'embourgeoisement theory' which enjoyed widespread currency a few years ago in sociology, and which argued that the 'working class', in Britain, were becoming more like the 'middle class' in their aspirations, consumption patterns and political views.[30] But it is important to note that there was no one study which established or refuted the theory. What studies did contribute to was its amendment, its clarification, its reinterpretation, its revision, its incorporation and almost replacement by other perspectives, in light of accumulating evidence from a wide range of studies. And this kind of process, one might add, is not untypical of the career of theories in natural science. Sudden death is rarely the fate of a theory; a slow ageing to redundancy is the more usual end.

CONCLUSION

The foregoing discussion has tried to make and illustrate the point that research methods cannot stand in isolation from the theoretical and conceptual issues which constitute the social sciences. While problems of method have their technical aspects – such as how many people should be interviewed? How long shall a group be observed? What is an acceptable chi-square value?, and so on – little of this will cast very much light on the crucial issues of method, namely what shall we study? What we study follows from theoretical or more broadly, disciplinary concerns rather than technical matters. We hope to show that methods are not, and cannot be, selected according to the qualities of the data they yield alone. The richness of the data sought by participant observation methods, for example, and the 'objective' and representative data sought by the survey are not, by themselves, virtues. The point is that they are deliberately sought because some reasoned theoretical considerations are felt to require them. Of course, such considerations may turn out to be erroneous; but the choice is, or ought to be, a reasoned one.

So far we have been raising rather large issues in an abstracted and certainly general fashion which, it is to be hoped, will become clearer as they are filled out in what follows by way of the discussion of specific methods of data collection. Finally in this chapter we want to return to the source of all social science data, and the ultimate object of social scientific investigation, namely the members of society. Social science is concerned to understand, explain if you will, the social origins, context and consequences of what the members of society do, the relationships they form, what they believe in, think about, pray to, fight about, collaborate on, discover, create, build, buy and sell, produce, and so on. Although the various social sciences take different interests in such matters and differ also on how such an understanding of them can be achieved, they do at least share this common source of data; that is, what the members of society have produced, and are producing, in the way of artifacts, social groups, institutions, documents of various kinds, systems of conflict and co-operation, records, and so on. Very generally we can categorise what this source produces by way of data into the following elements: first, what people do, their acts and behaviours; second, the thoughts, beliefs, aspirations, values and motives that people hold; third, their speech, either verbal or written, which accompanies both of the above. With respect to all of these elements there are widely different interpretations both as to their nature and as to the relation between them; all of which have profound methodological consequences. However, conventionally, which is not to say correctly, modes of social scientific explanation tend to see these elements as analytically separate orders of phenomena and, accordingly, data. On this view, one of the more important problems of methods is to relate these various elements together through some inferential apparatus in systematic ways. Thus, the interview is often used to inquire into the beliefs and values of a particular social group on the supposition that these are crucial to the explanation of the behaviour of the members of the group. This could arise, for example, in researching into the voting behaviour of, say, white-collar workers, or the differential rates of absenteeism among workers within a particular plant. The beliefs are seen as influencing, at least in significant part, the behaviour in which the members of the group engage and which distinguishes them from other groups who hold different beliefs. The methodological problem arises because beliefs, attitudes, values and other so-called subjective states cannot be directly inspected. They have to be inferred usually from some form of verbal behaviour, such as responses to attitude scales, or to questionnaire items. In turn this leads on to the problems to do with the extent to which, and the conditions under which, respondents accurately report their beliefs, attitudes and, ultimately, to the extensive and impressive technology of interview and attitude measurement.[31]

Some of these issues we shall deal with more fully in Chapter 5 on the interview. The point we want to make for immediate purposes has to do with the way in which methodological problems arise from particular conceptions of the 'order of things'. In other conceptions, for example, problems of the kind just reviewed do not arise. It is argued that the distinctions noted earlier are by no means clear and that behaviour cannot be identified in isolation from speech and so-called 'internal mental states'. Such elements are not, logically speaking, analytically independent.[32]

There is a further theme to do with the collective nature of social life. All the social sciences are predicated on the notion that individuals are not isolated like so many Robinson Crusoes – who, in any case, was already a social creature by the time he was shipwrecked on the island – but are related to others in complex ways. Human beings form economic relations of many kinds with one another, involve themselves in political relationships or religious ones, live within many kinds of groups, and so on. As Durkheim and others have tried to demonstrate, these relationships seem to have an independent existence over and above the individuals who compose them. Individuals live and die, but economic, political and religious systems, for example, show durabilities that go beyond the lifespan of any one individual. The methodological problem arises, it is argued, because all we can observe and gather data from are individuals. Only individuals can fill out questionnaires, be interviewed, respond to attitude scales, be observed, and so on, and yet, very often, these are used as evidence for, or descriptions of, the supra-individual phenomena to which we have just referred. Accordingly, some theoretical and methodological grounding for this transformation needs to be provided. As we shall see in Chapter 4, it is the absence of this grounding that opens some methods to the charge of excessive individualism.

There are many problems here and we cannot hope to deal with all of them adequately, not simply because of limitations of space but, more importantly, because many of them are, as yet, problems to which there are no satisfactory answers, no clear solutions or, very often, many possible solutions but no clearly superior one. What we hope to have shown so far, if only in a general way, is the vital link between theory and method which is so essential to a fuller understanding of methods of data collection.

Chapter 3 begins a discussion of one inferential structure that is predominant in social research, namely variable analysis and its approach to data, measurement and theory building. This is important since it informs much of the discussion of substantive methods which, these days, are associated with this mode of social research, namely the survey and the interview.

NOTES

1. Umberto Eco, *The Name of the Rose*, London, Picador, 1988.
2. A. Sayer, *Method in Social Science: A Realist Approach*, London, Hutchinson, 1984, for example, contains no references to methods as conventionally understood. In this sense method is best understood as a logical-cum-epistemological system for sociology.
3. This is a simplification of Schutz's phenomenologically based distinction between the natural attitude and that of science. Here

we do not intend or imply anything more than noting such a difference between the sciences and the attitude of ordinary life. See, for example, A. Schutz, 'Concept and theory formation in the social sciences', in M. Natanson (ed.) *Philosophy of the Social Sciences*, New York, Random House, 1963, pp. 231–49. Also R.J. Anderson, J. A. Hughes and W. W. Sharrock, *Philosophy and the Human Sciences*, London, Croom Helm, 1986.

4. To advance a claim that human beings ought to do what is in their own best economic interests is to turn a methodological assumption used by economics into a moral injunction.

5. Disciplines may well vary in the extent to which there are arguments about basic phenomena or disciplinary interests. Physics, for example, while carrying on the search for sub-atomic particles which will decide between specific theories about the constitution of matter, does not display the kind of arguments that go on in, say, sociology about what its fundamental concerns ought to be. Whether this represents a difference in kind or is simply a difference in degree is a moot point.

6. There is clearly much more that could be said in reference to both these figures. But see E. Durkheim, *The Rules of Sociological Method*, ed. G. Catlin, New York, Free Press, 1966, and M. Weber, *The Methodology of the Social Sciences*, trans and ed. E. Shils and H.A. Finch, New York, Free Press, 1949.

7. H. Garfinkel, *Studies in ethnomethodology*, Englewood Cliffs, Prentice Hall, 1967. N. Fielding, 'Observational research on the national front', in M. Bulmer (ed.) *Social Research Ethics*, London, Macmillan, p. 81. The full research is reported in N. Fielding, *The National Front*, London, Routledge & Kegan Paul, 1981.

8. As Goffman himself said, 'I ask that these papers be taken for what they are: merely exercises, trials, tryouts, a means of displaying possibilities, not establishing fact', *Forms of Talk*, Oxford, Basil Blackwell, 1981, p. 1. See also P. Drew and A. Wootton (eds), *Erving Goffman: Exploring the Interactional Order*, Oxford, Polity Press, 1988.

9. In biology, for example, the taxonomy of species and fossils is informed by the requirement to display evolutionary relationships. However, meeting such a requirement is not straightforward. Indeed, there is an intense debate between the advocates of 'numerical taxonomy' and 'cladistics' as to the principles of taxonomy. See J.M. Smith, 'Dinosaur dilemmas', *New York Review of Books*, 25 April, 1991.

10. Mulkay makes the fascinating point that the single most prestigious biological theory had its origins in a rejected social theory first expounded by Malthus in the preceding century. See Mulkay's *Science and the Sociology of Knowledge*, London, Allen & Unwin, 1979.

11. Another good and worked-through example is to be found in M. Goldstein and I. Goldstein, *The Experience of Science*, New York, Plenum, 1984, in their discussion of Snow's discovery of how cholera was transmitted, and its importance in discrediting the then plausible 'effluvia' theory of the transmission of disease. His work was important in laying down the foundations of the later germ theory of contagious diseases.

12. The term 'corpus' might imply that there is a strongly identifiable and determinable unity to the knowledge of a discipline. This is far from being the case. Any attention to the state of a discipline at any one point in time will show some problems being picked up, others dropped, others ignored, in a shifting kaleidoscope of activities.

13. See R.J. Anderson, J.A. Hughes and W.W. Sharrock, *The Sociology Game: An Introduction to Sociological Reasoning*, London, Longman, 1985, for a discussion of the idea of sociology, and philosophy, as argument subjects.

14. The literature on the philosophy of science and social science is voluminous. See, for example, J.A. Hughes, *The Philosophy of Social Research*, 2nd rev. and enl. edn, London, Longman, 1990.

15. The originator of this was K. Popper in his *Logic of Scientific Discovery*, London, Hutchinson, 1959. See also Hughes, *op.cit.*, for an exposition of Popper's ideas and their connection to more recent philosophies of science. See also, R.J. Anderson, J.A. Hughes and W.W. Sharrock, *Philosophy and the Human Sciences*, London, Croom Helm, 1983.

16. These developments owe much to the work of Thomas Kuhn, *The Structure of Scientific Revolutions*, 2nd edn, Chicago, University of Chicago Press, 1970. See also his 'Second thoughts on paradigms', in F. Suppe (ed.) *The Structure of Scientific Theories*, Urbana, University of Illinois Press, 1974.

17. See R.J. Anderson, J.A. Hughes and W.W. Sharrock, (eds) *Classic disputes in Sociology,* London, Allen and Unwin, 1987, for a review of some of these philosophies.

18. This is, of course, debatable within philosophy and within the social sciences themselves where many see the solution to philosophical problems as the key to making progress in social scientific knowledge.

19. This is the burden of argument of the newer sociologies of science in its inquiries into the social bases of science. We are not implying here that there is any sort of conspiracy to take a subject in a particular direction. One of the features of any science is that, at certain times, particular problems predominate for perfectly respectable intellectual reasons and these tend to be those in which scientific eminence is likely to be gained so that, naturally, many scientists gravitate toward doing research on these problems. See, for example, selections in B. Barnes and D. Edge (eds) *Science in Context*, Milton Keynes, Open University Press, 1982, and B.

Barnes, *Interests and the Growth of Knowledge*, London, Routledge & Kegan Paul, 1977.

20. See M. Bulmer, *The Chicago School of Sociology: Institutionalisation, Diversity and the Rise of Sociological Research*, Chicago, University of Chicago Press, 1984, for an interesting account of how and why Chicago became the foremost research and massively influential department in the first quarter of the twentieth century.

21. L. Stone, *The Family, Sex and Marriage in England, 1500–1800*, London, Weidenfeld & Nicolson, 1977.

22. See P. Bridgeman, *The Logic of Modern Physics*, New York, Macmillan, 1937. More recently, R. Pawson, *A Measure for Measure: A Manifesto for Empirical Sociology*, London, Routledge, 1989.

23. See, for example, A. Bryman, 'The debate about quantitative and qualitative research: a question of method and epistemology', *British Journal of Sociology*, 35, 1984, pp. 75–92; D. Silverman, *Qualitative Methodology and Sociology*, Aldershot, Gower, 1985.

24. E. Durkheim, *Suicide*, trans. J. Spaulding and G. Simpson, London, Routledge & Kegan Paul, 1952.

25. See, for example, J.M. Atkinson, *Discovering Suicide*, London, Macmillan, 1978, for an extended discussion of these issues. Also P. Eglin, 'The meaning and use of official statistics in the explanation of deviance', in R.J. Anderson, J.A. Hughes and W.W. Sharrock (eds) *Classic Disputes in Sociology*, London, Allen & Unwin, 1987, pp. 184–212.

26. See Eglin, *op.cit.*, and also, for a different view, B. Hindess, *The Use of Official Statistics*, London, Macmillan, 1973.

27. Taken from Silverman, *op.cit.* p. 34.

28. This owes much to the work of P.F. Lazarsfeld. See, for example, 'A conceptual introduction to latent structure analysis' in his edited volume, *Mathematical Thinking in the Social Sciences*, Glencoe, Free Press, 1954.

29. I. Lakatos and A. Musgrave (eds) *Criticism and the Growth of Knowledge*, Cambridge, Cambridge University Press, 1970. For a review see Hughes, *op.cit.*

30. See, for example, J.H. Goldthorpe, D. Lockwood, F. Bechhofer and J. Platt, *The Affluent Worker: Industrial Attitudes and Behaviour*, Cambridge, Cambridge University Press, 1968; and the companion volume, *The Affluent Worker in the Class Structure*, Cambridge, Cambridge University Press, 1969.

31. See, for an alternative view, D. Zimmerman and M. Pollner, 'The everyday world as phenomenon', in J.D. Douglas (ed.) *Understanding Everyday Life*, London, Routledge & Kegan Paul, 1974.

32. See, for example, J. Coulter, *Mind in Action*, New Jersey, Humanities Press, 1989, for a review of some of the arguments here.

Variable analysis and social measurement

What we intend to do in this chapter is discuss the inferential structure that forms the backbone of many of the methods of data collection currently in use. Although, and it is important to stress this, most of these methods arose and developed from a diverse range of sources and traditions, their contemporary unity was a rather later achievement, as that collection of ideas we can refer to as variable analysis. Broadly expressed, variable analysis is the disposition to see and describe social life as a collection of variables which, potentially, can be quantified and the relationships between them also measured and described in quantitative terms. These days it is not unreasonable to present variable analysis as a relatively coherent approach to social research, some would say *the* approach, which embraces not only the technical matters to do with data collection and analysis but also, importantly, a way of thinking about theoretical and empirical problems. Some go so far, though this is an excessive claim, as to argue that variable analysis is the embodiment of the scientific method, while more, if less fulsomely, do make strong claims for it as the epitome of objective, rigorous empirical social research against which all others are to be judged. While we do not wish to go even this far, there is no doubt that it represents a powerfully persuasive tradition of social research. It is often equated with the explanatory social survey (as we shall see in Chapter 4) and although this may well be its prime expression, the logic and the impulse of variable analysis is somewhat wider than this being devoted to securing a more general basis for quantification in social research. A separate section in this chapter is devoted to the topic of measurement itself.

The key figure in the initiation and development of variable analysis was Paul F. Lazarsfeld, who worked at Columbia University from the 1930s to the 1950s and who, with colleagues such as Stouffer, Thurstone, Rosenberg and Guttman, pioneered what was to become the orthodox mode of social research. Their work had a considerable impact on both the thinking and the practice of social research, including some of the highly mathematised branches of social research. Indeed, as far as the latter are concerned a direct line of descent can be traced from the work of Lazarsfeld and his colleagues to the modern mathematical and statistical modelling of social data. Many of the techniques that came to be associated with variable analysis, the survey, cross-tabulation, indicators, covariation, to mention but a few, were not all invented by Lazarsfeld and his co-workers, though a number were, but begged, borrowed and stolen, from a variety of other fields and brought together as a distinctive and integrated way of constituting a theoretically informed and theoretically consequential empirical social research approach.[1] Of course, what became this major achievement did not happen overnight. Rather, it evolved in fits and starts as its various components were deployed in a variety of areas producing what quickly became classic studies and the base line for a growing corpus of social research findings. Here, it seemed, was a method capable of testing theoretically generated hypotheses by expressing the hypothesised relationship between two or more factors quantitatively and, so it was assumed, objectively. These days, of course, the relatively primitive Lazarsfeldian methods have grown into the full mathematical eloquence of causal modelling, factor and cluster analysis, and more, encouraged by the power of the modern computer to handle larger and larger data sets and their mathematical analysis.

However, Lazarsfeld, though primarily a methodologist, was no mere technician. He had briefly been involved with the Logical Positivists of the Vienna Circle and developed a strong leaning toward the importance of systematic empirical observation as the cornerstone of the scientific method, and a corresponding dislike of abstracted theorising and metaphysical speculation. Despite his European background he developed a detached, almost apolitical style of social research. For him, and ultimately consequential as one of the prime presuppositions of variable analysis, science does not deal with 'things-in-themselves' but with their manifested properties or attributes. It is the attributes or properties of some phenomenon that are exhibited, revealed, discovered and which are measured; never the 'thing-in-itself'. Science does not deal with its objects of study in their full concreteness.[2] Science's empirical connection to the world is an abstracted, or selective, one dealing with the properties, attributes or qualities of phenomena rather than with the phenomena themselves. We do not, for a simple example, examine heat directly but through, for instance, the property it has of causing certain metals to expand at uniform rates: a property which enables us to construct mercury thermometers which are capable, within reasonably precise limits, of measuring heat. In which case, and on this conception, a great deal of scientific activity, including its laws and theories, is concerned to measure and, through this, examine the observable properties of phenomena. Again for example, the property of heat to expand metal at uniform rates is a great advance on the common sense distinction between 'hot' and 'cold'. We can now speak of quantities of heat and use this to develop better and better theories and laws of thermodynamics. Developing better and more precise measurement of the properties of phenomena is the key to the progress of scientific knowledge.[3] But this process is two way: it is also better theories which allow us to develop more precise measurement.

In this respect the human sciences should be no different. Where they do differ is that they know a great deal less about the properties of social and psychological phenomena than do the natural sciences about the properties of the natural world. There were, and still are of course, immense difficulties in the way of quantifying human phenomena, some of which we shall touch on later. None the less, since antiquity there have been many efforts to describe features of the world, including the social, in quantitative terms, efforts which began to assume an even greater urgency and consequentiality with the rise of the modern nation state and its requirements for an accurate accounting of its resources.[4] The modern census is but one expression of this movement, as well as the development and vastly increased scope of economic statistics and other methods of social accounting. But none of these efforts, important as they were, amounted to a mathematised science in which theoretical relationships could be expressed mathematically or, less ambitiously, subjected to stricter testing through measurement. Nevertheless, a start needed to be made somewhere to build a cumulative and objective body of knowledge of the relationships between the properties of social phenomena as a prelude to the formulation of substantial theoretical laws. They did this by emphasising the development of measurement scales by which data could be systematically organised and available for various forms of mathematical manipulation. What was at stake was not merely organising data in this way, but this was an inferential structure that could be used to accumulate knowledge systematically and, little by little, develop laws of social life. It was to building this basis that Lazarsfeld and his colleagues devoted much of their energies.

Up to the 1930s the bulk of quantitative social research had been largely demographic in character. Although Durkheim had made use of official statistics and standardised arithmetic procedures, such as averages and percentages, for theoretical purposes, the connections he made between the data and his theoretical conclusions were largely impressionistic if, from his point of view, effective enough.[5] It was due to scholars such as Lazarsfeld in providing a logic of social research which encouraged the making of the connection between research problems in biology, particularly eugenics, which had stimulated the development of inductive statistics, and those of social research. This led to the incorporation of statistical techniques of inference into empirical social science.

None the less, it had to be faced that most, if not all, social science theories, with the possible exception of those of economics, left a great deal to be desired if quantification on the natural science model was to be achieved.[6] Most theories were little more or less-than an integrated set of concepts or too impossibly abstract to have much direct relevance for social research. The only route to more empirically grounded theories, according to what became the Lazarsfeldian programme of social research, was to develop suitably confirmed empirical generalisations across a range of studies and problem areas, and this would require the effective translation of concepts into empirical indicators; translate, that is, concepts into the publicly observable. To achieve this Lazarsfeld borrowed a notion from mathematics and logic, that of the variable, and used it to create a way of thinking about social science in both its theoretical and empirical aspects.

THE IDEA OF THE VARIABLE

Thinking of social organisation and processes in terms of variables is now commonplace. It is a common strategy, for example, to think of analysing or decomposing a construct into a number of dimensions or variables. A well-known example is Merton's suggestion that there are degrees of conformity to cultural goals, differences in the willingness of groups to innovate, and so on. The device of constructing typologies to distinguish and, then, compare and contrast phenomena, as well as efforts to measure such differences through organising relevant data, is a predominant feature of sociological thinking and research. Typologies such as traditionalism, rationalism, affectivity, industrialism, and many, many more, all reflect what is now known as variable analytic thinking.[7] So common is this way of thinking in social research that it is difficult to recapture its radical and innovative character. It is a way of thinking that is predominant in social research and to a considerable extent in social theory, too. For many, one of its important features is that, as a method, it is theoretically unspecific. It belongs to no particular approach but is a means of linking theory with empirical analysis to the betterment of theory. The basic requirement of the approach is to think about concepts as empirical variables which can be measured through indices. This enables the data to be searched for patterns so placing theories within the constraints of empirical evidence. Indeed, it is through data collection and searching for patterns in those data that theory is elaborated.

Lazarsfeld's contribution to the development of variable analysis was pivotal both as thinker and as teacher. His idea was that social phenomena can and should be measured in a way similar to the way physical properties, such as size, weight and temperature, are measured. He recognised that the metrication of these properties had to be constructed, that measuring devices, or units of measurement, had to be devised, and so it should be for social and psychological phenomena. On the Lazarsfeldian conception, people, or any unit for that matter, can be treated as objects displaying properties such as age, gender, social class, status, intelligence, attitudes or beliefs. But the trick was to think of these properties as mappable; that is, capable of being thought of as dimensions in space. To this end he used a metaphor drawn from mathematics, the variable, to create 'devices by which we can characterize the objects of empirical social investigation'.[8] The idea of a variable is simple enough. A variable, as opposed to a constant, is anything, any attribute, that can vary in value; that is, take at least two values. Such values can be 0 or 1, where 0 might indicate the absence of some property, and 1 its presence.[9] Thus, if a researcher was interested in the property of home ownership, 1 might indicate a 'home owner' and 0 a 'non-owner'. This is a very minimal level of quantification, if quantification at all, but at least we can add the frequency with which these values occur within some collection of persons. We could describe the distribution of the property among some population. If, in addition, we had a similar frequency count of another property, say level of income, and looked at their mutual distribution, their covariation in a word, we can see how strongly the two properties, the two variables, are related. Of course, other concepts, other properties and attributes, could make more significant use of the properties of number systems other than their ability to classify. 'Power', for example, is an ordinal attribute in which we might want to talk about individuals having 'more' or 'less' power than others and to reflect this in using the power of numbers to reflect 'more' or 'less' of some attribute in the same way that a higher number score on a test signifies a greater ability to do the test than a lower number. The point is that by thinking of concepts as variables we also begin to think of suitable ways of reflecting their character by numbers.

In significant respects, Lazarsfeld's proposals were both bold and radical. The route to quantification, he urged, could be secured through the notion of the variable; a format that could be applied not simply to properties which were self-evidently quantitative, such as money, but also to qualitative materials. By simply recording the presence or the absence of some property a level of quantification could be attained; certainly sufficient to allow for the examination of the joint frequency and occurrence of a property with others. One could go further and try to rank order properties, such as 'power' and 'status', which would give a yet higher level of measurement.

But the idea of the variable was only part of the revolution. What Lazarsfeld was after was a way of searching for patterns in data, patterns exhibited between variables, and patterns that, if confirmed regularly across studies, could stand as statements of empirical relationships between phenomena. Thus, we could begin to provide statements of the form 'The greater the X, the greater the Y', 'A's are associated with B's', 'Q is inversely related to P', and so on: statements which would be supported by, and indeed describe, quantitative relationships. To see this we need to look more closely at the essentially simple idea, taken from mathematics, of the property space.[10] A property space is simply a conceptually bounded area defined by one or more properties. Location in this space can be indicated by means of coordinates, a technique familiar to map-making, graphs, gunnery, navigation, and more. In a two-dimensional space, for example as on this printed page, every point can be fixed, and fixed uniquely, by two numbers derived from the scales measuring of the length and the breadth of the page. However, the dimensions on which we can locate units, such as people, in some property space can be of different kinds and certainly of more than two dimensions. We can use continuous variables, such as psychological test scores, qualitative variables, such as occupational type, or dichotomous variables such as voter/non-voter, male/female. Thus, if we take a unit and an attribute of that unit, say a person and home ownership, the property space is defined by two values: being a home owner and not being a home owner. These are the values the property can take and can be, as before, denoted as 1 and 0 respectively. If, for the same unit, we take another property, say trade union membership, then, similarly, this property space is defined as trade union member – not trade union member. Therefore, each unit can be classified in terms of these properties and can take one of four combined values: home owner/trade unionist; home owner/not trade unionist; not home owner/trade unionist; not home owner/not trade unionist. Each unit, that is, is uniquely described in terms of these properties by one, and only one, of the above categories. If we display the property space formed by these attributes with each attribute constituting an axis, then we arrive at Figure 3.1.

Figure 3.1 Property space of homeownership and trade union membership

	Home owner	Non-home owner
Member of trade union		
Not member of trade union		

Figure 3.1 shows the joint variation of the two properties we have been talking about, and, of course, the possible values which any unit can take. Each unit in some population can be allocated uniquely to one of the cells so giving, providing that we count the number of units

in each cell, the frequency with which combinations of the relevant properties occur. In social research this is the basic structure of the cross-tabulation or contingency table. As Lazarsfeld urged, cross-tabulation is the 'automatic' research procedure employed in social research when faced with a relationship between two or more variables.[11]

In actual social research such tables are generally more complex than the one illustrated here, often involving 'higher' levels of measurement than the simple dichotomous attributes in the example. None the less, they are based on this simple inferential structure which is the core of variable analysis. The point of the structure is to find patterns of relationship among variables; patterns which can, hopefully, become established empirical generalisations and, ultimately, strongly established theoretical laws. However, it is important to stress that this latter ambition is not one that Lazarsfeld, for one, felt could be quickly fulfilled. Variable analysis is very much a beginning by presenting theory with reasonably well-confirmed empirical relationships upon which to work. It offered, too, a way of testing hypotheses and theoretical predictions by providing a method for detecting whether patterns hypothesised by some theory were, in fact, supportive.

But, prior to any of the deployment of the inferential structure is the crucial issue of what properties, what variables to examine and how to reflect their character in measurement. For the Lazarsfeldian programme this is a matter, though not a simple one, of selecting and refining indices.

VARIABLES, PROPERTIES AND INDICES

Of course, aspects of social life have been measured for almost as long as history. Duncan reminds us of the antiquity of the propensity to quantify the doings of people in various ways.[12] There has long been the counting of people as one of the first activities of states (as we shall see in Chapter 4). There are voting, taxation, efforts to measure and record social rank, attempts to fix standards for weights and measures, and above all, money. Money is one of the more fascinating of social inventions which depends on counting as a capacity to express, in a word, measure, the social value of individuals, labour and commodities in society. The measurement of length, area, distance, weight, and such like, was achieved long ago as an integral part of day-to-day practical activities, and later to be refined within the context of modern science. It was within the latter context, that Lazarsfeld and his colleagues sought to apply a generic conception of measurement to social phenomena as a means of effecting the link between theorical concepts and the empirical world.

Lazarsfeld recognised that social science theories, currently and for the foreseeable future, could simply not match up to those on offer in the natural sciences. There were no adequate generalisations to build on, let alone laws, and certainly few, if any, solidly confirmed hypotheses. It was not so much a case of social science theories being senseless, misguided or absurd, but more to do with their serious lack of evidential support. What they had by way of this was largely impressionistic, qualitative and suggestive rather than confirmatory. This did not make such theories false, but it did prevent them being seriously developed as scientific theories. The only way forward was to develop the tools of empirical research, measurement scales to facilitate the description, aggregation and comparison of data; to provide good, solidly based findings on the lines just sketched. For Lazarsfeld, the research process began with a problem and a 'vague image' of some relevant concepts and their interrelationships. It was this 'vague image' which had to be translated into a form which could be explored, even tested, empirically using the pattern-searching techniques of variable analysis. And this meant translating the concepts into empirical indicators.

Take a common sociological concept, that of social class. This is a concept which belongs to a number of well-known sociological theories, including those of Marx, Weber and many commentators since. What we have are a number of ideas of what social class is as a phenomenon, sometimes overlapping, sometimes divergent. Marx, for one example, regarded class in capitalist society as a collection of persons who have in common a particular relationship to the means of production, namely, that of ownership or non-ownership. The bourgeoisie class own the means of production, the proletariat do not. Weber, on the other hand, while agreeing that class had much to do with a person's economic position within a social organisation of capital and labour, departed from this dualistic conception. For him a class was about life chances and included dimensions other than the ownership and non-ownership of the means of production. This alone could not take into account the much finer distinctions that it is necessary to look at when determining social class. Weber also gave more emphasis to status as a factor which, in some circumstances, could override the effects of class on social behaviour and ideas, often to the point of diminishing them entirely.

What we have here is a range of differences and similarities concerning a concept, and putative phenomena connected with it, that both scholars, and many more since, have argued and disputed over. But on the Lazarsfeldian view theoretical debate without systematically provided empirical evidence is essentially sterile not to say unscientific. It is, like most of the concepts in social science, a contested, relatively vague one that can only be made less vague, of greater theoretical relevance through systematic empirical exploration.[13] The task is to generate indicators of the concepts in order to see better just what empirical relationships the phenomena pointed to by the concept of class might be.

Thus, it is reasonable to argue, instead of trying to determine what class is by theoretical disputation, let us recognise that what we have here is a concept which probably indicates something significant about social behaviour, but precisely what that is is not clear. It has something to do with a person's occupation, the control and autonomy a person has, the amount of training required in order to do a particular job, the way occupation shapes life chances, income, style of life, the kind of social activities engaged in, the prestige a particular occupation attracts from others, and may be more. So, one reason why 'class' is a 'vague' and contested concept is because it is multi-faceted and, as a result, it is not always clear just what possible dimension, attribute or property is being used. Such problems, on the Lazarsfeldian view, can be sorted and clarified empirically only by, in this case, formulating indicators for each of the possible dimensions of the concept. Indeed, on the Lazarsfeldian conception we do not need to know what class really is. All we require is a collection of reasonable indicators which represent, to some degree which may be unknown, the concept of class. It is the behaviour of the indicators which enables us to unravel the conceptual and definitional ambiguities.

This process of elaborating a concept and moving toward empirical indicators is the crucial step in variable analysis. It is nothing less than the invocation of a two-language model of social scientific inquiry: that of theory and that of research; that of concepts and that of variables. Theoretical ideas are connected to the world by a translation into an empirical language more closely attuned to the observable world. The language of theory would be built using the terms and semantics of the language of observation. In a word or two, it is an empiricist strategy of theory construction and testing.

Of course, the choice of indicators is not a straightforward business even though, these days, there are available a number of fairly standard ones, such as occupation as an indicator of social class.[14] In fact, any concept is likely to generate a number of indicators with no very clear idea, in advance of empirical inquiry, what they 'stand for'. What Lazarsfeld proposed was essentially a trial-and-error process of winnowing out the poor, if promising, indicators of a concept in favour of ones which proved effective across studies. Finding patterns of association among indicators will enable us to determine which among them are the most significant.

It is important to recognise that the research itself, and its setting, inflicts its own contingencies on the choice of indicators: research using interviews will have to use indicators that are largely constructed out of respondents' answers to questionnaire items whereas observational studies, and Lazarsfeld did not preclude them from variable analysis in principle, would have to use others.[15] Similarly, depending on the setting, some concepts would require different indicators entirely.

It is not proposed that in every case a single indicator will suffice for a concept on every occasion, and it is not suggested that in every case an indicator will fully represent the concept it is to 'stand for'. The relationship between an indicator and the property of the underlying phenomenon it represents is a probabilistic one, though the parameters of the relationship are unknown since the phenomenon itself can never be directly inspected. It is made visible only through its indicators. However, this is no reason for despair since it is by examining and measuring the relationship between indicators that researchers can begin to get a better idea of what are good and what are poor indicators. If a number of studies are able to show that occupational type shows consistently stronger correlations with other variables, say voting choice, style of life, level of education or values, this is evidence that the variable occupation is a reasonably effective indicator of the important dimensions embodied in the concept of social class. It is some evidence, that is, that the concept of social class points to a real phenomenon with stable properties as reflected in the empirical relationships among the various indicators. Matters do not, of course, end there. Science is importantly a cumulative endeavour fuelled by a trial-and-error process of refining theories so moving toward theories of greater scope and explanatory power.

Of course, it may turn out that what these empirical relationships show is that some or all of the original theories were wrong or, at least, insufficiently precise. But this eventuality is exactly what variable analysis is intended to show. Effective theory building is from discovered empirical patterns or relationships. Armchair theorising may be a useful preliminary, a source of what may turn out to be interesting ideas, but for science to begin it must be secured to empirical results and its theories determined by them.

The connection between the world and the indices is effected by means of the interrelationships between indices and the strength and durability they display, if they do, from study to study. Indicators are, on this conception, what social research works with and they indicate something, however well or badly, if they show detectable patterns of association with each other.

As it happened, Lazarsfeld and his colleagues recognised that it was, and still is, difficult to develop indicators for many concepts used in social science. However, asking people to express attitudes was a relatively straightforward way of producing a large number of indicators on almost any subject that was of interest. Attitudes could be elicited aplenty and could, contra the views of many of the early survey researchers who thought them unlikely material for social research in being basically subjective opinions, provide valuable data if suitably measured. The key to this was developing attitude scales, many of them named after the researchers who devised them.[16] One consequence of this for social research (as opposed to psychology) was to make it very dependent on the survey as a means of data collection. As we shall see in Chapter 4, one of the first results of these ideas was to transform the social survey.

THE LOGIC OF PATTERN SEARCHING

The inferential structure of the pattern searching method of variable analysis made use of the idea of the property space and the covariation of property attributes. It also made more than passing obeisance to the logic of the experiment which, for many and wrongly, was taken as the *sine qua non* of the scientific method.[17] The great advances in producing the laws of physical science had come about through the application of a method, one which systematically simplified the messiness of the appearances of the world, to produce the pristine laws of natural science.[18] The experiment was regarded as the embodiment of that method. Essentially, the classic experimental design involves controlling all factors extraneous to the hypothesis of interest in order that this can be tested. It was realised that the ability to experiment in the human sciences was extremely limited for a number of practical and ethical reasons. Apart from branches of psychology, laboratory experiments in which factors were manipulated in order to achieve the necessary control were clearly impracticable when dealing with, say, the effects of educational attainment on voting choice. None the less, variable analysis was seen to offer a surrogate way of using the logic of experimental design engineered from the idea of the property space.

Imagine that we are interested in the effect of a new managerial style on output. In variable analysis the managerial style would be called the 'independent variable', or causal factor, and the output, or the effect, the 'dependent variable'. The simplest way would be to introduce the style and then see whether or not output increased or decreased or, even, stayed where it was. However, we know that there are potentially many factors other than managerial style, which could affect output: a more satisfied work-force, a better trained and more experienced work-force, increased pay for higher productivity, more investment in up-to-date machinery, greater morale among the work-force, and so on. Accordingly, to be sure that changes in managerial style have the effect found we need to take into account the actual or potential effects of all these other factors on the dependent variable, output. In the classic experimental design a control group would be used which was as alike in all respects to the experimental group (the latter being, in this example, the workers who experienced the new managerial style), save in this one respect; only the experimental group is subjected to the independent variable. In which case, if all the other factors have been adequately controlled, any difference in output has to be attributable to the independent variable since it is the only difference between the two groups.

In practice, of course, it is extremely difficult to establish such a design effectively. Normally a control group and an experimental group are constituted deliberately by matching subjects on relevant characteristics and then randomly allocating one of each matched pair to the control or the experimental group respectively. In this example, such an endeavour could prove practically very difficult, as it is in most social situations. Moreoever, even if one were to do this the fact of setting up the control and the experimental groups could well introduce a note of artificiality into the experiment.

None the less, for variable analysis such problems are by no means the end of the matter since the logic exemplified in the experiment can, it is argued, be replicated, at least sufficiently, by multivariate analytic procedures involving statistical controls. In multivariate procedures the controls are deployed as potential intervening variables. Such methods will be dealt with more fully in Chapter 4 on social surveys where the Lazarsfeldian conception became most firmly entrenched.

With hindsight, it is difficult to see quite the radical innovation variable analysis proved to be in social research. Its advent was auspicious in that following the Second World War the strenuous efforts of many social scientists, especially in the United States, to secure a more acceptable place for social science, which itself contributed to many of the techniques which became part of variable analysis, was served by a way of thinking which seemed to offer a way of emulating some of the crucial features of the scientific method. Sociologists, social psychologists, anthropologists and economists began to use and develop variable analysis in a series of what became classic studies. Lazarsfeld's own contribution lay in the study of voting choice and the studies on the effects of the mass media and, during the Second World War, collaborating on studies of Nazi propaganda and race relations, among others. These had a major impact in Britain and elsewhere and form the beginning of subsequent studies. Statistical analysis also developed apace making use of statistical theories which had their origins earlier in the century in the work of Pearson especially. Variable analysis welcomed, indeed required, an un-ashamed borrowing of regression and correlational statistics and, later, building these into causal models in which the weight of the effects of various variables could be determined.[19]

Of course, none of these developments took place overnight, but their growth to some maturity had much to do with the promise variable analysis held out that this was the route toward the scientific respectability of social research methods. Lazarsfeld's ingenious, if ultimately flawed, step toward the basis of quantification in social research, provided, for some at least, a realistic hope that social research, through measurement and hypothesis testing, could begin to develop serious empirically based theories.[20] It was not without its critics, of course. Symbolic interactionists were trenchant in their attack on variable analysis largely because of its failure to provide a sense of the processual and negotiated character of social life. For those, talk of variables smacked too much of talk of causes with no place for the human being as agent. (This particular criticism we shall deal with later, especially in Chapter 6.) For now we wish to go into some detail on one of the major planks of variable analysis, namely measurement.

MEASUREMENT AND VARIABLE ANALYSIS

The history of social measurement is a long and fascinating one, certainly too considerable to do justice to here. Our more immediate concern in this section is with measurement as understood within variable analysis. Variable analysis stipulates that the phenomena of social research be reflected in objective, observable indicators which 'stand for' the phenomenon. No direct inspection of phenomena is possible; they can be investigated only through their indicators. The problem here is an obvious one and has already been alluded to, namely how do we know how good an indicator is if we cannot compare the phenomenon with the indicator? The answer is that we cannot know or, rather, that there is no simple solution to this problem. All we have is a process of trial and error which, essentially, consists in seeing how well a particular indicator correlates with other indicators of the same concept and with other indicators of concepts presumed to be related in some causal connection. This process of refinement within and across studies will, it is argued, slowly build up our confidence that the indicators which work are measuring something, some phenomenon, that our concepts point to. This is never once and for all, but slowly and more or less surely.

The refinement of concepts and the steady march of trial and error depends upon not only thinking up good indicators for our concepts, but also on measuring them appropriately. Measurement is, in many ways, the point of variable analysis and is its inferential backbone. Measurement, and the reason why Lazarsfeld was so insistent on developing a social research format that permitted even a modest level of quantification, is one of the procedures that facilitates the mathematisation of theory, a feature which is the hallmark of the most advanced of the natural sciences, such as physics. A standard model of the progress of science sees it as a move from classificatory knowledge to knowledge which is more quantitative in character and able to express its laws in precise mathematical form. Quantification provides greater descriptive flexibility and subtlety than simple classification. Instead of 'warm' and 'cold', temperature scales allow for much finer distinctions. Relative ordering is possible; we can say that 70°F is warmer than 60°F. Greater descriptive flexibility makes for a greater flexibility in the formulation of laws. An increase in the temperature of a column of mercury accompanied by a proprotionate increase in the height of the column would be impossible to state precisely using classificatory concepts. Measurement opens up the possibility of using mathematics in which to state general laws and theories such as the relation between the height of the column of mercury and its temperature.[21] So, the advantages of rendering properties measurable, as contrasted with simple classifications, are manifested in both the descriptive and explanatory functions of science – if it can be achieved.

For our purposes, measurement can be characterised as the assignment of numbers to some property in such a way as to effect a one-to-one correspondence between the character of the numbers and the characteristics of the property being measured. For brevity, and without going into the axioms of the mathematics of number, the main features of numbers we need to note are order, distance and origin. Numbers are serially ordered (1,2,3,4 ... *n*) as are the differences between numbers so that, for example, the distance between any pair of numbers is greater than, equal to, or less than the difference between any other pair of numbers. The distance between 0 and 5 is equal to that between 5 and 10. The number series also has a unique origin indicated by the number 0. Accordingly, if it is possible to establish the necessary correspondence between these characteristics and the property of concern, then relationships between the numbers should reflect the relation between objects with respect to the property being measured. We could, to suggest an example, determine whether *A* has more, or less, or equal power, status, intelligence, or whatever, to *B*, assuming, that is, that we have suitable measures for these properties. If we can satisfy the stringent requirements of the number system then we have established a scale of measurement.

However, mapping the characteristics of the number system on to some property is not to be had for the wishing. One has only to think of the time it took and what was necessary to develop the now largely taken-for-granted temperature scales; an effort involving not only technological developments, but also developments in physics, thermodynamics, mathematics, and more. That the social sciences are a long way from devising scales which even approximate to the temperature scale is not to be wondered at. Nevertheless, this does not mean that measurement in the social sciences is impossible since, as Lazarsfeld endeavoured to establish, even lower levels of measurement offer a beginning.

The founder of the theory of scales which is commonly used as the basis for social measurement is the psychologist S.S. Stevens, whose ideas began to crystallise in the 1940s in response to a challenge issued, in 1932, by physicists and psychologists of the British Association for the Advancement of Science to 'assess the possibility of "quantitative estimates of sensory events"'.[22] Stevens identified four types of measurement scales: nominal, ordinal, interval and ratio scales.[23] The first of these, nominal scales, which some would argue do not involve measurement in any strict sense of this term, are classificatory schemes and are fundamental to any level of measurement. In classifying the aim is to sort objects by their selected properties into homogeneous categories. Placing individuals in the categories 'male' or 'female', 'working class' or 'middle class' are cases in point, though nominal scales need not be restricted to dichotomies. As long as the categories are exhaustive and mutually exclusive, the minimal conditions for the application of some counting or statistical procedure are met. Thus, if we have placed people into the various categories 'male' or 'female' we can count the frequency of the cases in each. Formally nominal scales have the properties of symmetry and transitivity. Symmetry means that a relation holding between A and B also holds between B and A, and transitivity that if $A=B$ and $B=C$, then $A=C$. Taken together these properties mean that if A is in the same class, or category, as B, B is in the same category as A, and that if A and B are in the same category, and B and C, then A and C are in the same class. These, complicated and ponderous though they may seem, are the basic rules of classification. What they are not, of course, are rules for the assignment of some number system. Although numerical values may be arbitrarily assigned to various categories, the standard arithmetic operations of addition, subtraction, multiplication and division are not permissible, though the frequency of cases within categories can be calculated. But, and to repeat the point, in assigning cases to a category one is not measuring the property except in some very truncated sense of the term.

Ordinal scales are used where it is possible to order cases in respect of the degree to which they exhibit a certain property or quality, even though it may not be possible to state precisely how much of that property they have. Socio-economic status is one such property where we can classify individuals as having 'more' or 'less' status but not be able to say how much more or how much less status one person has with respect to another. Formally, ordinal scales are asymmetrical in that if A is greater than B, B cannot be greater than A.[24] Transitivity still holds in that if A is greater than B, and B is greater than C, then A is greater than C. It is these properties which enable us to order cases along a continuum. But it is important to note that since nothing can be said about the magnitudes of the differences between the various elements along the continuum, none of the standard arithmetic operations can legitimately be used.

It is with interval and ratio scales that we reach a level of measurement which allows us to use the standard arithmetic operations. Not only can cases be ranked but also we know the distances between the rankings. What this requires is an agreed upon standard of measurement such that we can say that we have a unit of measurement and can give a precise quantitative expression to distances between the various points. Further, if it is also possible to locate an absolute zero point, scores can be compared by taking their ratios to assert, for example, that one score is twice as high as another. Also, we can transform one scale into another. Another property, concatenation, arises when we can add measures together: a feature which attaches only to ratio scales. The amount of money is a good example. This type of scale has a non-arbitrary zero point of 'no money', and we can add figures for the amount of money with respect to a particular unit be it a person, a country or a firm. Thus, we can add the joint income of husband and wife to obtain a total for that unit, whatever we choose to call it, whereas we cannot sensibly add their separate statuses to achieve a joint status for both of them unless we know a great deal more about how status is a distributive phenomenon and what its properties are. Ratio scales, to remind ourselves, contain all the properties of ordinal and interval scales with the additional one that they can be transformed one into another. The best known of such a transformation is probably that for turning Celsius temperature into Fahrenheit where F=32+9/70C, or, for another example, a conversion formula for turning imperial weights into metric ones.

These requirements represent an attempt mainly by social and psychological researchers to formalise the conditions for measurement in the social sciences, and one that has been remarkably successful judging by the extent to which such scale types are taken as the standard fare for methods training. There is a recognition in the notion of scale types that any effort to measure human attributes, be they psychological traits, attitudes or social properties, is unlikely to attain the standards of measurement typical of the natural sciences; indeed, they are seldom used in their most developed form. Basically, devising a scale involves three stages. The first is to generate a large number of test items designed to indicate the supposed social or attitudinal attribute. In a scale of authoritarianism (an example we shall look at in Chapter 4), a large number of items designed to produce responses that might be judged more or less 'authoritarian' are devised. These are tested in a number of ways to cull out those that seem less than clear or ambiguous, then they have to be scaled. The Thurstone procedure involves judges ranking the test items on a scale from 'most authoritarian' to 'least authoritarian' to establish which items are most indicative of different degrees of authoritarian sentiment. Finally, the test items selected are weighted accordingly and used in research contexts to discriminate groups of different degrees of authoritarianism and search for any correlates which might explain such differences.

The vast majority of social research employs ordinal data or, more rarely, the interval scale: even in such cases it is doubtful whether even the most developed of such scales actually satisfy the requirements. For example, even with the widely used psychological scales, such as those for measuring intelligence or extroversion, we cannot be sure that an IQ of 145 points is really greater than one of 144. As psychologists will readily admit, such scales are unreliable at the extremes because the cases they measure are so rare that the scales cannot be adequately calibrated.

However, even the best of these efforts, and they are perhaps in their fully fledged forms used more in psychology than in social research, do not reach up to the standards of measurement used in science or, less ambitiously, the higher levels of measurement represented by interval and ratio scales. None the less, for the inferential structure of variable analysis *some* level of quantification is required. This is precisely what the apparatus is designed to achieve. The very idea of the variable draws upon an analogy with the highly abstract structure of mathematics in which variables and constants are objects in a mathematical domain operated upon by the appropriate rules for manipulation. To apply a mathematical system, as in measurement, objects in the target domain (for brevity we can call this the social world) must be mapped on to objects, that is numbers, in the mathematical domain. If the mapping is successful then manipulation of the mathematics is equivalent to manipulation of the objects in the target domain. This is, for illustration, exactly what is done in a voting system. Each vote is weighted 1 and by adding, that is manipulating the numbers according to the rules of arithmetic, the result of the election is determined.[25] But in a scientific context matters become far less straightforward than this example suggests. In physics and other mathematised disciplines, there is an established homology of structure between the mathematics and the relevant substantive domain. This connection is normally secured theoretically and depends upon well-established law-like relationships which are not only expressed mathematically but also indicate measurement units, as in the case of the thermometer. Indeed, in such disciplines, measures are strictly derived from the mathematical theory; measurement being akin to engineering where the measurement devices, be they atomic clocks, watches, thermometers, lasers, electronic counters, dials, etc. are engineered instantiations of well-established theories. Thus, and again for example, the measure of velocity $v=d/t$ can be instantiated in a number of ways, in car speedometers, lasers bounced off the moon, radar, inertial navigation, astrolabes, etc. and can be expressed in various kinds of ratio scales translatable one into the other, such as feet per second, miles per hour, metres per second, and so on. As Duncan illustrates in a brief discussion of the development of temperature scales, it is not merely that in science measurement becomes more precise and reliable in the move to a new type of scale, say a shift from the nominal categories 'hot' and 'cold' to degrees of heat to the Fahrenheit, Celsius and, lastly, the Kelvin scale, but that the theoretical basis also shifts. It required much experimentation to determine the properties of air, mercury, alcohol and other thermometric substances, as well as devising methods for constructing and calibrating instruments. The story of temperature measurement has to do with the experimental determination of the quantitative laws of expansion as well as a greater theoretical understanding of heat and thermo-dynamics. Kelvin's scale of temperature, the only true ratio scale of temperature since it has a non-arbitrary zero point, is not simply a mathematically more powerful scale or one that is invariably more useful, as far as the latter is concerned quite the contrary, but it is one that 'incorporates a profound understanding of how a certain class of phenomenon works'.[26] As Pawson remarks more generally,

The very objective of measurement is to incorporate and embody within an instrument principles derived from theoretical science. Instrumentation is a branch of engineering, and engineering is nothing other than application of the laws, theories, hypotheses and principles of theoretical physics.[27]

Another feature of measurement in science worth noting is that although there are thousands of measuring instruments in daily use, the number of dimensions measured is actually quite small. In the human sciences, of course, again with the possible exception of economics, there is no system of units or standards for them equivalent, for example, to the quantities of mass, length and time.[28] Instead, what we have are literally thousands of measures in educational testing, social surveys, attitude research or statistical analysis, with little or no idea as to how any of them could conceivably be reduced to a few dimensions or compared with agreed-upon standards.

However, given the lack of such well-established theories in the human sciences, variable analysis proposed to achieve the homology between the mathematical and its substantive domains by working through the methodological stipulation that social and human properties be described in variable analytic terms and the measurement scales just discussed.

It should be no surprise that both variable analysis as a mode of sociological thinking and the use of scaling in research have been criticised. Some have expressed doubt that Stevens' scale types add up to a theory of measurement or, if they do, whether this approach is a useful one for social research as it currently stands. As Duncan rather carpingly points out, age is a ratio scale but it is hard to see any analysis of age as a variable which exploits this fact.[29] In other words, it is a moot point as to whether the effort to develop interval and ratio scale measures is really worth it, especially since it underplays the importance of counting and categorisation as perfectly respectable procedures which are possibly more beneficial in the long run.[30] Arguably more of a problem is the inadequate theoretical base upon which to devise measures even approximating to the standards of natural science. Effective measurement requires detailed knowledge of the properties of phenomena which are to be reflected or mapped on to some mathematical system. Without this social research runs the risk of imposing on its subject matter properties derived from mathematics for other purposes.

However, it is not unreasonable to argue that trying to meet the measurement standards of natural science is to inflict a crippling over-ambition on social research. If theory and measurement do go hand in hand, there is no alternative but a patient and directed effort to improve both. This is the burden of Blalock's views, one of the doyens of causal modelling and quantitative social research. For him, the only way to bridge the gap between theory and data is by the development of 'auxiliary measurement theories' which can better specify appropriate measures and their levels and, through this, contribute to theory development.[31] Others are less sanguine than Blalock, arguing that if quantification in social research is to proceed, there are some very fundamental problems to resolve first, not least describing accurately and effectively the properties of social phenomena.

A number of the latter arguments will be addressed in subsequent chapters, but the thrust of the critique has to do with the categorisation procedures employed in data gathering in order to meet the requirements of variable analysis measurement and their relationship to the properties of ordinary language and of social phenomena themselves.

A UBIQUITOUS LANGUAGE OF SOCIAL RESEARCH?

To repeat, these days it is hard to recapture the innovative and radical character of variable analysis since it is now so much the orthodox conception of what social research consists in. Its innovativeness did not so much lie in the originality of the separate ingredients but in the recipe itself. Most of the ingredients were taken from other fields and disciplines, but the achievement was to meld these into a way of thinking, both theoretically and methodologically, so that one, the latter, could provide a route for a more effective formulation of the other, namely, theory. As one textbook advises: 'It is necessary to translate your ideas ... into the language of variables before you can carry out or evaluate research. The experienced sociologist develops the habit of routinely translating the English he reads and hears into variables.'[32] Variable analysis is an inferential structure, a form of methodological reasoning, that has come to dominate social research.

One important feature of variable analysis, and for many its primary virtue, is that, as a method, it is theoretically neutral. It is the prisoner of no particular approach but is a ubiquitous way of thinking, capable of dealing with and being deployed in respect of the widest range of approaches. It is a format for thinking theoretically-in- research-terms. Its approach of quantification even allowed for dealing with qualitative properties and variables. The basic requirement of the approach is that concepts be translated into empirical indices. Its pattern-searching strategy resolves many theoretical issues by placing them within the constraint of empirical evidence. So, the elaboration of a theory is through not only the kind of conceptual elaboration spoken of earlier, but also elaborating the indicators through pattern searching. Variable analysis is the closest that social research has come to a generic method of social investigation.

There is a metaphysics of ontological realism underlying the conception of variable analysis, if only to the extent that it makes sense to talk of indices only if it is assumed that they 'stand for' something. Lazarsfeld's proposal is not to try to resolve methodological problems philosophically but to see what follows by way of research practice if we recognise that we can never investigate phenomena directly. If we have only indicators what his methodological reasoning suggests is that we look for patterns among indicators which might suggest that we have found something of substance and significance.

NOTES

1. Bulmer points out that although on the decline of the Chicago School, Columbia (where Lazarsfeld was) asserted a pre-eminence, many of the methods later associated with variable analysis, particularly the survey, sampling and the use of inferential statistics, had been pioneered at Chicago, largely under the inspiration of Ogburn. See his *The Chicago School of Sociology: Institutionalisation, Diversity and the Rise of Sociological Research*, Chicago, University of Chicago Press, 1984. Much of Columbia's expansion was centred around the Bureau of Applied Social Research under Lazarsfeld's leadership and stimulated by harnessing its research to the war effort.

2. P.F. Lazarsfeld and M. Rosenberg (eds) *The Language of Social Research*, New York, Free Press, 1955, p. 15. This collection is a testament to the pioneering and exciting early days of variable analysis, and is still a good introduction to its style of methodological thinking. See also D. Benson and J.A. Hughes,

'Evidence and inference', in G. Button (ed.) *Ethnomethodology and the Human Sciences*, Cambridge, Cambridge University Press, 1991.

3. The 'mathematisation of nature' marks what is referred to as the Galilean Revolution in science, though it probably owes as much to Descartes. As Galileo is reputed to have said, 'the book of nature is written in geometric characters'. See A. Koyre, *Metaphysics and Measurement*, London, Chapman & Hall, 1986.

4. See O.D. Duncan, *Notes on Social Measurement: Historical and Critical*, New York, Russell Sage Foundation, 1984, for a review.

5. Despite being educated and trained in a country renowned for its innovative statisticians, such as Quetelet and Le Play, Durkheim's efforts were motivated, in part, by an effort to distance sociology from social statistics as well as psychology.

6. On the mathematisation of economics see R.J. Anderson, J.A. Hughes and W.W. Sharrock, 'The methodology of Cartesian economics: some thoughts on the nature of economic theorising', *Journal of Interdisciplinary Economics*, 2, 1988, pp. 307–20.

7. Of course, typological constructs were used and deployed long before Lazarsfeld and his colleagues offered a formalised way of thinking about them. Also see A. Barton, 'On the concept of property space', in Lazarsfeld and Rosenberg (eds) *op.cit.*

8. Lazarsfeld and Rosenberg (eds) *ibid.*, p. 15.

9. Note that there is nothing about the numbers except convention to force us to use 0 for the absence of a property, and 1 for its presence. It could easily have been vice versa, if perhaps more confusing.

10. See A. Barton, 'The concept of property space in social research', in Lazarsfeld and Rosenberg (eds) *op.cit.* pp. 40–3.

11. P.F. Lazarsfeld, 'Interpretation of statistical relations as a research operation', in Lazarsfeld and Rosenberg (eds) *op. cit.*, p. 115.

12. Duncan, *op.cit.*

13. Of course, neither Marx nor Weber drew their ideas out of thin air. Both provided a great deal of empirical support for them. However, on the Lazarsfeldian conception, such empirical material was suggestive rather than systematically directed at confirming, or otherwise, the theories.

14. Strictly speaking, it is not the occupation that is the indicator, but particular aspects of it, especially whether it is classifiable as manual or non-manual; a classification itself which is supposed to reflect clusters of characteristics.

15. Cicourel argues that Lazarsfeld's thinking about variable analysis was much influenced by his predilection for survey research. See A.V. Cicourel, *Method and Measurement in Sociology*, New York, Free Press, 1964.

16. Thus, we have Thurstone, Guttman and Likert scales, all types of measurement scales which differ on the ways in which the underlying metric is constituted. See, for example, W.S. Torgerson, *Theory and Methods of Scaling*, New York, Wiley, 1967.
17. In fact there are many sciences which make little use of the experiment as classically understood, including some of the more advanced sciences, such as astronomy.
18. Which are neither pristine nor always exact. See J.A Hughes, *The Philosophy of Social Research*, 2nd and rev. edn, London, Longman, 1990.
19. See, for example, H. Blalock, *Conceptualisation and Measurement in Social Science*, London, Sage, 1982.
20. Variable analysis is often referred to as positivism whose demise has been announced now for a long time. Given the strength of this style of social research, it would seem premature to start holding its wake.
21. W. Torgerson, *Theory and Method of Scaling*, New York, Wiley, 1958, p. 10.
22. Quoted in Duncan, *op.cit.*, p. 121. Interestingly Duncan notes that measurement is one of those human achievements and practices that grew up and became taken for granted before any serious inquiry into its foundations began in the nineteenth century. See also M. Lynch, 'Ordinary and scientific measurement as ethnomethodological phenomena', in G. Button (ed.) *Ethnomethodology and the Human Sciences*, Cambridge, Cambridge University Press, 1991.
23. S.S. Stevens, 'On the theory of scales of measurement', reprinted in A. Danto and S. Morgensessor (eds), *Philosophy of Science*, New York, Meridian Books, 1960. Stevens's scale types have become standard in most methods books in social research.
24. Occasionally a category of partially ordered scales is distinguished where it is possible to get ties between cases, as is common in social research. Symmetry holds between the tied cases.
25. More complicated variants of voting systems do not alter the point being made here. Any system of voting can be treated as an institution designed to render a collective outcome of individual choices using the rules of arithmetic.
26. Duncan, *op.cit.*, pp. 148–9.
27. R. Pawson, *A Measure for Measures: A Manifesto for Empirical Sociology*, London, Routledge and Kegan Paul, 1989.
28. Duncan, *op.cit.*, p. 162.
29. Duncan, *op.cit.*, p. 150.
30. J.S. Coleman, *Introduction to Mathematical Sociology*, New York, Free Press, 1964, p. 73.
31. See H. Blalock, *Basic Dilemmas in the Social Sciences*, Beverly Hills, Calif., Sage, 1984.

32. J.A. Davis, *Elementary Survey Analysis*, Englewood-Cliffs, NJ, Prentice-Hall, 1971, p. 16.

CHAPTER 4

Social surveys

Most of us living in industrialised countries are familiar with social surveys of one type or another. Few of us would be surprised to find an interviewer on our doorstep asking us to give a few moments of our time 'to answer one or two questions' on our voting habits, which TV programmes we watch or which washing powder we use. Some of us may have taken part in an academic survey; most of us will have taken part in the census. Week by week we read of the latest opinion polls on this or that. Accordingly, while most of us may not be *au fait* with the technicalities of surveys, we are likely to have an intuitive grasp of what surveys are about; they are concerned with finding out how many people, within a defined social-cum-geographical area, hold particular views or opinions about things, events or individuals, do particular activities; possess particular qualities; and so on. In this chapter we shall be considering some ideas which inform the design and purpose of social surveys; we shall also say something about their origins and their applications. As the above introductory remarks suggest, the experience most people have of social surveys is through the interview. For the sake of convenience this will be left for Chapter 5 though it is essential to remember that the data collected through social surveys are almost exclusively obtained by means of this method.

We shall consider four types of surveys. The first we call the '*factual survey*', which aims at collecting facts about the conditions of populations. This was the first kind of social survey to be seriously used in the United Kingdom, a fact which was a consequence of a combination of historical and political factors. What the approach bequeathed is procedures for surveying large numbers of people at minimum cost, and a series of guides for eliciting 'factual' information from respondents in an interview. This may be contrasted with the second type, the '*attitude survey*', which aims at producing an accurate picture of people's attitudes as a guide to their likely behaviour. This type of survey was first developed seriously in the United States, and its importance can similarly be traced to economic and social factors peculiar to that country at a particular stage in its history. Among the inheritance of this type of survey are procedures known as the quota sample and the attitude questionnaire. The main aim of both these types of surveys was to effect, as accurately as possible, a description of the social structure or, in the case of the attitude survey, the current state of public opinion. This meant that issues to do with the representativeness of the sample drawn and interviewed were paramount since the objective was to gain an accurate estimate from the sample of the likely population characteristics. By contrast, the third and fourth types were more concerned with explanation and theory testing than with description. The '*social psychological survey*', for example, used survey designs and questionnaires to investigate the distribution of personality via various kinds of attitude measurement techniques. The '*explanatory survey*', as its name implies, is concerned to gain information from respondents in order to test some theoretical explanation and represents the full-blown expression of variable analysis in the survey tradition.

In an important sense the factual survey and the attitude survey were designed to achieve practical objectives rather than serve disinterested theoretically inspired research. The interests which stimulated their innovation and guided their development and use were primarily those of political administration rather than the strictly academic. Throughout the nineteenth century in most industrialised nations there had been a growing need for governments to obtain reliable knowledge about the state of their societies. In Britain, the first census of modern times was begun in 1801 and a series of government reports resulted in various inquiries into the state of the nation. In general, many of these inquiries were motivated by the need for what we would now regard as manpower planning, especially to do with the defence of the realms concerned. Governments, throughout Europe especially, found themselves, sometimes reluctantly as in Britain, sometimes with more enthusiasm as in Prussia, assuming an increasingly managerial role in economic life as the basis of political and military power. For this information about the 'state of the nation' became vital. However, such social research was not only governmentally inspired. Booth and Rowntree, in the late nineteenth century, carried out the first major surveys of income and consumption in London and York respectively, which laid the foundations for a style of social research which was, in the coming years, to play a major role in the formation of policy and social welfare legislation in the United Kingdom.[1] Booth's survey also had an influence on a similar movement in the United States, though its roots go back to the middle of the nineteenth century when a number of small surveys on the 'dangerous classes' were undertaken.[2] As in Britain, the early social survey belonged much more to a reform impulse than to an effort to develop an explicitly social science methodology.

One major presupposition of these early surveys was that it was preferable to study the whole population of a society in order to ensure the reliability and accuracy of the data collected.[3] Though Booth and Rowntree were wealthy industrialists, it was principally considerations of cost which led them to limit their study to the particular areas they did. If it had been possible to study the whole country cheaply and in sufficient detail they would have done so.[4] So, one key feature of these early surveys was the assumption that the greater the absolute size of the population studied and the closer this approximated to the total population of the country, the better. The higher the proportion of this population which could be contacted the better. It was developments in sampling theory from statistics which weakened the force of both these assumptions, and quite early on in Britain. Sampling theory showed that reliable estimates of population characteristics could be arrived at using appropriately constructed samples. Though the whole population remained the focus of interest, sampling techniques enabled it to be studied economically. But, none the less, the aim to study the whole population determined the scope and the character of both these types of early surveys and, in so doing, encouraged the search for new ways of doing so cheaply through innovations in the applications of statistical theory to the selection of samples.

THE EARLY 'FACTUAL' SOCIAL SURVEYS

Given the interests of the early social surveyors in investigating whole populations we must include among the forerunners the censuses of pre-modern times. The two best-known ones are the one undertaken by Augustus Caesar, which allegedly affected the birth of Jesus, and the Domesday Survey compiled at the instigation of William I. Both of these were attempts by an occupying power to extend its control over the population and, no doubt, record the spoils of victory. Data in each of these cases were sought by the central administration of the dominating power for taxation purposes, among other considerations, so that money and tribute could be more effectively extracted, and the rewards to loyal service allocated. It was this legacy of coercive intent along with centuries of suspicion toward central administration which, perhaps, encouraged resistance to attempts to introduce a census in Britain until the beginning of the nineteenth century.[5]

By the time the first censuses were undertaken in Britain, much had changed in the structure of society as well as in the nature of the state itself. By 1801, not only had the conflicts between monarch and nobility over the extraction and use of rents and taxes, and the respective rights and duties of each, largely been resolved and in the process made irrelevant, but also the industrial revolution was well under way, establishing the basis for the growing political ascendancy of the industrial classes over both monarchy and aristocracy. The character of the state had changed decisively from the coercive apparatus of monarchical power to the increasingly bureaucratic (but determinedly *laissez-faire*) administration of the first capitalist nation.

Indeed, the categories used in the censuses display many of the concerns of the governments of the day. In the first census of the nineteenth century, many of the concepts developed by the classical economists Smith, Ricardo and Malthus influenced the categories used.[6] Since then the assumptions underpinning, and the meanings attributed to, census data have changed a good deal. Nowadays, the census does not seek information about the numbers of people obtaining support from different factors of production, but has extended its range into a whole gamut of policy-related matters such as housing, education, income as well as occupation, and, very recently, ethnic status. The census has been for many years now an important instrument, among a range of such instruments, in the administration of the welfare state.

This particular development of the census, along with other official data and information-gathering techniques as an integral part of the welfare state, is a comparatively recent development in Britain. Much of the early social survey work was concerned with establishing the case for the need for nation-wide welfare provision along the lines now embodied in the modern welfare state. Also, the census was slow to be influenced by the techniques of survey method, both in the use of sampling designs and in the search for more appropriate data. A biographer has said of A.L. Bowley, the man who above all others took up the mantle of Booth and Rowntree in the early part of this century, that 'it was unfortunately not the custom in Bowley's day for the British Government to call outside experts. Undoubtedly British official statistics would have advanced more rapidly, particularly in the use of sampling techniques, if Bowley had had more to do with them.'[7]

Britain was comparatively slow in acquiring a welfare state by comparison with some other societies, notably Germany, and it is in the context of this struggle to achieve a more adequate provision of social welfare that the early uses of social surveys in Britain must be understood. The process of industrialisation not only began later in Germany than in Britain, but also Germany achieved spectacular economic success in a relatively short period of time. In the space of two decades Germany rapidly overtook Britain in industrial output. By the early years of the twentieth century, well before the outbreak of the First World War, Germany was increasingly challenging Britain's dominance as the world's leading industrial and imperial power. That Germany had also provided a comprehensive state insurance for sickness, accident, disability and unemployment for its people from an early date was thought by some to be implicated in that country's economic success. Also, the inability of Britain to sustain its economic growth from about 1870 onwards was partly explained by inadequate state welfare protection for its citizens. About this time a particularly long and deep depression hit the British economy, giving further impetus to the need to reappraise social and economic policy. British liberal political thought, hitherto contenting itself with a more or less straightforward advocacy of *laissez-faire* non-interventionist policies, began to transform itself into what has been called 'social liberalism'.[8] This, along with parallel doctrines such as Fabian Socialism, provided important ingredients to the intellectual context in which the pioneering social survey work was undertaken in Britain. Social liberals, like Booth and Rowntree, and Fabians, like Sydney and Beatrice Webb, may have differed in their views on the extent and the permanence of the provision of state welfare that they advocated, but shared an interest in what they saw as the factual demonstration of the extent of poverty which existed in what was still regarded as the major industrial and political power. They also advocated the use of social survey methods of research to show, accurately and in considerable detail, the actual extent and character of existing social conditions in a way that would be difficult to challenge.

While it would be going too far to claim that social surveys such as these by themselves induced major political change, it would be dangerous to ignore their significant contribution. In the circumstances in which they were used they powerfully augmented other forces of change by providing data on the state of society at a period when so little was known. This can be illustrated by the early surveys of Booth and Rowntree. At the time the prevailing view of poverty was that it was primarily due to personal inadequacy, especially laziness and moral turpitude; a convenient view for the orthodox political doctrines of the time which held that government intervention in either the state or the economy or society was invidious, and, what is more, likely to make matters worse by restricting liberty, constraining the rights of property and, in any event, useless. Governments could do little to turn immorality into morality, or bad characters into good. But the scale of the poverty revealed by the Booth and Rowntree surveys shocked late Victorian sensibilities. Both surveys showed that for many people poverty was a way of life even when they were in gainful employment. This struck at the root of the idea that nobody need be poor if they conscientiously engaged in economic activity. Poverty was merely the lot of the indigent. As a result, there came an increased acceptance of the view that persistent, and unacceptable, inequality and want might be built into the economic system unless the state made key interventions along the lines of the German model. The shift towards a greater acceptance of this point of view marks the emergence of social from *laissez-faire* liberalism, a shift assisted in no small measure by the early poverty surveys.

If liberalism was a spent political force in Britain by 1930, the kind of social survey to which it helped give rise was not. Sampling techniques were refined throughout the early decades of the twentieth century by Bowley, Hilton, and others. Such methods were increasingly copied and applied within the official investigations of the state itself, and became an important element in its maintenance and extension.[9] As Moser comments: 'By the middle of the 1930s surveys were beginning to assume importance in the field of town planning and reconstruction'.[10]

By 1941 social surveys on the lines pioneered by Booth, Rowntree and Bowley were fully incorporated as instruments of the welfare state, impelled further by the imperatives of planning for war. The Government Social Survey was created in the same year as an adjunct to the Central Statistical Office, more recently combined into the Office of Population Censuses and Surveys. The survey has changed from being an instrument devoted to demonstrating the need for a welfare state into a central feature of its maintenance and administration. As Moser revealingly wrote of the Government Social Survey: 'the survey exists to collect data required for administration, not for party politics'.[11]

While the ability of the factual social survey to provide large-scale pictures of prevailing social conditions within a community is important, it is less frequently used these days. To the extent that social research more generally has retained an interest in social reform this has been redirected in various ways. Increasingly, private pressure groups commission private survey organisations to focus on particular subgroups or issues and, as a result, deal with matters that go beyond material deprivation. Where such studies make use of the survey, they tend to be smaller in scale and more analytic in scope using directed samples.

CONTRIBUTION OF THE EARLY SURVEYS: PROBABILITY SAMPLING

In Britain the social and intellectual origins of the early surveys gave them a particular emphasis summarisable as generality and factuality. That is, the aim of describing the state of the society by gathering hard facts about the conditions of life from as many people as possible; hard facts to do with income, expenditure, consumption or living conditions. Little interest was evinced in gathering material to do with how people felt about their conditions, or their hopes and fears for the future. Facts were to do with the material conditions of life described as precisely as possible and counted as accurately as possible. In terms of the impulse for social reform which motivated many of these surveys, such facts were intended to be difficult to rebut by erstwhile opponents of reform.

Although in terms of later social science methodologies such an approach might seem naive, it did leave an important legacy for social research and survey data collection, namely sampling. The desire to survey the social conditions of the largest possible population proved difficult and costly, so methods were sought to reduce the costs of such surveys without, at the same time, sacrificing accuracy. Sampling was a means to achieve this objective.

Sampling techniques were adopted from statisticians working in the fields of biology and botany.[12] The statistical theories involved were designed to allow generalisations about a population on the basis of a sample of that population, within known margins of error. Thus a precise estimate of the average height of adult males in this country can be made on the basis of a representative sample of the total population of adult males. The problem is that without measuring the heights, and their frequency, of all adult males we will not know what a representative sample would be. While we can say that the average figure is likely to fall between 1 and 3 metres, since we do not know how many are 1.6 metres, 1.7 metres or 2 metres tall, we cannot calculate the average. What we can do, however, is take a sufficient number of adult males chosen randomly and use this as the basis of the calculation of the average, and take this as an estimate for the average of the population. Since the population of adult males in Britain is many million, there are obvious savings to be made using these techniques. It means that the population value of some characteristic, say, average height of adult males, can be estimated within range of error, from the values found within a suitably drawn sample of that population.

Although this is not the place to enter into a detailed exposition of the mathematics behind sampling theory, there are two questions worth dealing with. First, how large does a sample have to be for a given population? Second, how can we be sure that it provides for an accurate and reliable estimate of that population? As far as the first is concerned, without going into statistical details, generally the larger the population the smaller the sample needs to be. The ratio of sample to population is normally expressed as a fraction, known as the sampling fraction. In our example, estimating the average height of adult males in the British population, would require a sampling fraction of about 1/4,000, whereas to estimate the same parameter in a population of 200, a sampling fraction of ¼, or a sample size of 50, would be necessary. In other words, the sample in the latter case would have to be a greater proportion of the total than the former. Broadly, the reason for this is that in smaller populations the selection of an extreme value for the sample would have a greater effect on the calculation of any value for that sample if the sample was also small as a ratio of the population. So, to minimise the chances of this, smaller populations require larger sampling ratios.

However, this is not the only factor involved. Sample sizes cannot be decided independently of acceptable error since sampling cannot guarantee that it will provide the true population value. What it does offer is a way of calculating the probable size of the error in estimating that value. Probability has a precise meaning here. It will be possible for a researcher to know, for example, that there is a 99 per cent probability that the sample estimate falls within 3 per cent of the real value of the total population. Larger samples will increase precision, the less likely they are to vary from the population value, and the more confident we can be that our sample estimate of the population value is within a given range of accuracy. For any chosen sample size there will be a calculable range of variation within which an estimate of the population value falls, and an associated probability that the estimate will fall within that range. For any sample size there will be an inverse relationship between these; the smaller the range specified, the lower the probability of accuracy it will be possible to associate with it. Thus, for example, we may be 99 per cent sure that the true population value is within 3 per cent of the estimate, or 99.9 per cent sure that it falls within 10 per cent of the same estimate, or 95 per cent certain that it falls within 1 per cent of the estimate.

Accordingly there is a choice about the level of accuracy we want to accept. Confidence limits of 95 per cent and 99 per cent are conventionally used in most statistical calculations in social research, not only in descriptive studies of the kind we are presently discussing, but also in more analytic ones we shall be considering later in the chapter. In choosing a sample size, therefore, not only do considerations of accuracy enter, but also considerations of conventionally accepted limits.

A crucial assumption of the kinds of statistical calculations we have been referring to is that the sample has been randomly drawn from some population. Randomness, which again is something that has a precise meaning in this context and certainly not equivalent to 'take anyone that comes along', is necessary to ensure that the estimate of the population value is unbiased. In brief, what this means is that every individual comprising the population of interest should have an equal chance of being selected for the sample. This is not always easy to operationalise. Sampling lists, that is, a record which identifies and sets out the population from which a sample is to be drawn, may not always completely enumerate the population from which the sample is to be drawn, the list may follow some peculiar sequence, sections of the population may be difficult to contact or refuse to co-operate, and so on.

Unless care is taken to minimise biases of this kind, careful calculations of precision will be pointless; the estimate of the population value will be wrong. It is not enough for researchers to assume that if they do not make conscious decisions, try to be scrupulously fair when selecting their samples, that randomness will be assured. Biases can creep in in extremely subtle ways, and researchers can, quite unconsciously, favour some groups and disfavour others.

The only way to ensure randomness is to make sample selections independent of human judgement. There are several techniques for this, the most common being to select a sample from a list, called a sampling frame, according to numbers generated by tables of random numbers. If the researcher is confident that there is no ordering principle at work in the sampling frame, that the list is random in other words, then systematic sampling can be employed by selecting every nth item from the list as required. As we say, systematic sampling requires care if there is unwanted selectivity in the list.

On occasions simple random sampling procedures as just described do not meet the requirements of the research. For one thing, especially if the sample is relatively small, unlikely events can skew the sample. More likely, it might be that we need to ensure that particular subgroups are represented in the sample. To meet these possibilities, a technique known as stratification is employed: this involves dividing the population into groups or strata and sampling randomly within each. If the differences between strata are maximised and the variations within them minimised, the benefits from stratification can be considerable. It is a technique which can also help keep sample size down in the case of a large survey. Against this one must set the likelihood of increased travel and other costs arising from the greater geographical dispersion of the units in the sample. To obviate these an alternative to stratification is to concentrate the sample within selected subgroups, or clusters, of the population which makes interviewing more convenient by concentrating respondents together. This does, however, tend to reduce precision and leave room for biases. Nevertheless, there may be special reasons why clustering may be a useful technique, such as when an investigator is interested in certain subgroups of the population.

However, neither of these procedures recommended themselves to the early survey researchers, such as Bowley; his procedure was to compromise between administrative convenience and representativeness by using more than one stage of sampling. He chose a sample of towns for his study as a first stage, then selected smaller districts within these, and so on. Multi-stage sampling surveys of this kind are most effective when the sampling units are carefully stratified at each stage.

The great achievement of the early survey researchers was to provide and encourage the development of techniques for surveying large populations cheaply and within calculable degrees of accuracy; although to a large degree the emphasis in social science has shifted from descriptive to analytic surveys, the legacies of sampling and survey design remain.

We now turn to a consideration of the early use of social surveys in the United States. These were scarcely more analytic or explanatory in their approach but were interested in different kinds of data, and, as a result, developed different techniques for dealing with the problem of representativeness.

EARLY ATTITUDE SURVEYS

In Britain the early surveys were primarily concerned with discovering the material conditions in which the population lived. They showed little interest in attitudes or opinions which explains their insistence on 'factual questions', precise and exact, in order to claim that the research yielded 'hard' data.

In the United States, although a social survey movement not unlike the tradition of Booth, Rowntree and, later, Bowley, was prominent in the early years of the twentieth century, different political traditions, among other things, gave rise to a different use of social surveys. In this the concern was to measure public opinion as a guide to political action. In Britain, despite the development of forms of democratic political institutions, the idea of an independent and consequential public opinion had never been a very serious consideration. By contrast, the political culture of the United States, always more populist in character than the British, took seriously the notion that public opinion was there to be wooed, cajoled, seduced but never ignored. As Abraham Lincoln is reported to have said, 'With public opinion on its side, everything succeeds. With public opinion against it, nothing succeeds'.[13]

It was against expectations and conceptions such as these that two of the early surveys were developed in the United States – the *market research survey* and the *pre-election poll*. The presumption was that whatever people said about their tastes, feelings, beliefs, attitudes or opinions was a reliable guide to how they would behave or how they would act. So surveys could be used to predict behaviour, for example, how the electorate would vote or whether people would buy a new product. Or they could be used to design new strategies; useful, for example, to politicians trying to get a policy on the agenda, or a sales manager trying to market a new product.

This kind of survey arose in a political culture very different from that which gave rise to the factual survey. It was a political culture which emphasised the democratic assumption that opinion was not merely of passing interest but an important guide to understanding how people would react to various policies. It recognised the power and the autonomy of the public as a force to be reckoned with; predicted but never ignored. By contrast, the British use of surveys involved finding things out about people in order that representations could be made on their behalf by their 'betters'. In addition, in the United States the view prevailed that it was neither possible nor desirable to attempt to influence social and political behaviour very much. However, one need not be overly cynical to realise that having a good idea of what masses of people are likely to do in response to certain policies gives a competitive advantage to politicians and businessmen alike.

The early American public opinion surveys were probably little influenced by British social survey work by contrast to the reformist social surveyors. Market research surveys were probably the first type of opinion survey to be used and as early as the first decade of the twentieth century. Abrams explained this in terms of a particular configuration of economic factors affecting the United States at this time. American firms were among the first to confront a national mass market since the market for consumer goods was huge, the whole of the country being a free trade area for business firms.[14] For business people the question of what consumers wanted and how their products could be most effectively marketed was a vital one spelling the difference between success and failure. As a consequence many large firms began to conduct their own market research until, more recently, it has become the specialised trade of advertising agencies and professional market research organisations.

Attempts to survey political opinions came rather later, though they did have not dissimilar aspirations to those of the market surveyors; however, they were rather less well conducted. Until the Three Mile Island nuclear accident, Harrisburg, Pennsylvania, was notorious only for the earliest perpetration of a 'straw poll' attempting to predict the outcome of the 1924 presidential election. Similar polls conducted by various newspapers became notorious for their frequent and lamentable failures to come even close to accurate predictions of electoral outcomes. The most famous débâcle was the Literary Digest Poll of 1936. Despite the success of an earlier poll in 1932 and the distribution of over 10 million questionnaires to respondents selected from telephone directories, the poll failed to predict the election of F.D. Roosevelt.[15]

However, far from discrediting such polls, it encouraged efforts to make them more effective predictors of outcomes and preferences. One of the more important of these was the quota sample, an attempt to approximate to random sampling methods but in a way that minimised the practical difficulties often involved in selecting and contacting respondents, so offering considerable advantages in cost and convenience. The other important innovation was the rise of the professional opinion research agency offering its services and expertise in opinion polling.

CONTRIBUTIONS OF THE EARLY ATTITUDE SURVEYS: QUOTA SAMPLING

Instead of seeking a random sample from a population in which each member has a known, calculable and non-zero probability of inclusion, the quota sample proceeds by deliberately selecting a sample which reflects the known composition of the target population. These days much is known about the socio-economic composition of the population thanks largely to the national census. It is possible, therefore, to construct a sample so that it has the same distribution of characteristics as the population as a whole or, if necessary, selected portions of it. By selecting for a sample a definite 'quota' which reflects the proportion of different types of people in the target population, which can, of course, be the whole population, we have, prima facie, reason to assume the sample as representative. The criteria most commonly used to establish how many people we should have in a sample are such characteristics as age, gender, marital status and socio-economic status, although various other criteria may be used as appropriate. These criteria are called 'quota controls' because they are used to limit the number of respondents chosen within predetermined quotas.

Strictly speaking, of course, this kind of sampling does not allow the deployment of statistical analysis in order to make inferences to population values from the sample, since the selection of cases within quota categories is not done according to random sampling procedures. For this reason, the method has attracted heavy criticism from a number of statisticians and methodologists; however, it can be argued that quota sampling is informed by sociological principles at least. For one thing it takes into account the fact that people in different social circumstances are likely to have different views and different opinions; the sample is chosen so that the more salient features and differences that are thought to exist are proportionately represented. To some extent this aim can be achieved by stratifying a random sample appropriately. But there are often insurmountable practical difficulties in doing this given that, under most random sampling procedures, it is individuals who have to be contacted not types of individuals who satisfy the quota controls as in quota sampling. Also, it is very difficult to stratify the electoral register (a frequently used sampling list) by social class or by education. Random sampling, it can be argued, makes rather few concessions to the fact that human populations are not normally socially well-mixed: indeed, they tend to develop distinct homogeneity within subgroups. Quota sampling, intelligently used, can deal with these difficulties reasonably effectively.

Instead of all the problems of finding or developing an appropriate sampling frame, and of drawing the sample randomly from the list, the quota sample is usually drawn by the interviewer. The researcher goes out looking for respondents who conform to the quota requirements, either by knocking on doors or by asking people in the street to participate: it must be stressed that the point is not to interview everyone who happens to live on the street or who happens to pass by, but only those who conform to the quota controls and in the proportions specified. Selecting respondents in the High Street on a Monday would include an excessive proportion of women of child-bearing age unless the quotas are strictly adhered to. Working the High Street on the day in question, an interviewer will probably fill the quota of married women 20–35, and possibly men and women over 65, but will most likely have to look elsewhere for men and women of other ages, marital status and socio-economic grouping.

The contact procedure is usually to begin with a number of preliminary questions to ensure that the people contacted do fulfil the quota requirements. If they do not then the interview is politely broken off. There are, of course, great temptations for an interviewer to classify respondents into categories where they are most needed rather than where they really belong, especially when the job is nearly complete and respondents from particular categories seem rare or, perhaps understandably, at the end of a long day in the rain and the cold.

None the less, when properly used, the quota sample can avoid the kind of gross errors made by attitude surveys in the past. On this point it seems that the Literary Digest Poll and others committed two errors. First, non-response was high and it is now known that, as a category, non-respondents are often very different in a number of relevant respects from those who do respond. Second, the telephone lists actually used for the sample were unrepresentative of the electorate. Owning a telephone, for example, implies a certain minimum of income and life-style, and using telephone owners as the sampling list would seriously over-represent the better off and, presumably, the more politically conservative sections of the electorate.

In view of the comparatively greater possibilities of error, it is perhaps surprising that the early polls came as close as they did in predicting electoral outcomes. After all, the Literary Digest Poll for the 1932 election came within a tiny margin of the actual result. This heightened expectations for the accuracy of the prediction for the election of 1936. Looked at against the background of the difficulties in the way of achieving a representative sample, the close result of 1932 was a fantastic stroke of luck; and errors of 4 per cent or so, as produced in 1936, are only to be expected. However, as quota sampling methods became more widely used much greater levels of accuracy were routinely achieved. On the basis of relatively small samples, only a few thousand in each of selected states, it proved possible to make accurate predictions of the electoral outcomes. This is quite an achievement in view of the size and the regional diversity of a country such as the United States. In 1948, three of the main polls wrongly predicted the outcome of the election of that year. Truman won (taking 49.5 per cent of the votes cast) against Dewey (45.1 of the votes). The Gallup Poll predicted 49.5 per cent for Dewey and 44.5 per cent for Truman. Although as a prediction of the electoral result this was incorrect, the estimates were only a few per cent out. For purposes other than electoral forecasting such close estimates would be regarded as highly commendable.

Since the interwar period, when quota sampling was first developed in the United States, it has been refined to a high art by commercial research organisations in many countries. Its chief merits are its cheapness and convenience. Such samples can be interviewed very quickly at a fraction of the cost of full-scale randomly chosen samples. Thus, for certain purposes, such as market surveys and pre-election opinion polls, they are probably not to be improved upon. In the 1980s there have been attempts to develop random sampling procedures as quick and as cheap as quotas. However, there is little evidence to suggest that these give better estimates of opinions which are any more accurate for these purposes than those yielded by carefully chosen quota samples. Indeed, for some purposes its cheapness and speed make quota sampling a procedure which could be more extensively used in some academic research where a general indication of the attitudes extant in a specified population is required. Moreover, it is possible to incorporate elements of randomness into quota sampling by rejecting numbers of possible respondents according to a random sequence.

We have described two uses of the survey method which originated outside academic circles. Moreover, by today's standards they both adopted rather naive assumptions regarding the nature of and the relationship between behaviour, ideas and respondent reports of these. For the early British researchers, surveys were a means of obtaining from large numbers of people reports on their conditions of life, while for the American surveyors, more interest was expressed in attitudes and opinions which predispose people to behave in certain ways. Today, and at least in academic circles though not solely these, both of these uses have been developed by a greater use of social scientific theory and by more advanced statistical techniques.

In both these developments it was largely scholars in the United States who took the lead. There social science and social research had become an established and thriving part of the academic community from the beginning of this century. The requirement of a PhD for an academic post marked the early professionalisation of social science. By contrast, social science in Britain, with the possible exception of economics, was largely unrecognised and underfinanced having little or no foothold in the elite establishments of higher education. In those institutions where the social sciences, especially sociology, were taught, principally the London School of Economics (LSE), it was a theoretical tradition rather than a social research one which was encouraged. This theoretical tradition was that of social liberalism developing the evolutionary and organicist elements of this approach into elaborate bodies of theoretical ideas. As a result, there is an unbroken strand of social liberal philosophy from Hobhouse, Professor of Sociology at the LSE from 1903 to 1929, through Ginsberg (1929–54), down to Marshall in the immediate post-war period.[16] The outlook of these men, particularly Ginsberg and Hobhouse, was evolutionary and comparative, scarcely connecting with the strictly factual investigations of Bowley, Boyd, Orr and Caradog-Jones. In Britain, it was mainly left to social anthropology among the social sciences to sustain a theoretical development based on empirical research.

The contrast with the United States could not be sharper. In that country three great universities (Chicago, Columbia and Harvard) had pioneered the development of sociology. Sociology had a major presence, though of variable quality and intellectual traditions, throughout the university sector before the Second World War.[17] Peel, reviewing the development of the social sciences, suggests that 'sociology was made a reasonably unified subject by the Americans who welded together very diverse streams', which, by the 1940s, 'was being synthesised into a mainstream of theory to which most ongoing research was related'.[18] It is certainly true that the most active social science departments gave rise to the approach to social science which became associated with participant observation, the more extensive use of the survey method as a means to examine attitudes and personality and, last but not least, the modern sociological use of the survey as a tool for the development of theory as in variable analysis.

The divide between theory and empirical data had long been a recurrent and problematic one for the social sciences, not least within sociology. Indeed, arguments about the relationship constituted much of the core debate as is evidenced by the attention given to it by classical figures such as Weber and Durkheim. However, it is fair to say that despite these distinctive efforts, and one reason why such people are now regarded as classical contributors, for most within the early social survey tradition the divide seemed unbridgeable or irrelevant. Indeed, in the early quarter of the twentieth century in the United States, interest in social survey research was far stronger among academics and activists in social welfare and social policy than it was among sociologists. For them, theory consisted of broad speculation which seemed to need little in the way of systematic data collection, while for empirical research on social life, such theories seemed to be of little relevance. Certainly, the British survey researchers saw little or no need for theories; hard facts were what was important and so with the early opinion researchers in the United States. So despite the widespread acceptance of social science in the United States by the early years of the twentieth century, it is possible to produce a sizeable list of American sociologists, all eminent figures in the history of the discipline, who seldom undertook on their own account, systematic data collection of any kind. In the main they relied upon their own convictions and inspirations and on secondary sources of various kinds. Such a list would include Sumner, MacIver, Giddings, Small, Sorokin and Cooley. They were eclectic in the data they sought and, by some standards, relatively unsystematic in their use of the data.

None the less, important foundations were being laid in the period immediately following the First World War. The University of Chicago, under Park and Burgess, had begun to move sociology toward becoming an empirical social science. Though this period of Chicago's history is normally associated with the more ethnographic, qualitative tradition of social research, both Park and Burgess were aware of the work of the social survey movement both in the United States and in Britain.[19] Though the social survey method was not extensively used in Chicago-inspired studies, and there was some scepticism about what it could achieve for sociology compared to field research, with the appointment of Ogburn in 1927, a statistically trained sociologist, the pace of the development of quantitative methods quickened.

Martindale charts the intellectual history of American sociology from the interwar period to post-Second World War as a movement from the dominance of social behaviourism as a perspective to that of functionalism. He suggests that shifts in the social and political climate in the United States may have had something to do with this change:

the very dates of the steep rise of interest in functionalism among sociological theorists also suggests that it may have some ideological import. It rose after 1940, and with particular speed after the Second World War. Moreover, its ranks have been increasingly swelled by deserters from social behaviourism – an evidently liberal position. The rise of sociological functionalism thus coincides with the return of the Republican Party to power, the return to religion, the rise of McCarthyism, and other typical manifestations of a postwar conservative reaction.[20]

Whether or not post-war social science was more conservative than its predecessors it is difficult to say: the character of social science is strongly influenced by its social, political and economic context. There are additional factors important in this case, however. In the United States during the period we are discussing there were powerful moves for the professionalisation of sociology and social science. The main manifestations of this were the insistence on education to doctorate level for recruits to the discipline, and the development of theoretical and methodological orthodoxies in teaching and in research. The orthodoxies which eventually established themselves were function-alism and, in methods, the survey.[21]

Prior to the culmination of these changes in the institutionalisation of American social science, the various branches of social behaviourism were well represented in the major American universities. As is to be expected, there were differences of viewpoint, sometimes major, both within and between institutions. Indeed, only by holding to a very diffuse and very general understanding of social theory is it possible to see many of these views and their exponents as representatives of the same general theoretical approach. This diffuseness was paralleled by a marked degree of confusion over the appropriate research methods to use in empirical studies. Indeed, in what is perhaps a more healthy attitude to such matters, a diversity of methods and investigative postures was the order of the day. The social survey was, in fact, only a minor player in the research game. Symbolic interactionism, as it became known, was perhaps the most vigorous of the variants of social behaviourism having a firm foundation at the University of Chicago.[22] Although this branch years later became closely associated with participant observation, during this period researchers in the Chicago School made use of a variety of methods in their research, including observation and, to a degree, survey type methods.

Perhaps one can gauge the relatively carefree attitude to data and their analysis from a seminal study from the period in question, *The Polish Peasant in Europe and America* by Thomas and Znanieki.[23] The bulk of the data used for this study were documentary in origin: letters from Polish peasants to relatives living in the United States, the archives of Polish newspapers, and the records and periodicals of Polish *émigré* organisations. Also included was the autobiography of a young Pole, running to some 300 pages in length. This material forms the basis of an account of the social changes in rural Poland, the attempts on the part of emigrating peasants to retain elements of their cultural identity, and their eventual imperfect integration into American society. There is no attempt at any systematic statistical analysis of the documents, either of their numbers or their content; there is also no attempt to supplement this material with interviews, though from the text it is clear that both authors talked to many Poles in the course of their investigations. However, the point to notice is how the data seemed ideal for the investigation as conceived: intimate life-histories are central to the project.

An equally celebrated study in its day, and one deserving more attention even today, was that undertaken by Robert and Helen Lynd working from Columbia in 1924–5.[24] This was a study of life in Muncie, Indiana, and typified by an eclecticism of data sources. They undertook the extensive analysis of various documents, compiled statistics of their own, made use of officially provided statistics and other materials, such as records, participated in community events and organisations, interviewed various members of the community in depth as well as administering a standardised questionnaire to various sets of people. Although the survey does make an appearance it is very much an adjunct to other methods of data collection. It was by no means the most important of the social research methods used; participation in the social life of the community and the consideration of documentary material is given far greater prominence.

However (as we indicated in Chapter 3), between the mid-1920s and the mid-1950s in the United States there was the marked and dramatic shift towards the dominance of survey methods in social research. A study of the kind of research, published in the official journal of the American Sociological Association for the years 1962 to 1969, showed that 90 per cent of the articles and research notes presented data taken from social surveys using questionnaires. A small number of studies did make use of observational methods, but a high proportion of these also included supplementary interview data 'to bolster their conclusions'. Brown and Gilmartin also report that 'Other anthropological techniques were completely ignored. Life histories and personal documents were seldom gathered'.[25] Associated with this rise to prominence of the social survey method were new modes of theorising about social action and social organisation. As Turner and Turner note, the 'history of social thought' as a subdivision of the discipline dropped out of view as the 'relentless propagandizing for the scientific method' and the identification of science with metrication gathered pace. Survey research became the paradigmatical method of sociology.[26] For one thing, the business of developing theory that was responsive to empirical investigation became a much more serious business as did the whole enterprise of methodology as a specific and distinctive branch of sociology and social research. Parsons's efforts to build a general theory of action, though criticised in some quarters, did at least provide an ambition for social research as something it could and ought to contribute to. As part of this a rather different kind of social survey emerged and with it new kinds of data.

THE SOCIAL PSYCHOLOGICAL SURVEY

During the 1930s the interest in public opinion polling germinated a more academically oriented interest in attitudes, in part as an attempt to resolve some of the problems arising from electoral prediction. At this time, and throughout the 1940s and 1950s, a series of attempts were made to take the problems of attitude measurement, and the related issue of the relationship between attitudes and behaviour, very seriously indeed. And, given its tradition, one of the problems to which this effort was first directed was toward the understanding of voting behaviour and the prediction of election results.

In the United States, what we now recognise as social psychology has always been a rich vein of thought. Not only have Americans made seminal contributions to the origins of this discipline, but also many American sociologists, and social researchers more generally, have been imbued with an interest in small-group phenomena and in personality and attitudes. Scholars such as Giddings, Cooley, Mead, Thomas and Znanieki are often considered as contributors to some of the basic ideas of social psychology as well as to sociology. Scholars in this field had for some time been engaged in a debate over the importance of acquired and inherited personality traits in behaviour. Attitude research was the property of no school in this respect and constituted a set of problems to which all might contribute.

At this time, too, the vigorous and largely indigenous current of thought and research in social psychology in the United States was given a powerful boost by the influx of expatriate German scholars, liberal democrats most of them, fleeing from the Nazi regime. Lazarsfeld and Adorno are, perhaps, the best known of these (as we suggested in Chapter 3) as major figures in the development and application of scaling methods in social research. The work of these men, which was primarily pioneering, though concerned with social surveys as a method, also contributed to American social psychology by suggesting new theories of personality and personality formation inspired by a very different European tradition of thought.

Also in the 1930s and 1940s, as has been argued in the last chapter, such scholars as Lazarsfeld, Thurstone, Likert, Stouffer and Guttman had begun to develop a quite different approach to attitudes than had previously been considered.[27] Instead of taking attitudes as relatively straightforward guides to behaviour and expressed as opinions, they sought to measure attitudes more as dispositional and rooted deeper in the personality. They reasoned that an attitude held by an individual is a unique value on a continuum of possibilities or scale, rather than something which is simply present or absent. Hence, instead of asking a voter whether or not s/he intends to vote Republican, they would ask a battery of questions bearing on many aspects of policy. In itself this was not so radical a departure from polling methods, and soon Gallup and other agencies began to adopt the same methods. But the procedures involved were more than attempts to improve the sensitivity of attitude measures; they also involved no little reformulation of the theory of attitudes. It was assumed that what was being measured was a property of the personality. Here we have, in fact, a developed form of the variable analysis discussed in the last chapter. Scholars were seeking to measure attitudes at a high level, and to infer from this different accounts or models of the personality by reference to which behaviour could be explained. This logic is common to many scaling procedures currently in use, and, of course, incorporates what later became known as the logic of variable analysis in reasoning from observable indicators to some theoretically defined construct.

The study which pushed the techniques discussed here furthest in the direction of theorising about personality on the basis of attitude survey data was the celebrated work of Adorno and his colleagues reported in *The Authoritarian Personality*.[28] In this study several discrete attitude scales were used: the so-called Anti-Semitism, Ethnocentricity, Political Conservatism, and Fascism scales. The scales were devised using a method originally devised by the American social psychologist, Rensis Likert. The questionnaire for the survey began with a few brief factual questions about personal details, and a second, more important part of the schedule contained batteries of questions aimed at measuring an individual's standing on the scales mentioned earlier. For the authors of this study there was a clear expectation that individuals would commonly produce patterned responses which could be ascribed to a particular personality type. The type they were most interested in was exemplified by persons scoring highly on each of the scales, which they called the 'Authoritarian Personality'. Such personalities were seen as objectifying within the personality a particular sort of social and political ideology, which was the product of determinable social processes.

CHIEF LEGACIES OF SOCIAL PSYCHOLOGICAL SURVEYS

These developments in social psychology and social research made available a whole series of highly sophisticated techniques for measuring attitudes and other social properties. Though attitude surveys were never widely used in Britain, none the less, the achievements of these researchers have inevitably influenced the work of modern survey analysts in the design and the analysis of questionnaires. The social psychological survey embodied the practical use of scaling techniques by which the attitudes of respondents were held to exemplify positions on basic dimensions and, in this respect, has profoundly affected the way in which social researchers think about the constitution of 'things' that constitute the social world.

Not only was it the structure of attitudes which concerned these scholars, but also they were interested in the dynamics of attitudinal change. Attitudes can change, can be changed, can be responsive to many kinds of stimuli, such as election campaigns, advertising, interactions with others, and so on, and sometimes such changes are crucial to understanding and predicting the outcome of events. Elections, for example, are not decided by those electors whose support for particular parties is relatively fixed, but by those relatively uncommitted individuals whose attitudes and voting choices may not set until nearer polling day. Presumably on many issues, and in many situations, attitudes in everyday life do change, and may change quickly. Recognising this problem led scholars in the area to make the first serious use of what are called longitudinal studies.

The surveys we have discussed so far in this chapter have all involved taking a single cross-section sample of a particular population. But, given an interest in attitude change, a survey taken at a single point in time is not very useful, for no matter how carefully chosen, one sample will fail to capture changes. Administering, as part of a cross-sectional survey, a series of attitude questions to a sample of respondents, we will not be able to determine which of them are expressing fairly firm attitudes from those responding out of some whim or other, or who have changed, or who simply want to please the interviewer or get rid of him. Moreover, in a volatile period, such as the run-up to an election, all kinds of events may predispose some people to change their minds and their attitudes, and it may well be important to chart this movement in order to decide if it is systematic, persistent or spasmodic. In an effort to meet these kinds of problems, Lazarsfeld and his colleagues devised the 'panel study'.[29]

In this type of survey a sample of people is recruited to a panel and their attitudes are surveyed at different times. This has the merit of allowing researchers to identify changes in attitudes among a population in a more reliable way than random sampling where variations might simply be due to variations between samples. Provided that the panel is selected on a random basis in the first place, we can be sure that the changes identified are real changes in the group and, within a given limit of reliability, in the population as well. A major problem to guard against is the effect of the research itself. Repeatedly interviewing the same people can sensitise them to the research, and this may have unknown effects on their responses. They might, for example, become more interested in the topics the attitudes concern than they might otherwise, or, conversely, become bored. Another factor is sample mortality. During the normal course of events people move, die, drop out of sight or get involved in other things, and such events are likely to affect the panel subjects. To obviate these effects sometimes a series of control samples are randomly selected and interviewed alongside the panel sample to check on the likely consequences of these effects, if any.

Panel studies are an example of longitudinal studies which are not, of course, confined to attitude research. In the form of 'cohort studies', that is, following single age groups through successive periods, they have proved extremely useful in medical, environmental, educational and policy-related research. They are also costly which is, perhaps, the major reason why they tend to be little used when compared with the cross-sectional, single survey.[30]

THE EXPLANATORY SURVEY

In Chapter 3 we outlined the logic of the experiment underlying the inferential structure known as variable analysis which achieved its full flowering in connection with the final type of survey we wish to discuss, the explanatory survey. In a way all the survey types we have been discussing have been concerned with explanation, at least in the wide sense of this term. Even the 'factual' survey provokes, at some point, the requirement to explain why the facts are as they are. What we have in mind here, however, are uses of the survey method which are explicitly designed to test particular theories or explanations. As such, it involves using the survey as a method which, through its design, allows for the testing of theoretically derived hypotheses: this was partly consequent upon the development of statistical methodology.

Just as an earlier generation of social survey researchers in Britain had made use of developments in statistics, so did the post-war generation of social scientists in the United States, though building on work done prior to this period. The eventual outcome of these innovations was the emergence of the social survey as the dominant method of social research using principles derived, and extended, from experimental designs in biology and botany, and in psychology.

For many years biologists and botanists had been concerned with developing methods for eliminating extraneous variables in their research in order that the factor in which they were primarily interested could be more effectively gauged as to its effects. For example, in evaluating the yield of a particular hybrid plant, they had to be certain that all the factors which, taken collectively, and variably, affect growth, such as climatic conditions, fertility of the soil, moisture, disease resistance, and so on, were adequately controlled so that the yield of the hybrid could be stringently compared with that of the non-hybrid. In this way observed differences in yields, or whatever property was under investigation, could be accounted for. The techniques which emerged to deal with this kind of problem owed much to the pioneering work of R.A. Fisher, and others, and involved elaborations of the classic form of experimental design.[31]

In Chapter 3 we reviewed some of the main principles of experimental design in which a control group is used to assess the relationship between some causal factor and its presumed effect. In trying to determine the effect of, say, a new teaching style on academic attainment, factors extraneous to this relationship but which might have a bearing on attainment, need to be excluded or controlled in some fashion in order to assess the effect of teaching style. In this case a control group would be selected which matches as closely as possible, member for member, the characteristics of the people constituting the experimental group. The presumed causal factor, normally referred to as the 'independent variable', is withheld from the control group and administered only to the experimental group. So, in our example, it would be the experimental group which was exposed to the new teaching style. Since the two groups are as alike in all respects except that one of them, the experimental group, has received the supposedly causal treatment, the new teaching style, then any differences in academic attainment between the two groups must be due either to chance or to the causal factor. There are a whole set of statistical techniques for assessing the probability that the observed differences between the two groups could have resulted from chance. Such statistical tests yield statements of probability about the likelihood of a particular result having occurred by chance. This is what is meant when it is reported that a result, according to a particular test, is significant at, say, the 0.001 level. That is, the probability is 1 in 1000 for the result to have occurred by chance. Because this is a low probability the researcher could feel justified in accepting the result of the experiment as, at least, probably demonstrating a causal connection.

Of course, one major problem is ensuring that the experimental and the control groups are as alike as possible in all relevant respects. Accordingly, the researcher needs to know a great deal about likely extraneous factors so that they can be controlled. In the example here it might plausibly be supposed that the age of the pupils might well influence attainment or otherwise modify the effect of the causal factor. In which case it would be verging on the absurd to have one group composed of 8 year olds and the other of 16 year olds. In this case, the researcher has the choice of restricting the samples to one age-group, or increasing the sample size to include wider age ranges.

But assuming that matches can be achieved on all the known likely factors, there may well be others that could affect the main relationship of interest that are not known about. Accordingly, in allocating each of the matched subjects to either the control or to the experimental group, and to ensure that there is no surreptitious influence determining this allocation, the researcher randomly allocates one of each matched pair of subjects to one or the other group. In this way the effects on any unwanted and unknown factors are randomised and should exert no untoward effect on the outcome of the experiment. Matching and randomisation are the two key principles here.

The logic instantiated in this research design has been used to effect in some branches of psychology and medicine as a method for testing causal explanations. It is also a design adopted by some survey researchers, though in a truncated form. The degree of control of human populations required by the design, especially in the random allocation of subjects to experimental and to control groups, and subjecting one but not the other to the causal treatment in the field, is practically impossible. This is quite apart from any moral objections that might arise. So, only approximations to the classical model can be achieved. In place of the random allocation of respondents to the control and experimental groups, survey analysts have to be content with random samples from different groups which occur 'naturally' in the population.[32]

In place of the controlled administration of a 'treatment', survey analysts have to ensure that individuals with different experiences or attitudes or characteristics are represented in the sample by stratification, or similar, procedures. Neither practice has the rigour of the design of the classical experiment. In fact, much of the use of the logic of experimental design in survey work takes place at the data analysis stage through elaborations of the cross-tabulation technique (described in Chapter 3).[33]

Although this use of the survey seemed to offer to social scientists a more scientific way of approximating closely to a natural scientific model of research, incorporating measurement and quantification, hypothesis-testing, generalisability and theory relevance, it has not been without its problems and controversies. One such concerned the validity of the statistical tests upon which much of the power of the method seemed to depend. Another, more prolonged and more significant, concerned the very foundations of variable analysis, and by implication the explanatory survey, namely its empiricist inspiration.

The first of these, the statistical test controversy, arose in the 1950s when a group of American scholars vigorously attacked the use of such tests, pointing out the difficulty of surveys meeting the strict mathematical requirements demanded by the statistical theory, especially those to do with randomness.[34] The random selection of units was vital. Unless this condition was met inferences about relationships within the sample could not be statistically secured. The standard defence against this charge was to concede the statistical point but, none the less, argue that such measures were valuable indicators of *possibly* significant or interesting relationships in the data. Both sides, however, agreed that the use of statistical tests without a well-thought-out theory was little more than useless. In other words, statistical testing should not be used as a substitute for theoretical ideas by simply dredging the data for any statistically significant relationships that happen to be present. It is the theoretical significance that is important.

In fact, the statistical significance test controversy was the precursor of concerns that turned out to be rather more fundamental to variable analysis; concerns that were not voiced by such as Becker and other Symbolic Interactionists who wanted no truck with a sociology derived from variable analysis (and whose criticisms we shall review later in this chapter), but by advocates of variable analytic and survey approaches. In brief, such doubts centred around the use of experimental designs in this context and, related to this, the nature of the knowledge such an empiricist research strategy was capable of producing.

We raised the matter of theory in connection with the explanatory survey: the testing of theory was the point of such a research tool and the rationale behind the inferential structure of variable analysis. The testing of theories or, more accurately, hypotheses derived from theories, was to be done using principles of experimental design and statistical testing. Unfortunately, in a number of respects explanatory surveys failed to match up to the strict requirements of the logic required.

The normal practice of surveyors is to select groups of interest and sample within these using an appropriate list giving full coverage of the population to be sampled. It is at the analysis stage that the logic of the experiment is deployed: in an important sense, this is too late a stage. The classic experiment requires both a control and an experimental group to which subjects are randomly allocated. In this respect, and prior to the experimental treatment, the two groups are as alike, in all relevant respects, as they can be. However, in field conditions nothing like this is ever attempted. Instead, random samples, simple or stratified, are taken for the survey. Then, when the data have been collected, the respondents are grouped into homogeneous categories according to their scores for selected variables. Thus, occupational type might be used, and for ease of exposition, the categories manual/non-manual. Clearly, although respondents so grouped will have this property in common, they will undoubtedly also vary on lots of other factors, such as level of education, income, attitudes and beliefs, number of siblings, ethnicity, age, gender, and many more. These, or at least the more salient ones, the analyst will try to control by partitioning, that is dividing each of the original occupational categories into, subgroups with other possibly salient characteristics in common. In this way, it is proposed, the effect of occupation on, say, political affiliation, can be explored by holding constant marital status, level of education, etc.

However, it is necessary to note that there is a limit to the number of variables that can be held constant in this way. These may be practical limits, but are real enough. The main ones are as follows. First, a survey can ask only about a limited range of matters. Kinsey, in his pioneering studies of human sexual behaviour in the late 1940s, may have made use of eight-hour interviews, but in the vast majority of surveys these are out of the question.[35] The point is that data analysts can control only for those factors on which they have data. This is true of the experiment but, by the random allocation of subjects to the control and the experimental groups, any effects of the unknown factors are randomised. This cannot be assumed so easily in variable analysis. Second, statistical partitioning requires expected cell frequencies of, roughly, between ten and twenty cases otherwise tests of significance and measures of association become unstable and unreliable. This constraint means that even with large samples of, say, 1,000 respondents, controlling for three or four factors at once means the analyst is likely to run out of cases very soon. Third, using the example of occupational categories again, even assuming that a researcher has selected the sample randomly, only later dividing the group with respect to the property of occupational type, this is hardly the randomisation required by experimental design. To repeat, in this randomisation is intended to neutralise the effects of all confounding factors, while in the case of the survey this is not so. The random selection of cases is an approximation to experimental randomisation if it can be assumed that the population from which the sample is drawn is homogeneous: a reasonable assumption when dealing with a population of seeds, plants, germs, etc. It is less reasonable, we suggest, when dealing with the social properties of human beings.[36] Moreover, it is one of the founding presuppositions of sociology, one might say of social science more generally, that individuals are related to each other rather than isolated. They are members of groups, associations, cultures and subcultures, families, neighbourhoods, work groups, organisations, and have many other affiliations. It simply cannot be assumed that samples selected for their distinctiveness on one variable will vary randomly on others. The sociologist makes the opposite assumption.

There are a number of complex issues bound up with this particular matter, ontological and epistemological, practical as well as theoretical. Sampling individuals for, say, opinion polling prior to an election is a reasonable procedure since the act of voting is an individual one.[37] The outcome of the election is, at least in simple majority systems, a direct arithmetic consequence of the individual votes cast. From this point of view, the factors which influence an individual's voting choice are less relevant: what matters is the choice and its distribution. But the objectives of an explanatory survey are not likely to be so straightforward, and it may be that sampling individuals, though convenient, does not sample the phenomenon of interest.

Sampling theory is aimed at providing a mathematical justification for inferences to some population value on the basis of knowledge of a subset, or sample, of that population. In this regard, achieving a representative sample is the objective. It is this requirement which requires a listing of the population members, or units, from which the sample may be drawn using a random procedure. Accordingly, if one wishes to produce a sample to estimate the prevalence of certain characteristics in the population of the United Kingdom, in principle one has to be able to list that population. In cases such as this substitutes to this ideal are used, such as electoral registers, lists of households, etc., with the proviso that such lists, while convenient, may not include, for any number of reasons, all the units that belong to the population of the United Kingdom. Given that we can adequately define who to include as belonging to the category 'the population of the United Kingdom', and providing that we have convenient lists which do not seriously under-represent significant subgroups, then reasonable estimations of population values can be made from the sample.

However, such a procedure is not always suitable for explanatory research since, in this case, the aim is to achieve sufficient cases for analysis rather than a representative sample of some population. Indeed, in many such cases, it is not at all clear what the parameters of the population, of which the sample is a subset, actually are. 'Deferential conservatives', 'militant labourites', 'alienated workers', 'authoritarian personalities', are types that are a sample of some population, but we could not list that population in advance. In most cases of explanatory surveys it is perhaps less appropriate to speak of samples at all in the strict sense. What explanatory surveys require are cases which possess characteristics relevant to the problem of the research. Thus, selecting cases needs to be done on the basis of theoretically informed criteria rather than those to do with representativeness. This may require targetting particular, and known, subgroups of the general population in order to obtain sufficient cases, or respondents that will contain sufficient cases.

There is an additional point worth noting here. The social survey makes use of the interview and/or the questionnaire, a method of data collection obviously designed to be administered to individuals. As a result, the sampling units are ultimately, even if stratification or a similar strategy is used, individuals. It is the responses they provide which constitute the data recorded and analysed. It is individuals who, in one capacity or another, appear on lists used by surveyors to select as their samples. However, it is this which is a possible disjunction between the instrumental presuppositions of the survey and various theoretical conceptions of the phenomena that are the subject of social research. It is a crucial postulate underpinning all the social sciences that individuals are related through associations of various kinds. In short, it is not so much the isolated individual, or even a large number of isolated individuals, that is the focus of interest, but individuals-in-relation-to-other-individuals. In this respect, then, it can be argued that the survey is too individualistic, not only in the sense that only individuals can respond to questionnaires, but also in that every individual is assumed to have as much importance as every other. As Galtung puts it, in surveys every individual is 'made to appear in the sample as a society of one person to be compared with other societies of one person'.[38] The only way in which such a procedure might be excused is if the societies from which the samples were drawn were homogeneous – an assumption which is hard to sustain. Although individuals may be grouped on the basis of various variable scores, this is almost always without regard for their position within the social structure. In other words, and as Lieberson stresses, there are selectivity processes at work in almost all social settings that vitiate, in the end, the idea of random sampling.[39]

There are, of course, ways of attempting to counteract this excessive individualism of the survey. For one, the sampling procedure could be designed so that individuals are selected according to their position within the social structure or social group. Such purposive sampling could sample individuals along with other individuals with whom they are significantly related, such as members of their family, stated friends, work-mates, or whatever is appropriate. This is in fact the implicit approach of some observational methods as we shall see in Chapter 6. Another method is to collect information on structural and other contextual properties and to use these as a basis for sampling. In any event, surveying becomes a much more complicated business and much more difficult to execute satisfactorily. Purposive sampling, for example, could not be effectively done in advance of interviewing, since significant others could only be guessed at without the informant furnishing more detailed information.

Galtung suggests that the individualistic survey method may well yield results that reflect conditions prevailing in one type of society only, that is societies which rate highly both on individual mobility, geographic, horizontal as well as vertical mobility, and on inner-directedness.[40] Thus, the traditional survey based on random samples from populations of individuals and the effort to account for what they do in terms of an interaction between attitudes, personality and general background structural factors, implies that we have an adequate understanding of the relative importance of social position, personality and the relationship between the two. Galtung goes on to suggest that social science needs a much richer conception of what constitutes the social unit, bearing in mind that these may well need to change from society to society. The counterpart of the survey is the election. The democratic principle is one person one vote, as is the principle of statistical analysis. Thus a democratic bias is introduced which may be inappropriate where individuals do not count equally.

CONCLUSION

There can be little doubt that the survey since its modern inception has had a major impact on social research, and any history of social research has to award it a salient place. It is probably the method most associated with the idea of social research constituting the source of much if not most of social science data. What is also of interest here, and this relates to a point Galtung makes, are the historical and social conditions which make the survey, like any method of social research for that matter, possible as instruments of data collection. This is not only to do with the intellectual innovations that led to the idea of the first factual surveys through to the social psychological and, finally, to the explanatory surveys incorporating variable analysis, but also to do with what is indicated about the nature of society and social life. Surveys, we might say though all too briefly, depend upon mores that allow individuals to be interviewed about their private lives, their feelings, attitudes or beliefs, without feeling unduly threatened, intimidated or insulted. The survey requires, too, an institutionalisation of the individual as an autonomous member of civil society with rights and obligations and a conception of the same individual as a distinctive agent in the social process. The individual is the provider of material and data, is sought after for this purpose, is the bearer of social forces and is the agent of society itself. Indeed, one could hazard a further, and more general, observation that the possibility of social research itself is an indicator of the character of society; to paraphrase Lieberson, social conditions not only determine the data of interest but also shape the availability of those data.[41]

Celebrating the importance of the survey in the history and contemporary milieux of social research is one thing; but this importance does not place it beyond criticism as a method of social research. As we indicated in the discussion of sampling, the survey method, especially the explanatory survey, has been subjected to severe criticism and from social researchers whose own careers have been forged within the tradition of variable analysis. Lieberson in a powerful and detailed critique of experimental thinking in social research, after all one of the cornerstones of variable analysis, argues that although most data in social research are non-experimental in origin, they are 'treated as if they were truly experimental data ... sliced, chopped, beaten, molded, baked, and finally artificially coloured until the researcher is able to serve us proudly with a plateful of mock experiment'.[42] As should be clear, this is precisely the objective of variable analysis and the explanatory survey, that is to emulate the experimental method in the collection and analysis of non-experimental data. Lieberson goes on, 'we are still totally oriented to the experimental model'. Researchers without very much thought, continually try to manipulate non-experimental data so as to approximate as closely as possible to the kind of experiment held to epitomise natural science. But to do so, he maintains, they are obliged to make impossible assumptions that 'generate analyses that are completely off the mark'.[43]

Although the details of Lieberson's argument are often statistical, formal, carefully wrought and complicated, the burden of his complaint is that controlling in most social research ignores, or fails to deal with adequately, selectivity in the controlled variable. This is a not dissimilar point to the one we made earlier concerning sampling individuals from a social world which is relationally organised. To put it briefly: in social science one is dealing with situations in which people, ignoring their birth, have not been randomly assigned to their respective social universes. The social world is an organised world.[44] In which case, the absence of random assignment, to use Lieberson's rendering of the problem, presents special difficulties if 'there is reason to believe that the subjects thereby placed in each condition differ in other ways that themselves have a bearing on the outcome of interest to the researcher'.[45] For example, suppose a researcher wishes to determine the influence of military service on later civilian earnings. Simply comparing the incomes of those experiencing military service with those who did not will not do. There are good reasons to think that military service is not a random event, irrespective of whether there is a draft system in operation or simply voluntary service. Social processes operate, 'selectivity' in Lieberson's terms, such that volunteers, draftees or those never serving, will differ from one another on factors that will have a bearing on life chances, hence income, later on. It cannot be assumed, as can reasonably in many experiments in natural science, that units are identical. Selectivity affects variables or attributes that influence the outcome or the dependent variable: the problem is, if using the experimental mock-up, to separate out this initial selectivity from the impact of the institution, in this case, the military.[46] Matters are made worse if different selectivity processes are operating for each subgroup. Thus, to continue with the example, different processes, or the same processes with different magnitudes, may well operate between volunteers, draftees and those with no military experience. Such unmeasured selectivity processes are operating in most social research. The reason why Lieberson is doubtful about the control variable approach is the selectivity processes are probably operating within the control variables themselves and involve factors which affect the dependent variable but in unmeasured ways. In a series of examples, Lieberson goes on to demonstrate that under a variety of conditions, unmeasured selectivity can produce wrong answers and identify wrong patterns. That is, the assumption that by controlling a researcher can move closer to the truth, or is at worst a benign procedure, cannot be sustained.

Another set of problems that has serious implications for the social survey involves issues to do with data analysis rather more than collection but, none the less, does have a bearing in getting us to understand the limits of the survey and of variable analysis. Most social surveys are cross-sectional, for obvious reasons of cost, even though the topic of the research may well be social processes of various kinds, such as attitudinal change, changes in life-style and life chances. Many of the techniques, and importantly the theories, used to analyse such data make assumptions about the nature of such processes, particularly that they are symmetrical and reversible. Suffice it to say that the cross-sectional survey is not well attuned to handling processes, but this is a much more serious matter if one abandons the assumptions of symmetry and reversibility. In examining, for example, the influence of X on Y, it has to be considered whether shifts to a given value of X from either direction have the same consequences for

Y. Does it matter, that is, whether *X* has increased or decreased to reach its present level, or whether the relationship is asymmetrical in that different values of *X* do not have a uniform effect on *Y*? Further, a great deal depends upon whether processes are reversible or irreversible. A reversible process would be one in which changes in *X* cause an increase in *Y* and a reversal in *X* produces a decline in *Y*. An example of this would be the move toward a more punitive style of management in a factory (*X*) which increased absenteeism (*Y*) which declined when a move is made to a more indulgent management style. An example of an irreversible process would be Weber's essay on the influence of Protestantism on the development of capitalism. Once the attitudes toward the acquisition of material goods and worldly signs of success had been acquired, then any decline in religious beliefs would leave the attitudinal changes unaffected.

The point that Lieberson is making is one concerning multivariate analysis but also has lessons for the cross-sectional survey. First, theory needs to be explicit about whether it is dealing with symmetrical or asymmetrical, reversible or irreversible relationships. Second, whatever is determined about this, it is crucial to determining whether or not the data produced by the cross-sectional survey can provide accurate estimates of the relationship of interest. This Lieberson doubts.[47]

We have spent some space reviewing Lieberson's arguments because he provokes an important critical reaction which is necessary to uproot the widespread belief that the survey is the answer to social research's dreams. The early proponents of the explanatory survey felt that they could, through the logic of variable analysis, closely approximate to the experimental model using non-experimental data and, through the patient accumulation of findings discover law-like relationships about the nature and processes of social life. This hope it begins to appear, admittedly with hindsight, looks to be one that must remain unfulfilled using current methods. For one thing, the Lazarsfeldian method is empiricist, that is concerned to discover empirical regularities or patterns among phenomena. While not denying that this has an important role to play in any science, it is not clear that it is the method responsible for the discovery of natural laws. To quote Lieberson once again: imagine an inquiry, using the logic of social research, into why objects fall. The strategy would be to find that different objects fall at different rates and, likely as not, determine that two variables were mainly responsible – size and the shape of each object. Both of these would account for most of the variations in the different rates of fall. It would not, in other words, discover gravity. The strategy could not make, nor sustain if it could, the *ceteris paribus* conditions such as the idea of a perfect vacuum in which objects fall at a constant rate of acceleration whatever their size and shape. In 'real' conditions where friction, for example, can affect the rate of fall, we would have a parallel situation to that of the social scientist.

This does not, of course, have any bearing upon whether or not there are such laws of social life to discover or imply that the survey method ought to be abandoned. Certainly there are many who would concur with at least the gist of Lieberson's, and others', criticisms but argue that more effort should be directed at improving methods of data collection and analysis to meet these kinds of objections. There are others, (we shall meet some of them later) who would argue that this urge to emulate the natural sciences in this way is premature. In any event, the idea that Lazarsfeld had discovered a ubiquitous method of social research has to fall by the wayside.

NOTES

1. See, for example, T.S. Simey and M.B. Simey, *Charles Booth, Social Scientist*, London, Oxford University Press, 1960; A. Briggs, 'B. Seebohm Rowntree: 1871–1954', in A. Briggs and J. Saville (eds) *Essays in Labour History*, London, Macmillan, 2 vols, 1960 and 1971; C. Booth (ed.) *Life and Labour of the People of London*, London, Macmillan, 1892; B.S. Rowntree, *Poverty: A Study in Town Life*, London, Macmillan, 1901.

2. See M. Bulmer, *The Chicago School of Sociology: Institutionalisation, Diversity and the Rise of Sociological Research*, Chicago, University of Chicago Press, 1984, p. 65. Also P.V. Young, *Scientific Social Surveys and Research*, New York, Prentice-Hall, 1939.

3. This was also an assumption of the early attitude researchers in the United States.

4. Booth, in particular, studied census data before he began his own more detailed investigations. See his 'Occupations of the people of the United Kingdom, 1801–1881', *Journal of the Royal Statistical Society*, 1886. For some comments on Booth's life and contribution to social science, see G. Easthope, *A History of Social Research Methods*, London, Longman, 1974, pp. 49–55.

5. D.V. Glass, *Numbering the People: The Eighteenth Century Population Controversy*, London, Gordon & Clemonisi, 1973.

6. B. Hindess, *The Uses of Official Statistics in Sociology*, London, Macmillan, 1973.

7. R.G.D. Allen in *The Dictionary of National Biography, 1959–61*, Oxford, Oxford University Press, 1971.

8. The term is taken from G.H. Sabine, *A History of Political Theory*, 3rd edn, London, Harrap, 1960. For an interesting commentary on the relationship between sociology and liberalism, see S. Collini, *Sociology and Liberalism*, Cambridge, Cambridge University Press, 1979.

9. See M. Abrams, *Social Surveys and Social Action*, London, Heinemann, 1951, ch. 10.

10. C.A. Moser, *Survey Methods in Social Investigation*, London, Heinemann, 1958, p. 23.

11. *ibid.*, p. 25. Incidentally, Moser himself, who identifies survey work very much with the tradition of national sample surveys, became Director of the Central Statistical Office, so prolonging the tradition of Booth and Rowntree.

12. D. MacKenzie, 'Eugenics and the rise of mathematical statistics in Britain', and M. Shaw and I. Miles, 'The social roots of social knowledge', in J.L. Irvine, I. Miles and J. Evans (eds) *Demystifying Social Statistics*, London, Pluto, 1979.

13. Quoted by G. Gallup and S.A. Rae, *The Pulse of Democracy*, New York, Simon & Schuster, 1940, p. 6.

14. Abrams, *op.cit.*, pp. 55–62.

15. Abrams, *op.cit.*, offers some perceptive remarks on the Straw Poll, see especially pp. 64–5.

16. T.H. Marshall, 'A British sociological career', *British Journal of Sociology*, 24, 1973, pp. 399–408.

17. L.L. Barnard and J. Barnard, *Origins of American Sociology*, New York, Crowell, 1943; J. Madge, *Origins of Scientific Sociology*, London, Tavistock, 1963, especially ch. 1; K. Wolf, 'Notes toward a socio-cultural interpretation of American sociology', *American Sociological Review*, 11, 1946, pp. 545–53; S.P. Turner and J.H. Turner, *The Impossible Science: An Institutional Analysis of American Sociology*, Newbury Park, Calif., Sage, 1990.

18. J.D.Y Peel, *Herbert Spencer: The Evolution of a Sociologist*, London, Heinemann, 1971, p. 249.

19. Bulmer, *op.cit.* Burgess wrote, 'The social survey provides a unique opportunity both for investigation and for social construction, both for the analysis of mental attitudes and for the control of forces in ... improvement'. E.W. Burgess, 'The social survey: a field for constructive service by departments of sociology', *American Journal of Sociology*, 21, 1916, p. 499, also quoted in Bulmer, *op.cit.* p. 73. For a description of modern survey methods see C. Marsh, *The Survey Method*, London, Allen & Unwin, 1982.

20. D. Martindale, *The Nature and Types of Sociological Theory*, London, Routledge & Kegan Paul, 1960, p. 520.

21. Writing in 1959, C.W. Mills suggested that American sociology was dominated by 'grand theory', which was largely Functionalist, and 'abstracted empiricism', which was predominantly the statistical manipulation of survey data. See his *Sociological Imagination*, New York, Oxford University Press, 1959, which is still worth reading.

22. See, for example, R.E.L. Faris, *Chicago Sociology, 1920–30*, Chicago, University of Chicago Press, 1967; P. Rock, *The Making of Symbolic Interactionism*, London, Macmillan, 1979; Bulmer, *op.cit.*

23. W.I. Thomas and F. Znanieki, *The Polish Peasant in Europe and America*, New York, Knopf, 1927.

24. R.S. Lynd and H.M. Lynd, *Middletown: A Study of Contemporary Culture*, New York, Harcourt Brace, 1929.

25. J. Brown and B.G. Gilmartin, 'Sociology today: lacunae, emphases and surfeits', *American Sociologist*, 4, 1968. See also D. Phillips, *Knowledge From What?* New York, Rand McNally, 1971, ch. 1.

26. Turner and Turner, *op.cit.*, pp. 124–5.

27. Bulmer, *op.cit.*, pp. 178, traces the influence of Thurstone on Stouffer's work and the connection through the latter of the British statisticians Pearson, Yule and Bowley at the University of London where Stouffer spent 1931–2.

28. T.W. Adorno, E. Frenkel-Brunswick, D.F. Levinson and R.N. Sanford, *The Authoritarian Personality*, New York, Harper, 1950. See also R. Christie and M. Jahoda, *Continuities in the Authoritarian Personality*, New York, Free Press, 1954, for an evaluation and assessment of the study from within a similar tradition.

29. See, for example, P.F. Lazarsfeld, B. Berelson and H. Gaudet, *The People's Choice*, New York, Columbia University Press, 1944.

30. For an account of panel and other types of longitudinal studies see W.D. Wall and H.L. Williams, *Longitudinal Studies and the Social Sciences*, London, Heinemann, 1970.

31. See R.A. Fisher, *The Design of Experiments*, Edinburgh, Oliver & Boyd, 1937.

32. See, for early formulations, S. Stouffer, 'Some observations on study designs', *American Journal of Sociology*, 53, 1950, pp. 355–61; D.T. Campbell and J.C. Stanley, *Experimental Designs and Quasi-experimental Designs for Research*, Chicago, Rand McNally, 1963.

33. See N. Bateson, *Data Construction in Social Surveys*, London, Allen & Unwin, 1984.

34. H. Selvin, 'A critique of significance tests in survey research', in R. Henkel and D. Morrison (eds) *The Significance Test Controversy*, London, Butterworth, 1970.

35. A.C. Kinsey, C. Pomeroy, B. Wardell and C. Martin, *Sexual Behaviour in the Human Male*, Philadelphia, Pa., Saunders, 1948.

36. Indeed, one such property is the effects of the experiment itself which, according to Boring, is the rationale behind the development of the control group itself. See E.G. Boring, 'Prospective: artifact and control', in R. Rosenthal and R.L.

Rosnow (eds) *Artifact in Behavioural Research*, New York, Academic Press, 1969.

37. Many factors do, of course, influence voting choice. But the act of voting for a party, the phenomenon of interest to pollsters, is an individual one. The point is that attention must be paid to the problem being addressed in judging the reasonableness of any methodological procedure.

38. J. Galtung, *Theory and Methods of Social Research*, London, Allen & Unwin, 1967, p. 150.

39. S. Lieberson, *Making it Count: The Improvement of Social Research and Theory*, Berkeley, University of California Press, 1985.

40. Galtung, *op.cit.*, p. 151.

41. Lieberson, *op.cit.*, p. 230.

42. *ibid.*, p. 4.

43. *ibid.*, p. 6.

44. Understanding the nature and origins of this organisation is, it could be said, one of the fundamental problems of social science. Talcott Parsons spoke of it as the Hobbesian problem of order and it is the site where many of the theoretical disputes occur.

45. Lieberson, *op.cit.*, p. 15.

46. Note that selectivity is not a problem if it does not affect the variable under consideration.

47. Lieberson, *op.cit.*, ch. 4.

CHAPTER 5

Interviewing

Interviews are encounters between a researcher and a respondent in which an individual is asked a series of questions relevant to the subject of the research. The respondent's answers constitute the raw material to be analysed at a later point in time. Usually a questionnaire, sometimes referred to as an interview schedule, is used in the interview and contains the questions that the interviewer puts to the respondent. Questionnaires are sometimes used without an interviewer, the respondent completing the questionnaire without any assistance other than the guidance provided by the written instructions on the questionnaire itself. Questionnaires depend on the use of some verbal stimuli – normally a question, but sometimes a statement expressing an attitude or an opinion – designed to elicit a verbal response which is recorded and subsequently analysed along with other responses from other interviewees.

Interviews are normally, though not exclusively, used in surveys. Respondents are selected according to some sampling procedure to be representative of some group, collectivity, attribute or process. For example, a researcher interested in the factors responsible for differing rates of absence from work may well interview groups of workers randomly selected from lists of employees in large factories and small ones, factories which have high or low overall rates of absence, or factories which involve different kinds of production processes. Any one, or a combination of these, may be chosen as the basis for choosing the work-places from which a sample can be selected. Similarly, a researcher interested in the determinants of voting choice might select respondents to interview from an electoral register. Each of the sample members would then be interviewed and the results cross-tabulated to see what differences, if any, there are in the replies from each of the sample collections.

However, interviewing is not the exclusive preserve of survey research. It is not unusual, for example, to find participant observers using interviews. In such cases the interview is used to collect illustrative material to complement other material and findings. In such cases the issue of representativeness is of less concern than in the sample survey. Yet the interview, especially of the formal and standardised type in which questionnaires are used, is more commonly used in connection with survey research, which means that standardised interviews using questionnaires are the most frequently used social research technique.

There must be few people in modern industrial societies who have not taken part in an interview for a social survey for the purposes of market research, public opinion polling or academic research (see Chapter 4). Of all the methods available to the contemporary social researcher, the interview, in conjunction with the sample survey, is the one most typically associated with social research itself. For some, social research and the sample survey are the same: most reports of academic research published in the field of sociology make use of the interview as a means of data collection.[1] There are, of course, some obvious practical benefits in the use of interviews and questionnaires in surveys; the main one being that they are an economical way of obtaining data related to the behaviour and attitudes of large and sometimes scattered populations.

There is now a considerable body of lore and detailed research on the interview method devoted to understanding the dynamics of interviewing and how, in practical terms, its effectiveness as a data-gathering instrument can be improved. Some of this we shall be looking at in this chapter. As with survey techniques, interviewing practices have also evolved. Indeed parallel with developments in the methodology of the survey, there has been a similar effort to make the interview a much more standardised, methodical and effective instrument of social inquiry. Much of this, if not all, has been within the tradition of variable analysis discussed in Chapter 3; that is, making the interview serve the requirements of objective and quantifiable data in the variable analytic format.

The early surveys sought factual information about people and tended to ask straightforward questions to elicit this information. They specialised in questions which, to quote Bowley, 'required an answer of "yes" or "no" or a simple number or something equally definite and precise'.[2] Contemporary surveys also make use of such questions, especially to do with face-sheet information about a respondent, such as age, marital status, and so on, but usually in conjunction with other types. The social psychological survey also left a legacy in the attitudinal questions which are very often contained in questionnaires. With the explanatory survey and the refinement of variable analysis as a way of thinking about social research, the interview and the questionnaire have become most important instruments in achieving the dream of a quantitative social science: it is this which has also modified the character and the rationale of interviewing and questionnaire design.

A great deal of valuable work has been carried out on the interview itself. In the past, the interview tended to be regarded as simply a means of collecting factual information from respondents and, by itself, of little interest. Today, however, there is a much greater realisation that the quality of the data is important to their precision and quantification and, in this regard, it is important to be able to assess the validity and the reliability of those data by understanding the nature of the collection instrument itself, the biases that it is heir to, and the kinds of instrumental corruptions that can affect the quality of the material it provides. In order to understand better the data produced, it is necessary to understand better how and in what ways the instruments that produce those data work.

In this chapter we shall, first, consider the rationale of the interview as offered in contemporary social research. Second, we shall look at the types of interviews and the way in which they commonly feature in social research. Third, we shall address some of the problems associated with interviewing and the use of questionnaires in the context of variable analysis. Fourth, we shall also look more fully at some of the implications of the recognition that the interview is a social process as much as it is a research technique; implications which are, potentially, far reaching.

THE RATIONALE OF INTERVIEWING

The foundations of interviewing lie in the mundane observation that individuals can report on what they feel, are, have, tell others about their lives, disclose what their hopes and fears are, offer their opinions, state what they believe in, say what they did last week, how much they spend on food, who they see regularly, and so on; in short, they can impart masses of information about themselves. The point of the interview is to make full and systematic use of this to gather data for research purposes. In its way, this unremarkable fact about human beings has, in the hands of skilled researchers, created a remarkable instrument of social research. Using as data what respondents say about themselves offers the social researcher access to a vast storehouse of information. Researchers are not constrained to what they can observe or experience directly, but are able to cover as many facets of as many people as resources allow. Nor are researchers limited to studying small numbers of people, as is the case with participant observation, but can, in principle, investigate many thousands. After all, the census questionnaire is intended to cover the entire population of the country. Researchers are not limited to studying only members of their own society but can interview people in other societies including people who may be illiterate and therefore leave no written record of their activities. Using verbal reports offered by respondents, the investigator has access to an almost infinite variety of information that would be impossible to gather by any other means. When reports are analysed using the various methods of statistical treatments available, they can be used to describe fundamental features of society, its nature and changes.

We can now begin to see a little more clearly some of the instrumental presuppositions on which interviewing depends. For one, the method is predicated on a claim that answers offered by a respondent to questions proffered by an interviewer are indicators of whatever aspects of the respondent's social life and being that are the subject of investigation. That is, to put it at its most basic, the respondent is at least an adequate reporter of his or her attitudes, beliefs and other subjective states, his or her relationship with others, past, present and intended behaviour, and about objective features of the respondent's life. This presupposition may seem an uncontentious one but it is far from that.

TYPES OF INTERVIEW

The most common criterion for classifying interviews is in terms of their degree of standardisation; that is, according to the extent to which the interviewer is allowed to vary both the content and the order of the questions asked. At one extreme is the *structured interview* in which interviewers use a schedule to which they must strictly adhere for all respondents. The same questions and the order in which they appear on the schedule would be administered, in a survey, to all respondents by all interviewers in the same way: this is to standardise stimuli. That is, in an effort to ensure that any variations in replies respondents provide are not artifacts of variations in the way in which the questions were asked, each respondent should be given the same questions in the same serial order. Thus, if an interviewer were to ask some questions of a respondent in one way and to another in another way, the researcher could not be sure what effect this variation in the administration of the questions had on the responses received. A question asked early in the interview may affect answers to subsequent questions, and if this order were to be altered it becomes difficult to detect the effect this might have on the replies. Of course, it is necessary to assume that the questions, however they are phrased, are understood in the same way by all respondents whatever differences they may have in other respects, such as level of education or gender. Unless all respondents share a single interpretation of a question their answers cannot be compared. (This is a point to which we shall return.)

However, there is a place in social research, and a very important one, for the type of interview which stands at the other extreme to the structured one, namely the *non-standardised interview*. In this type interviewers work from a list indicating, often in some detail, the kinds of topics to be covered in the interview. Interviewers are free to ask questions in whatever way they think appropriate and natural, and in whatever order is felt to be most effective in the circumstances. Both interviewer and respondent are allowed much greater leeway in asking and answering questions than is the case with the structured interview. Such an interview almost amounts to a conversation. Flexibility is the keynote and is a feature often recommended in pilot studies preliminary to a full-scale study. It is also particularly useful where highly sensitive and subtle matters need to be covered, and where long and detailed responses are required to understand the matters the respondent is reporting on. In a pilot study it allows researchers to test out various lines of questioning, different ways of phrasing questions, gauge the tenor of likely replies, and so on.

The *focused interview* is closely related to the non-standardised or unstructured interview, and differs mainly in the extent to which the direction of the interview is controlled by the interviewer.[3]

Between the two extremes of standardised and non-standardised interviews is the large category of *semi-structured interviews*. As their name suggests they combine, or attempt to do so, the advantages of both of the two polar types. The interviewer is normally required to ask specific questions but is free to probe beyond them if necessary. The relative weight of standardised and non-standardised items can vary from research to research. The most common arrangement is to use the standardised format for 'face-sheet' information, such as age, sex, marital status, educational experience and other relevant data of a demographic character. The less standardised section is used to elicit information more varied and qualitative in character.

Each type of interview is designed with a particular research task in mind. The non-standardised type is most suitably used in exploratory studies where little of any systematic nature is known about the topic. In studies such as these the researcher might interview a small group of people in a fairly free-ranging manner with the intention of gaining useful guidance for the construction of more systematic and standardised interview schedules. The researcher will be looking for indications of the salience of topics, the extent to which questions are understood by different classes of respondents, the likely range of replies to given questions, and so on. These pilot studies are often of immense value in the design of more systematic and more extensive social surveys.

There is a limit to which the non-standardised interview can be used with larger samples. It is extremely costly in time and money since such interviewing can easily take two hours or more, and the data produced are not easy to code and analyse. In fact, pilot studies using the non-standardised format are a useful guide to the coding categories a researcher might use in a larger survey. Accordingly, where large samples are necessary, the structured or semi-structured format provides a number of advantages. They are less costly in time and effort to administer, more straightforward to code and process, and can be used by interviewers not fully conversant with all the fine details of the research. Further, the quantitative form in which the results of standardised interviews can be cast makes it especially important for the testing of hypotheses.

QUESTION AND QUESTIONNAIRE CONSTRUCTION

In designing questions and questionnaire schedules for use in standardised or semi-standardised interviews, the first question that needs to be addressed concerns the objective of the study. What information is the questionnaire intended to elicit from the respondent? Whatever theoretical ideas inform the research will have to be translated into questions, or statements, which can be administered to a relevant respondent. One obvious constraint here is that the questions must be cast in a form understandable to the vast majority of respondents. There would be little point, for example, in asking about 'social integration' or 'anomie'. Concepts such as these will have to be translated into readily understandable questions, the answers to which can serve as indices of the more abstract and theoretical concepts.

There is an art to the design of questions and questionnaires. Apart from the content of the questions decisions will have to be made on the form of the question-and-answer unit. Basically there are two choices here, between 'open-ended' and 'closed' or 'fixed-alternative' questions.

The 'fixed-alternative' question provides respondents with a selection of answers, 'yes' or 'no' or 'don't know' being the simplest, from which they have to make the choice which best reflects their answer to the question. In some cases such multiple choice items form attitude scales in which each alternative is given a numerical weighting so that a set of such items can be cumulated to give the respondent an overall score on the scale. For example, a questionnaire designed to investigate attitudes towards work may provide respondents with a list of statements indicating a point of view to which they have to express a level of agreement or disagreement (see Figure 5.1).

Figure 5.1 Forced-choice item

'Most of the time I find my work fulfilling'

Strongly Agree	Agree	Undecided	Disagree	Strongly Disagree

Depending on the particular dimension being measured, the degree of agreement may be given a higher weighting and that of disagreement a lower one. A scale like this will normally consist of a series of such statements tapping the same attitudinal dimension. The cumulated score over all statements constituting a particular scale provides the researcher with a quantitative means of describing respondents in terms of their scores which can then be correlated with other variables of interest to the research.[4]

The 'open-ended' item allows respondents the freedom to provide an answer in whatever form they choose. For example, 'What do you think about Mr Gorbachev?' or 'Who do you think is going to win the next election?' Unlike 'fixed-alternative' questions, the coding categories of 'open-ended' items have to be decided after the interviewing stage of research is complete in order to see the range and kind of answers produced by the question. It also takes longer to ask 'open-ended' questions and to record the responses. However, sometimes the richness of the responses makes this a price well worth paying. It is not unusual for questionnaires to contain a mixture of both types of questions. In the main, 'open-ended' questions are best used, conventional wisdom argues, in exploratory surveys when a researcher needs to elicit the respondent's frame of reference without undue constraint by the format of the question. They do also help to achieve and sustain rapport and stimulate the respondent's thinking.[5]

The wording of the question is as important as the form. A question should be free of ambiguity, precise and clear; each question should express a single idea. Asking a question such as 'Should Britain spend more on defence or on education?' and requiring a single response one way or the other does not cover those cases where a person might feel that more should be spent on both, or, for that matter, less on both. The question begs other questions and is potentially leading and confusing. Loaded questions should also be avoided, although in statements comprising attitudes scales such 'loading' is often deliberately intended to express a strong point of view with which the respondent can concur or not. Questions should also be as short as possible, be easily understood, and avoid esoteric language. They should be specific about events and topics: instead of asking, 'How often have you been off work?', ask, 'How many times in the past two months have you been off work?' In this way a standardised frame is provided for all respondents alike making comparisons easier and more sensible. In phrasing questions it is as well to remember to protect the self-esteem of the subject by avoiding subtle hints as to what is an appropriate or desirable answer. Also, it is necessary to avoid giving the impression that the respondent's answers are in any way exceptional no matter how hair-raising. In the case of 'fixed-alternative' questions, the alternatives provided should be exhaustive covering all possible ranges of response including 'don't know' or 'no answer', and be mutually exclusive.[6]

The order of questions is another matter which needs careful attention: initial questions may predispose answers to later ones. A technique known as 'funnelling' in which more general questions are followed by more specific ones amplifying the general ones can be useful in guiding the interviewer through the schedule and encouraging the respondent to give fuller answers. Using this mode of question organisation, a respondent and an interviewer can often be guided through subsets of questions. For example, questions of relevance only to married women can be prefaced by a general question about marital status followed by an instruction for those who have answered in a particular way to move to the relevant subset.

Sequencing questions can play a helpful role in easing the respondent into the interview. Uncontroversial and fairly routine questions – not always easy to spot – should normally come at the beginning, leaving personal and more intimate ones for later. By then the interviewer and respondent will, hopefully, have established sufficient rapport. Closing the interview can be eased by using less challenging questions.

One final point as far as the design of questionnaires is concerned. An interview can last anything from fifteen minutes to a few hours, though normally one hour is considered long, so it is essential to maintain the informant's interest and attention for the duration. This means that the designer must avoid long unbroken sequences of questions demanding little thought or deliberation from respondents, otherwise they are likely to grow bored and inattentive and provide ill-considered answers to get the interview over with. This can be especially serious in the case of attitude scales where respondents by simply offering the same answer to the series of items produce a 'response set' so distorting the score. The judicious use of 'open-ended' questions can go some way to mitigating these effects by making the questionnaire more varied and interesting. But the designer must not go too far in the other direction by filling the schedule with deeply sensitive and thought-provoking questions so that the respondent is exhausted after a short period. Many of these difficulties can be anticipated and corrected by testing the questionnaire in field conditions prior to the full-scale study.

THE PROCESS OF INTERVIEWING

Although the interview, in some form or another, has been a data collection instrument in social research from the earliest empirical researchers, the main development over the years 'has been the increasing systematisation of the interview techniques'.[7] The early interviews were rarely deliberately engineered and designed encounters. These days, however, there is a considerable body of lore and experience concerning the method and its application.

A fact about most social research data collection methods, and one which is often lost sight of, is that they involve the researcher in social encounters with their subjects; the interview is no different in this respect. Indeed, the validity of the data collected by the interview depends upon the effective establishment of a particular kind of social relationship between the interviewer and the respondent. The task of the interviewer is to obtain information, often of a highly personal and private nature, from a respondent who is a stranger with little or no obligation to spend time and effort answering questions. A respondent is free to refuse to give an interview and capable of breaking off at any moment. Nor is there any guarantee that the respondent will tell the truth or furnish information required. To avoid all of these problems, and more, the interviewer must be exceedingly careful, and training manuals spend a great deal of effort devoted to proper and effective interview conduct.

The interview encounter is normally divided into phases. The first, that of initial contact, is especially crucial. Obviously if this fails there is no interview. Getting respondents to consent to an interview is not always a simple matter. Appointments made over the phone are relatively easy to refuse or break. Personal contact is much better but by no means foolproof. At the outset the interviewer must ensure the co-operation of the intended respondent. This means that interviewers must quickly establish their credentials. Academic researchers are not the only ones to make use of interviewing: pollsters, government researchers, market researchers, sales people also do so as a cover for some sales pitch, and so on. Individuals differ in their estimations of the utility, to them, of spending time answering questions. As far as academic research is concerned, there is only one rule: honesty. This may not result in a higher rate of acceptances, but is required as a way of showing respect for the subject. The interviewer must give the respondent sufficient information about who the interviewer is, why he or she is there, how the respondent came to be selected, what the questions will be about, assurances must be given as to confidentiality, and permission sought for the interview to take place. Any form of bullying is out.

If this results in an interview being granted, the next phase requires the interviewer to establish a suitably relaxed and encouraging relationship with the respondent: one normally described as a relationship of rapport. The interviewer must communicate trust, reassurance and, even, likeableness to the respondent so that the latter's interest and motivation are sustained. Interviewers should never threaten respondents or destroy their confidence in the relationship. Many manuals recommend that interviewers use 'small talk' to ease the situation a little before embarking on the interview proper. Benney and Hughes, in discussing the 'behavioural conventions' of the interview, refer to the norm of 'equality' which should govern interviewer-respondent relations.[8] 'Equality' assumes that information is more likely to be valid if freely given. Therefore, from the outset the interview should be a relationship freely entered into by both parties, but especially by the respondent. Benney and Hughes liken it to a contractual relationship such that for, allowing the interviewer to direct the relationship the respondent 'is assured that he will not meet with denial, contradiction, competition, or other harassment. As with all contractual relations, the fiction or convention of equality must govern the situation.'[9] This means, too, that the interviewer should try to minimise any inequalities of age, gender, intelligence, social status, expertness, and so on, which may exist between the interviewer and respondent. Clearly, it is not always easy to adhere to this convention which is why, on occasion, attempts are made to match interviewers to some of the social characteristics of respondents; for example, using black interviewers to interview black respondents, women to interview women, and so on.

What happens in detail during the interview itself will, of course, vary with circumstance and type of interview. If the interview is non-standardised or contains a significant number of non-standardised items interviewers should aim to relax respondents as soon as possible so that they feel free enough to talk at some length. It is also a good idea to ask relatively innocuous questions early so that both parties can become used to each other more quickly. If the interviewing method is the standardised type, while every effort may be made to relax the respondent, the questions should be administered in the form and the order as set out. In this case the second convention noted by Benney and Hughes becomes pertinent, that of 'comparability'. This convention is designed to minimise the immediate and unique features of a particular interview encounter so that only those aspects which are generalisable across interviews remain salient. In this way what the interviewer receives from the respondent as answers are treated as variable about social properties, rather than as details about a particular person in a particular social encounter. None the less, it is important in both types of interview that the interviewer treat each encounter as a separate experience to guard against the surreptitious influence of prejudgements about typical responses and, of course, for the very practical reason to be able to accommodate any contingencies that might arise.[10]

A major goal of the interview is to gather relevant replies to the questions asked. Accordingly, an interviewer must be quick to recognise whether an answer is adequate given the question's objective, and must be ready to probe further or encourage the respondent to elaborate or reformulate an answer should it be required. This might amount to a simple, 'Yes, I see' or 'That's interesting', but may require a more standard probe of the kind, 'Could you be a little more specific about that, please?' or 'What do you mean by that exactly?' These must be offered in a friendly and reassuring way without threatening the respondent or implying that he or she is a fool. Among the most difficult responses to cope with are 'don't know' ones. Such an answer might imply genuine ignorance, that the respondent does not understand the question asked, is embarrassed by what the answer might imply, or any number of things. Only delicate probing can illuminate such an answer further. In some cases interviewers are instructed on how many and what types of probes to use with particular questions.

Such careful preparation and conduct on the part of the interviewer will be wasted if the answers given are not recorded. With the structured type of questionnaire the interviewer has to make sure that the category given is correctly and clearly marked. With open-ended questions all the words spoken must be taken down, avoiding as far as possible paraphrasing or précis.

The final stage is bringing the interview to a close and disengaging from the scene. This can often be harder than it looks, especially if the relationship has been a rewarding one for the respondent. Although, initially, many people express a reluctance to be interviewed, once they begin this often disappears making it harder for the interviewer to keep within reasonable time limits, which is not difficult to understand. The interviewer is giving the respondent a chance to talk anonymously without fear of contradiction, signs of boredom, disagreement, disapproval, and so on, often about deeply personal matters, a temptation few find difficult to resist. Accordingly disengagement may have to be delicately handled. What must be avoided is giving the respondent the impression that now the interviewer has got what he or she came for, the respondent is of no moment. A good compromise is to be fairly business-like or professional in attitude, stressing the value of the interview to the research, thanking the respondent for all the time and effort, and politely withdrawing from the encounter. Abruptness should be avoided except in emergencies.

Interviewing is not an easy matter. It can often be a harrowing and frustrating experience and needs skill and experience; reasons why, perhaps, academic researchers, funds permitting, are making increasing use of accredited agencies and their professional interviewers. Training can certainly increase success rates and efficiency, which is especially important where large numbers of people have to be interviewed.

Evaluation of the interview as method

The aim of the interview is to obtain information from a respondent. Clearly, to be of any use for social research the interviewer and researcher must be confident that this information is accurate. It is to achieve this end that all the conventions of interviewing and questionnaire design are directed. It is known that people can lie, say things intended to put them in a good light, try to avoid offending others, and so on. All of these, and many more, can lead to bias in the information gathered; also the interviewer is not immune from various sources of bias. One salutary study illustrating this point is reported by Hyman.[11] Fifteen people were ostensibly hired for a special study, even though they had little or no experience of interviewing. Each was sent to interview a series of people, among them planted respondents: one, a 'punctilious liberal' simply would not give unqualified responses; another was a 'hostile bigot' who was unfriendly, aggressive, highly suspicious, and rude; and, finally, an 'alternative respondent' who offered him or herself in place of the respondent who was not, at that time, available. Interspersed among these plants were uncoached respondents. The interviews with the plants were secretly recorded. Errors of various kinds were found. For example, confronted with the 'hostile bigot' some interviewers, not perhaps surprisingly, did not ask a large number of questions, hoping, no doubt, to terminate the interview as quickly as possible. A typical error was to record answers consistently with other answers the respondent had provided, even though the particular answer given was ambiguous. Instead of probing further the interviewers tended to interpret the question in terms of what they expected it to be. Again, an early study by Edwards found that the 'social desirability' variable affected responses to questions.[12] Personality traits judged desirable in others were more likely to find their way into self-ratings than were items judged to be less desirable. A similar finding appears in a study concerned with the effects of social class and ethnicity on mental health, in which it is suggested that many of the responses about the prevalence of mental health symptoms reflected cultural differences in the social desirability of modes of expressing distress and a willingness to report it. Puerto Ricans, for example, regarded many of the items indicating mental distress as less desirable than did members of other ethnic groups.[13]

It is findings such as these which raise nagging doubts about the interview method; doubts which that great innovator of method, W.I. Thomas, also expressed in the early 1920s. Although the method would seem to offer many advantages to the social researcher in that it substitutes what respondents say about their behaviour for detailed, and often unobtainable, observation of actual behaviour, it is also a well-known fact of life that people often do not do what they say they will do, or have not done what they report they have done. Even with so-called factual questions, large errors can occur. For example, some studies have reported errors of 20 per cent or more in respondents reporting whether or not they voted in a previous election.[14] These are not difficult to understand. After all, the situations in which people find themselves often change in unanticipated ways, and whatever one might say in an interview isolated from those very processes which impinge on courses of action, it is another matter when one is confronted with situations which call for action. Thus, in an interview respondents might agree to all kinds of high-minded principles only to find themselves providing excuses or justifications when confronted by a conflict between what might otherwise be construed as self-interest and principle. In light of this it is perhaps not so surprising to find widespread condemnation of trade unions among the very people who are just as likely to come out on strike when their wages are at issue as are those who do not express such condemnation. Or to find large sections of the population expressing sentiments in favour of racial equality, but agreeing with immigration controls especially when there is a generalised threat to unemployment.

Before becoming too cynical about the level of principled behaviour among the British, or any other population, we do need to look rather more closely at the sociology of the interview itself in relation to the instrumental presuppositions which inform its use as a method of social research. The point is not simply that people are often inconsistent as between what they say and what they do, which they often are, but whether the relationship between saying and doing, to put it crudely, is adequately conceptualised in the presuppositions of the method itself.

The potential offered by the interviewer in allowing a researcher to cover a wide range of topics, to explore the past, present and intended behaviour of respondents depends upon respondents being truthful in what they report: determining this accounts for much of the research done on the method to identify likely sources of bias which can influence both the respondent and the interviewer. A slightly different but no less important problem has to do not so much with whether or not the respondent is being truthful, but with what can be inferred from the responses. As pollsters know only too well, the public can at times express keen dissatisfaction with the government of the day, but this is a far cry from being translated into a vote against the government come election time. In other words, there are issues to do with whether or not the data collected by interview on such matters as attitudes, beliefs, actions, and so on, are adequate surrogates for data about actual activities.

Researchers are aware of problems such as these as all the efforts devoted to questionnaire design, interviewing styles, and the study of interviewer effects attest to. One of the biggest problems arises from the fact that the interview is an occasion isolated from most of the matters with which it concerns itself. It is isolated from the respondent's past and from the future. With regard to the past the problem facing the researcher is to judge how much of what is reported by the respondent is refracted through the lens of the present. Isolation from the future creates problems no less difficult. To repeat a point made earlier: though individuals may express strong support for all kinds of sentiments in the relative comfort of the interview, when actually confronted with situations where these sentiments might have relevance, they are no longer isolated from all the factors which impinge on behaviour and, accordingly, may well act in ways 'inconsistent' with the beliefs and attitudes expressed in an interview.

What should be fairly obvious is the intimate connection between technical methodological problems and theoretical issues and how closely the instrumental presuppositions are interwoven with the theoretical. The interview is a social encounter and, as researchers have shown, cannot be exempted from the normal social processes that govern such encounters. This is why such stress is laid upon interviewing and questionnaire design techniques, as well as the management by the interviewer of the interviewer–respondent relationship. What is being claimed is that a particular kind of social relationship is likely to result in more adequate and truthful replies. But more than this is the question of the extent to which information gleaned by the interview can be used to generalise and infer to social processes and relationships outside its environs. One can look at the problem as one of licensing various interpretations based on data collected from a social situation which we have already suggested is both isolated and artificial. There are many facets to this issue that it is only possible to deal with a few of them in general terms.

The modern interview has evolved out of the rather free-ranging encounter that was typical of the first days of social research into a much more systematically organised instrument. Over the years the techniques have been refined, honed and sharpened in an effort to improve the interview's reliability and validity. Some of the principles we mentioned earlier are only a small part of the lore of interviewing: practices developed in response to some of the difficulties and problems we are highlighting here.

One of the features of the interview that has become clearer, and this parallels a point made in connection with the survey method of which the interview is an essential part, is that the conception of the interview encounter is not simply informed by instrumental considerations. It is not self-evident, for example, that the establishment of a 'warm and trusting relationship' will necessarily get the respondent to tell the truth. It seems plausible to argue that it could, just as likely, result in the respondent avoiding potential conflict and controversy, offering instead blandness and deceptions designed to maintain conviviality.[15] Certainly few police interrogators or even job-selection panels would necessarily subscribe to the method proposed by social research interviewers as the best method for getting at the truth. Even in social research other interview relationships have been used. Kinsey, for example, in his studies of human sexual behaviour, used the model of a prosecuting lawyer rather than that of the faceless and inoffensive social researcher. By all accounts his strict, direct and aggressive manner seemed to work.

The procedures of interviewing are, of course, as much infused with ethical sensibilities as they are with instrumental concerns. While academic social researchers do not need licences to ply their trade, public opinion would be rightly outraged if interviewers were to appear on a respondent's doorstep at 8.00 a.m. backed by five or six 'heavies', threatening dire consequences for the respondent's family and career if the questionnaire is not completed by 8.30! Though this example might appear rather fanciful, it does illustrate that the interview method of data collection, and some of the instrumental presuppositions on which it is based, derive their plausibility from wider cultural conventions. One can put this more strongly and claim that the interview, as a method of social research, depends very heavily upon particular cultural conventions prevalent in some types of social systems. It presupposes, for example, a fairly stable social and political order in which potential respondents do not feel particularly intimidated by requests for interviews, and can either accept or decline to take part without further hazard. Further, on acceptance they must feel confident that their private remarks will not be disclosed to others who have no right to know what has transpired in the interview. To the extent to which conventions such as these do not prevail within a society or group, then doubts will be raised about the ability of respondents to express themselves freely in an interview. Similarly, the interview itself, as a social relationship, depends on other cultural conceptions which give it legitimacy as a social encounter. It would be hard to imagine interviewing, for example, a Viking raider, an Elizabethan soldier or, more contemporaneously, a Kalahari bushman or a Sicilian peasant. We are not saying that one could not interview such respondents but would suggest that, at least, they may find it difficult to see the point of an activity which presupposes a very different kind of social order; one in which literacy is widespread, personal viewpoints deemed significant, private lives investigated by duly authorised people, extensive public accounting procedures, and a confidentiality equivalent to that of the confessional, to mention but a few.

None of this, of course, necessarily invalidates the interview method, except when it is used in societies or groups where the kind of cultural underpinnings just mentioned do not obtain. And, moreover, these are not always to be found in exotic and less developed regions of the world. In our own society, it is not easy to interview, for social research purposes, meths drinkers, tramps, members of the IRA, the heads of large industries, senior civil servants and other holders of elite positions. But social researchers who use the interview are aware of these kinds of constraints and concede the general principle that any method of data collection has to be evaluated in terms of the general social conditions that prevail, as well as in terms of its technical adequacy for the research problem in hand. Indeed, knowledge of the society and its culture, as well as variations among members of that culture, is essential for a researcher to evaluate how best to go about interviewing, how the effect of particular characteristics, such as age, gender, social class, level of education, ethnicity, and so on, may be assessed, and more. The convention of 'equality' by which the interviewer should try to minimise any inequalities arising from, for example, age, gender, ethnicity, social status, and so forth, is not always easy to meet, yet it is useful to know how such social characteristics might affect responses. What, for example, would be the 'interviewer effects' of using 'black' interviewers to interview 'black' populations as opposed to 'white' interviewers?[16] Does the topic of the interview make a difference to the authenticity of replies? Questions such as these are not easy to answer, but what is more certain is that the method itself and an assessment of any 'interviewer effects' on responses presupposes a wide knowledge on the part of the researcher of the society and the culture in which the method is used.

Not surprisingly there has been much research on the effect of interviewer characteristics on the interview situation and on the qualities of the respondent's replies. Interviewers, of course, cannot but influence respondents since not only is it their job to do so, but for the additional reason that people react to characteristics they perceive in others. Among those characteristics are those especially salient in the culture or society concerned, such as age, gender and social status. In some societies, such as the United States, ethnicity must also be counted among these. In 1968, just after the assassination of Martin Luther King, Schuman and Converse interviewed 619 black residents of Detroit using a mix of black interviewers, mainly older women with experience as interviewers, and white, male and female, graduate students.[17] It was found that black and white interviewers obtained significantly different responses to over 25 per cent of the questions asked. Yet, perhaps more significantly, against expectations, some questions did not produce strong race-of-interviewer effects. In other words, the effects of race, and by implication other characteristics too, are not always in the direction that might be expected: we cannot always assume that black respondents are more likely to tell the truth to black interviewers than they are to white. In this case, while respondents might distort their answers in a more integrationist and less racially hostile direction to please white interviewers, they may also express more militant sentiments to please black interviewers. It appears, too, that differences in response to the race of the interviewer were greater among the low-income and less educated respondents.

Among other interviewer characteristics, status has been found to have variable effects. In some cases, equivalence of status can result in greater rapport but this does not always result in more truthful answers.[18] Once again no coherent general picture emerges from the research. Similarly, with respect to other interviewer characteristics, religion, gender, age and so on, the effects are highly variable suggesting no simple rules whereby these factors can be systematically controlled.

A twist to all this is added when interviewing is used as part of cross-cultural research which has, in recent years, become more common. Here matters become more complicated by the fact that a researcher is dealing not just with one culture but with two or more. This raises the possibility that the conventions governing the interview encounter may vary as between cultures. But not only is the interview itself affected, so, too, are the questions themselves. It cannot be assumed that the same words and sentences mean the same thing within different cultures even if the same language is spoken.[19] As Deutscher remarked, 'a vocabulary is not merely a string of words; immanent within it are societal textures'.[20] The lexical equivalent of the English word 'friend' is 'Freund', but whereas the latter is reserved for a few long-standing intimates, the former can be applied to a wider circle of acquaintances.

Problems of translating questionnaires across cultural boundaries are not, of course, insuperable. By careful translation by bilinguals many of these kinds of problems can be detected if not eradicated. But the point is, once again, that these efforts require knowledge, often of a detailed and precise kind, of the society and culture to be studied by the method.

We have been discussing the kinds of biases that can arise from the interview itself, such as the various sorts of 'interviewer effects', the factors which encourage or discourage a respondent not only to be forthcoming but also to tell the truth. It is also important to note that none of these adds up to a wholesale condemnation of the method. Quite the contrary. Over the years knowledge gained of the method and the kinds of biases and influences it can be subjected to have been used to improve the technique as well as to evaluate the validity of the results obtained.

However, this is not the whole story. So far we have been discussing the interview, and the problems which arise from it as an instrument of social research designed to retrieve information from a respondent under the stimulus of questions put to that respondent. But it needs to be remembered that an interview is normally part of a social survey inquiring into the beliefs, attitudes and relationships of collectivities of people, and its assessment as an instrument of social research needs also to take this into account.

The objective of the interview, especially but not only in the context of a social survey, is to obtain information from a respondent who represents a category of persons deemed relevant to the research. Thus, and for simple example, Joe Smith is interviewed not because he is Joe Smith but because he represents, say, a 'working-class Conservative voter', a 'skilled worker' or an 'unemployed person', a 'council tenant' or whatever. Joe Smith may, in fact, be a member of a number of such categories. Of course, the interview encounter is designed to be an encounter between people, as indicated by all the advice on how to conduct a successful interview. But how does Joe Smith come to represent a category? Basically in the following ways: first, by being selected as such using some appropriate selection criteria and sampling scheme, and second, by aggregating the responses taken individually from people deemed to have the relevant categorical properties in common. Thus, if Joe Smith is a 'working-class Conservative voter' then he, along with others belonging to the same category, will be grouped together. It is then up to analysis to see if this category is associated with other variables, say, level of education, home ownership, or whatever.

One effect of aggregating responses in this way is to cancel out non-systematic variations in each particular interview. If the assumption that there is no systematic bias operating across all the interviews more or less equally can be sustained, then the accumulated data can be searched for patterns. To a degree, cancelling out individual variation through aggregation does seem to work under some circumstances. Pollsters at election times do reasonably well on the whole in predicting the outcomes of elections by relying on sufficiently large representative samples. Some of those interviewed may change their minds, even at the last minute, may not even vote at all, may even lie about their intentions, but in the aggregate, such variations tend to cancel each other out to provide a reasonably accurate estimate of the likely result.[21] However, election prediction is not necessarily an appropriate model for other kinds of social research which make use of the interview method.

We began this evaluation of the interview by posing the problem as one of licensing inferences from data gathered in the interview to what we might bluntly term 'real life' social processes. Matters of bias are important here, but there are other dimensions to consider as well. The methods of good interviewing recommended by practitioners can be seen as interpersonal devices to encourage the respondent to speak authentically; to get respondents to say what they truly think, feel or believe about certain things, report accurately on what they have said or done, relationships entered into, and so on. This is essential if the verbal data collected in the interview are to be regarded as an adequate substitute for observation of the subject over a long period of time. But, even if the interviewer has performed magnificently and is convinced that the data obtained are as authentic as possible, there still remains the question of the relationship between this interview encounter and the 'real life' processes we referred to earlier. Deutscher referred to this as the relationship between 'words' and 'deeds'.[22] What Deutscher is mainly concerned with here is the oft-remarked-on discrepancy between what we earlier referred to as attitudes and behaviour; frequently people do not 'put their moneys where their mouths are'. However, there is another way of looking at this problem which does not rely on charging whole sections of the population with inconsistency or bad faith.

We need to remind ourselves of the processes of designing an interview schedule, the techniques of interviewing and, in so doing, will try to bring together a number of disparate themes raised in the earlier discussion. In designing an interview schedule we remarked that the researcher has to choose between a standardised format or a non-standardised one, or a mixture of the two. In making this choice a number of considerations will, no doubt, play their part: the ration of interviewers to sample size, cost and methods of data analysis; the nature of the sample population; knowledge already available; whether the research is mainly exploratory or hypothesis-testing, and so on. But whatever the eventual choice made, this will place constraints on the interview and the sense that can be made of the responses. If it is decided to use mainly fixed-choice items in an effort to standardise stimuli across interviews this will, inevitably, restrict the ability of the interviewer and the informant to amplify responses. This does not merely mean a sacrifice in richness, but one also in the extent to which responses can be clarified. Though respondents can and do answer questions given to them in terms of categories provided, this is not the same thing as saying that these categories adequately reflect the respondent's meaning. What, for example, would we infer about a respondent who replied 'AGREE' to a question such as that in Figure 5.1? The question itself asks about 'most times' (and such questions are not rare in questionnaires), but how does the interviewer know what 'most times' means here? Is X's reply equivalent to Y's who also chose the 'AGREE' response?[23] The point is that the structure of the question format imposes a version of meaning, or set of criteria, to assess the respondent's replies that may or may not equate with the meaning the respondent would wish to subscribe to in other circumstances or from a different style of questioning. There is no guarantee that the stimuli offered to respondents in the collection of interviews are interpreted in the same way by all respondents. No matter how interviewers try to play the role prescribed for them by training manuals, respondents also bring expectations of various kinds to the interview encounter and it is not known in advance what these might be. For these reasons it is hard to see in what ways the standardised stimuli in the form of prestructured questions, standardised behaviour on the part of the interviewer, and so on, can result in a set of interviews equivalent in all respects, and the researcher has no business treating them as if they could be.

If the researcher decides to use open-ended questions in a non-standardised interview format, richness is gained but at the expense of what is commonly taken as the standard of inter-interview comparability. But this may be a large and significant gain for some purposes. The interviewer can probe more freely, ask for clarifications, pursue interesting matters in more depth, and so on. These will, of course, vary between interviews, often significantly.

What, hopefully, we are beginning to see here are more of the consequences of seeing the interview as a social encounter in all its particularities and complexities. It is this quality of the interview which gives rise to the investigative dilemmas reflected in the choice between a standardised versus an open-ended format: the choice, to put it another way, between generality and richness or between reliability and validity.[24] Errors, it is claimed, arise because the researcher and the actual questions used are both potentially misinterpreted and misinterpreting. The efforts to maximise reliability result in standardised methods which, it can be argued, seriously misinterpret the respondent's meaning by imposing a formalised structure on to the responses using methods designed to elicit those very meanings. Indeed, the notion of 'bias' implies a standard against which to judge the truth or the authenticity of replies, but whose standard is this? It may be that such standards owe more to achieving the appearance of reliability than they do to a serious attempt to determine the meanings the research is designed to uncover. On the other hand, efforts to maximise richness seriously militate against the purposes of the interview survey by emphasising the particularities of each interview encounter.

The proponents of the interview method have devoted no little effort to developing compromises between these alternatives. At bottom, of course, this is a theoretical question as much as it is a technical one. Some would claim that the interview method embodies an inadequate theory of social action which, among other things, glosses, even ignores, the way in which meanings are created and used in social situations. In terms of the model referred to in Chapter 2, for example, the interview presupposes that words uttered by a respondent in an interview could stand as indicators of inner thoughts, attitudes, and opinions, and of social activities. However, the relationship between these various elements is not straightforward. The attempts to remove biases which can arise because of the profound social nature of the interview encounter are, in part, a recognition of this complexity. But to speak of 'biases' is to presume that the task of the interview is to get as close as possible to what the truth of the matter is: whether it be what respondents truly feel, what they have done, who they associated with, and what they will truthfully do. If, however, we look at this from another sociological tradition, the achievement of this task becomes much more problematic than simply making a list of contaminants which interfere with the attainment of some ideal interview. Interactionists, for example, argue that social action is situated, in that what meaning it has for the participants is achieved on a here-and-now basis in the course of interaction. The interview is a social encounter to which both parties bring expectancies, presuppositions, beliefs and experiences; without some understanding of these and their interplay we shall be unable to understand the social dynamics of interview encounters. What we cannot do is assume that a particular interviewing style will work with all respondents alike. We cannot assume that what appear from our point of view to be inconsistent responses are, for the respondent, inconsistent at all. We cannot afford to prejudge the question of whether standardised items are, in fact, treated in the same way by all respondents. We cannot assume that similar responses necessarily mean the same thing, and so on.

CONCLUSION

The discussion of the interview method has taken us to the point where we need to look again at the instrumental presuppositions on which the method is based as sociological theories proposing specific models of the social actor and society. To do this we can take a leaf from one of Garfinkel's methodological recommendations; to whit, and to paraphrase, one way of examining how good a sociological theory is is to turn it into a set of instructions for producing social action.[25] In which case we can treat the prescriptions of interviewing as a set of instructions on how the respondent and the interviewer should interact in order to achieve the aims of scientifically collecting verbal data. It is these instructions, or, to release the metaphor for a moment, models which, in effect, license the inferences that are drawn from data gathered in the interview. If the models can be doubted, then the inferential structure that underpins the interview must also be doubted. Related to this are issues intimately bound up with the point of the interview, namely obtaining answers from respondents. It is not answers from Joe Smith that are of interest, but answers from a category of persons of which Joe Smith is a member and representative. It is at this juncture that we need to refer back to some of the principles of variable analysis discussed in Chapter 3.

In survey interviewing responses have to be codable into predetermined categories in order that they can be counted: this is why use is made of standardised questions. This procedure presumes that the responses provided are allocatable into equivalence classes; that is, that respondent R1's answer to a question is the same as R2's answer, up to Rn's answer. In other words, that similar responses form an equivalence class. If they do not and yet we count the frequencies of these responses, then we have failed to count since, in effect, we shall not be counting the same things. Yet, the categories generally used in social research are diffuse and inexact. This is recognised in variable analysis by its stress on the need for multiple indicators on the supposition that no one indicator is likely to capture all that a concept might mean or a property show.

But the fact remains, people do answer questionnaires, researchers offer findings based on them which are, most of the time, not without sense. They gain a 'real worldly' status as 'objectively extant phenomena'.[26] According to Cicourel, this link is forged by researchers implicitly using common-sense knowledge about the social actor and about the social world in which s/he lives as a resource to secure the connection between an indicator and a concept. Fixed-choice questions, for example, are designed to elicit common-sense meanings from a respondent but, at the same time, provide a format for categorising responses into a small number of alternatives to facilitate categorisation and, through this, data processing. The form of the question is an integral part of the classification procedure. It is an instruction on how the meaning of the respondent's reply shall be categorised. It is a formalisation of both the question and its response through 'obvious' and 'reasonable' coding procedures and which 'thereby manage, through progressive classification operations, to keep one foot in the commonsense world of everyday life and the other foot in the quasi-acceptable (in a practical sense) measurement procedures'.[27] The classification procedure required for social research is imposed on 'data' elicited from respondents who are reporting on their experiences in a manner detached from the circumstances in which they were made relevant, and played their part, in constructing social activities. But all we know about their experiences is how they look through the imposition of the format of questioning.

The rules of interviewing are practical procedures for managing a social encounter in order to get the interviewing done and achieve meaning equivalence in the material. Thus, the interviewer and, later, the coder, out of all the interchanges that take place on the occasion of the interview, have to select those which can be treated as valid replies to the questions asked, reject those which are 'chatter', make judgements about the consistency, or otherwise, of the replies, and so on. So, the neat tables that are the end result conceal the vast amount of interpretative work done by interviewers and coders in doing their best in accordance with the rules. 'Resolving ambiguities', 'letting certain remarks pass', 'allow propriety to constrain lines of questioning', 'hold meanings in reserve', 'giving the benefit of the doubt', and more, all involve the interviewer's use of his or her common-sense knowledge of social structures to make sense of the replies, the coding task and, later, make sense of the tables produced.[28] The very activity of categorisation upon which counting depends, the determination of 'this' as an instance of 'that', as another case of 'this' accomplishes the necessary equivalence characteristics. These are features of local decision-making about the particularities encountered in the course of the interview as the 'same' or 'different' so accomplishing what Baccus calls 'interphenomenal integrity'.[29] So, an important part of what interviewers are doing is making use of their common-sense knowledge in order to get the work of interviewing done according to the format required. The complexity of the world, in this case what a respondent says on the occasion of the interview, is reduced in compliance with the requirements of the format.

If we take these arguments on board, then this has some major implications for the inferential structure which underlies interviewing as an instrument within the variable analysis tradition. What the format of interviewing provides is a way of mapping the properties of phenomena – 'what people say in response to questions asked' – on to a mathematically conceived 'property space' which allows for the use of inferential apparatus of quantification and statistics. It is not, of course, the case that interviewing is devoid of any reference to the social world; quite the contrary. It is always stressed that indices, questionnaire items, attitude scales, and the rest, have to be based on observables. But this 'visibility' is a function of the format and the use of common-sense knowledge on the part of interviewers and coders.[30]

Clearly these arguments go beyond mere technical criticism of the interview method, though they do raise important points to ponder in this regard. What is at stake is nothing less than the phenomenon the interview method, as with any method of social research, is concerned to tap into or uncover. The attitude toward the method will depend, to put it briefly, upon whether the interview is seen as a method for tapping the 'true value' of some attitude, belief or opinion, or as a way of exploring such matters by encouraging respondents to talk about themselves. We mentioned earlier that interviewers make use of their own common-sense knowledge about society in order to get the interviewing done. In this they act no differently from the ordinary members of society in doing their own day-to-day business as members of that society. They, too, categorise and reason and inquire into the social world around them in the course of their construction of social activities. It is these that the interview is designed to uncover and display. But its format makes the assumption that we know how individuals use categories and their common-sense knowledge in advance of inquiry into these procedures of practical reasoning. For variable analysis the point of categorisation is to identify those factors which best explain the distribution of values on some dependent variable.[31] What is concealed are the ways in which members use the categories they do in order to make the social world visible and organisable in ways relevant to them. Dorothy Smith, for example, alludes to this in connection with the term 'single parent'.[32] This kind of term could well occur on a questionnaire, be asked in any interview or be the answer provided in response to a question in an interview. But the point Smith makes is that the term is not one which has the features of a generalised description usable on indefinite occasions, though it can be made to appear so. Rather, it has a particular set of loci of use. One such place is in relation to 'parenting' and 'schooling':

This category 'single parent' names, from the perspective of the school, a particular type of defect in the conditions of effective classroom work organisation. The category provides an interpretative procedure regardless of the mother's actual practices.[33]

Generalising the point, the categories devised and used in variable analysis provide a common-sense basis for the interpretation of statistical results without ever once coming to grips with the actual organisation of social activities for which these categories may or may not be relevant. To treat these categories as 'properties of objects' operating in conjunction with other 'objective properties' is to claim that these categories have a trans-situational quality independently of how real persons use and make relevant or disattend to such features in the accomplishment of social activities. Thus, for example, how the category 'single parent', or any other category, is made relevant within an ongoing organisation of scenes and activities is assumed rather than addressed.

In sum, then, what variable analysis does is turn the interview method into a format for describing social phenomena objectively, quantitatively, in order to determine the patterns among phenomena empirically. It is this apparatus which enables a researcher to make claims about the social world and how well theories do or do not correspond to it. But, on the arguments just reviewed, the requirements of objective data, measurement systems, consistency and the like, lead to a disguise of the phenomena by the format. Yet, in order to get the format to work, there is a necessary and unavoidable reliance by the format for its sense, its intelligibility, its very ability to do the work required of it, on the ordinary knowledge of social life as understood and accomplished by members but which is not made into a topic in its own right.[34]

The arguments we have just reviewed are arguments about one theoretical context of the interview, namely variable analysis as a method of data collection in social research: arguments about one inferential structure in which the method is implicated. It also has to be stressed that this is not the only context of interviewing. Sometimes, and this is as worthy a social research endeavour as that proposed by variable analysis, interviewing is done just to find out what people have to say, what they do and think about various things. Respondents act as reporters on their life or, more likely, aspects of their lives. Such material is rarely encumbered by the requirements imposed by variable analysis and is rarely the sole material used. It becomes part of the picture which the research is trying to paint.

In Chapter 6 we turn to methods of data collection which have come to be seen as part of a very different tradition of social research and social theory, namely observational and ethnographic methods, which belong to a qualitative rather than a quantitative strand of social research and, as such, are part of a very different theoretical context.

NOTES

1. J. Brown and G. Gilmartin, 'Sociology today: lacunae, emphases and surfeits', *American Sociologist*, 4, 1969, pp. 283–91, reported that 91 per cent of the research articles published in the two major American sociology journals had gathered data by means of the interview/questionnaire; it is very unlikely that this has much changed since.
2. A.L. Bowley, *Elements of Statistics*, 3rd edn, London, Curtis, 1937, pp. 20–1. Interestingly, why 'yes' or 'no' should be more precise is not self-evident. If the question is vague, so will the answer be whether categorised as 'yes' or 'no'.
3. R.K. Merton and P. Kendall, *The Focussed Interview*, New York, Free Press, 1951.
4. A.N. Oppenheim, *Questionnaire Design and Attitude Measurement*, London, Heinemann, 1966.
5. A. Orenstein and W. Phillips, *Understanding Social Research*, Boston, Mass., Allyn & Bacon, 1978, p. 222.
6. If there are a large number of 'don't know' or 'no answer' responses, this is normally taken as an indication that the range of alternatives provided is failing to tap the range of possible responses.
7. J. Madge, *The Origins of Scientific Sociology*, London, Tavistock, 1963, p. 532.
8. M. Benney and E.C. Hughes, 'Of sociology and the interview', *American Journal of Sociology*, 62, 1956, pp. 137–42.
9. *ibid*.
10. H.H. Hyman, *Interviewing in Social Research*, Chicago, University of Chicago Press, 1954, pp. 238–40. The point about contingencies is an important one since many interviews take place in respondents' homes where many things can happen to detract from the attempt to encourage a relaxed and serene interview.
11. *ibid.*, pp. 238–40.
12. A.L. Edwards, 'The relationship between the judged desirability of a trait and the probability that the trait will be endorsed', *Journal of Applied Psychology*, 37, 1953, pp. 90–3; see also D. Crowne and D. Marlow, *The Approval Motive*, New York, Wiley, 1964.
13. D.L. Phillips, *Knowledge From What?*, Chicago, Rand McNally,

1971, pp. 39–47, contains a summary of many such studies. See also his *Abandoning Method*, San Francisco, Jossey-Bass, 1973, chs 2 and 3.

14. C.G. Ball and W. Buchanan, 'Reliable and unreliable respondents: party registration and prestige pressure', *Western Political Quarterly*, 29, 1966, pp. 37–43; D. Calahan, 'Correlates of response accuracy in the Denver validity study', *Public Opinion Quarterly*, 32, 1968, pp. 607–21.

15. See A.V. Cicourel, *Method and Measurement in Sociology*, New York, Free Press, for an extensive critique of the interview method.

16. Hyman *et al., op.cit.*

17. H. Schuman and J. Converse, 'The effects of black and white interviewers on black responses in 1968', *Public Opinion Quarterly*, 35, 1971, pp. 44–68.

18. B.S. Dohrenwend, J. Colombotos and B.P. Dohrenwend, 'Social distance and interviewer effects', *Public Opinion Quarterly*, 32, 1968, pp. 410–22.

19. See, for example, E. Scheuch, 'The cross cultural use of sample surveys: problems of comparability', in R. Rokkan (ed.) *Comparative Research Across Cultures and Nations*, Paris, Mouton, 1968.

20. I. Deutscher, 'Asking questions cross-culturally: some problems of linguistic comparability', in H.S. Becker *et al.* (eds) *Institutions and the Person*, Chicago, Aldine, 1968, pp. 318–41.

21. Of course, pollsters tend to interview a number of times in the run up to an election which gives a better indication of the aggregate movement of voting intentions.

22. Deutscher, *op.cit.*

23. See J. Heritage, 'Assessing people' in J. Armistead (ed.) *Reconstructing Social Psychology*, Harmondsworth, Penguin, 1965. For a more general critique see D. Benson and J.A. Hughes, 'Evidence and inference', in G. Button (ed.) *Ethnomethodology and the Human Sciences*, Cambridge, Cambridge University Press, 1991.

24. See Cicourel, *op.cit.*

25. H. Garfinkel, *Studies in Ethnomethodology*, Englewood Cliffs, NJ, Prentice-Hall, 1967.

26. H.D. Baccus, 'Sociological indication and the visibility criterion of real world social theorising', in H. Garfinkel (ed.) *Ethnomethodological Studies of Work*, London, Routledge, 1986.

27. A.V. Cicourel, *Theory and Method in a Study of Argentine Fertility*, New York, Wiley, 1973.

28. Cicourel, *Theory and Method, op.cit.*

29. Baccus, *op.cit.*

30. Baccus, *op.cit.* pp. 4–5. Also Benson and Hughes, *op.cit.*

31. There is often a confusion here between theoretical and statistical explanation. The latter is concerned to account for the variance which may or may not be relevant to the theoretical explanation required. This is, as always, a complex matter. See S. Lieberson, *Making It Count: The Improvement of Social Research and Theory*, Berkeley, University of California Press, 1985.
32. D. Smith, *The everyday world as problematic*, Toronto, University of Toronto Press, 1988, p. 173.
33. *ibid.*, p. 173.
34. D. Zimmerman and M. Pollner, 'The everyday world as phenomena' in J.D. Douglas (ed.) *Understanding Everyday Life*, London, Routledge & Kegan Paul, 1974.

CHAPTER 6

Observational methods

Although, until recently, among the least frequently used of social research methods, observational methods have been used from time immemorial and are beginning to come into their own under the umbrella of qualitative methods.[1] Early examples are travellers' tales of their life and experiences in foreign lands; a tradition preserved, though in a much refined form, in social anthropology. It is also a method which we all, as members of society and inquirers into our own society and culture, have experience of in the sense that such an ability to observe and reflect on what is going on around us is an essential part of our being competent in our culture. Of course, as a research method used in social research, observation aims to go beyond this. Nevertheless, there are common elements in the skills and knowledge required for ordinary interaction and observational methods.

The most well-known of the observational methods is participant observation, which requires researchers to involve themselves in the lives of those being studied – looking, listening, enquiring, recording, and so on. Although participation may involve encounters similar in scope and intensity to the interviewing associated with the survey, it cannot be disassembled into a series of discrete practices following some preset sequence. By contrast to the survey, participant observation involves the researcher in a series of engagements in quite ordinary social situations in which the research aim of the encounters is concealed or, at least, not paramountly the point of the encounter. As Becker and Geer define it, participant observation is that 'method in which the observer participates in the daily life of the people under study, either openly in the role of researcher or covertly in some disguised role'.[2] This can be compared with a research situation in which subjects are simply observed, as in the case of the now little-used Bales technique for observing group interactions within a confined setting or in a laboratory setting. The participant observer normally takes on a role which can credibly be accommodated in a social group or organisation being studied. This is often a matter of very fine judgement (as we shall see later). But the aim of the method is to build up, over a period of time, an account of the way in which participants being studied manage and organise their lives as natural social actors, rather than as the homunculi of some sociological theory. In short, the researcher tries to obtain an 'insider's' view of the world as seen by the members of the social group concerned.

Forms of observation, and participant observation at that, have been recurrently used in social research. Charles Booth, for example, lived for a period among the poor so that he could better understand the lives that they led.[3] Although the earliest studies in anthropology relied upon the reported experiences of explorers and colonial administrators, modern anthropology has developed methods of immediate observation to a high art.[4] A major study in this vein which extols the virtues of participant observation is Malinowski's study, *Argonauts of the Western Pacific*, published in 1922.[5] No doubt in sharp reaction to the early practice of relying on the vicarious accounts of 'primitive tribes' and their exotic customs, Malinowski elaborates the advantages of participant observation. Though he himself did not use the term to describe his method of research, his book is a powerful statement of the benefits to social research of direct observation. The peoples he (and other) anthropologists studied did not generally have written records. Accordingly, sociological accounts of these societies were (and still are) dependent upon what the members of these societies do and say, and how they interact with each other in the present. By trying to see the world from the natives' point of view by learning to live within their society, so holding in abeyance the preconceptions natural to one's own society, the investigator can better identify the relationships, rules and values through which the society is organised. Since Malinowski's time, participant observation has become the standard method of anthropological inquiry.

However, although the point of direct observation or ethnographic methods is similar in some respects in both anthropology and sociology, it does involve differences of emphasis and practice as well as stemming from different theoretical and methodological traditions. For one thing, the anthropologist can seldom plausibly adopt the role of another participant as sociologists might do by becoming bread delivery drivers or machine operators as the 'cover' for their research roles in our own society.[6] For the anthropologist, adopting some sort of 'outsider' role is usually inevitable unless it is an anthropological inquiry into a society that is similar to the researcher's own. But the differences do not entirely turn on accidental factors such as this. For many years, roughly the period from 1920 to 1950, social anthropology in the west was dominated by a structural-functionalist approach. The institutions and groups in society were seen as having a function within the total social system, and the anthropological recommendations about the use of observational methods reflected this orientation.[7] By contrast, although sociology did have a long period, especially in the United States, when it was dominated by a structural-functionalist perspective this did not particularly encourage the use of participant observational methods. The practice of participant observation in sociological research arose out of a very different tradition, and later became associated with yet another: the sociological and the anthropological uses of participant observation reflect different theoretical specificities.

THE ORIGIN AND RATIONALE OF PARTICIPANT OBSERVATION

The early development of participant observation arose almost accidentally out of Chicago in the 1920s and 1930s as a result of the innovative work of Park, Burgess and Thomas. At this time the city of Chicago was growing rapidly, changing dramatically as influxes of immigrants from abroad and from within the United States itself flooded into the area. Sociology had been taught at the University of Chicago since before the turn of the century, and was soon established as the foremost research school in the United States.[8] The early work done there (in the first decades of the twentieth century) had been primarily conceptual, analytic and speculative. Small had pioneered the theoretical analysis of society; Dewey had reoriented psychology towards the analysis of interaction and communication; and Cooley, at nearby Michigan, developed a powerful conceptualisation of institutions and groups. Park, Burgess and Thomas represented a second wave of sociologists at Chicago, one more concerned to couple theoretical speculation with empirical study. Indeed, a major contribution of Chicago sociologists during this period was the pioneering and development of a variety of sociological research methods including the survey, the use of personal documents, intensive fieldwork, the use of documentary sources, ecological analysis and ethnography. The changing milieux of Chicago at the time, accommodating wave after wave of immigrants, as well as developing a major manufacturing and processing centre for the Middle West, must have seemed a challenging prospect for study.

But the roots of these sociologists' interests did not only have to do with the character of Chicago during this period: they lie deeper in their intellectual ideas and motivations. The development of American sociology paralleled the development of sociology in Britain as a transition from economic to a more general and social liberalism. This is a major theme of two studies of the development of sociology in the United States.[9] It is a change reflected in the work done in Chicago in the period concerned. Herbert Spencer's ideas, which to some extent were seen as extolling the idea of economic competitiveness as the natural social condition of humankind and central to social progress, had found powerful advocates in the United States, most notably W.G. Sumner.[10] Social progress as a natural outcome of economic competition and development, as Sumner proposed, can be seen as a continuing theme in much of the early sociological writing produced in the United States. A similar preoccupation runs through the work of the second generation of scholars in Chicago who first undertook sustained study of the city itself. The little communities springing up at the time were regarded as 'natural' communities, social entities which were largely self-regulating, in no need of externally imposed control.

To the American mind the small community was the natural unit of social organisation despite the presence of growing conurbations such as New York, San Francisco, Los Angeles and Chicago itself. It is important to note, as C. Wright Mills pointed out, that many of the contributors to the debate about social pathology which began in the United States about this time, were born and raised in small towns.[11] It is probable that the outlook produced by such origins helped shape much of the sociological thinking about urban and occupational life. The slums, the rooming house districts, even the delinquent groups of the city, tended to be measured, implicitly at least, against the standard of the 'natural' community. Rock writes that each of the areas studied 'was treated as a symbolic world which created and perpetuated a distinctive moral and social organisation. Each was subjected to interpretative analysis which attempted to reproduce the processes by which that organisation was brought into being'. He goes on to suggest that comparison was frequently drawn between these 'natural' processes and structures and 'those structures produced by planning and science'.[12] If we add to this concern with the minutiae of change in the community, American pragmatism, with its disdain for highly rationalistic and formalised theories in favour of first-hand and workable knowledge, two important ingredients of the style of social research that emerged are in place. Anderson's study of the hobo was one of the first to be published in 1923, followed by Thrasher's study of gangs, Cressey's study of 'taxi dance halls' and many more. At this time, too, Lindeman's exposition of research method, which first makes use of the term 'participant observation' was also published.[13] The research for these monographs was carried out under the supervision of Robert Park and Ernest Burgess, following on from W.I. Thomas, during the 1920s, and made major contributions to urban sociology, criminology and deviance, the sociology of the family, and the sociology of social problems. Though in some ways case studies, the intention was to place them within a generalising scientific framework by trying to 'understand social problems in terms of the processes and forces that produce them'.[14]

The development and use of participant observation can be roughly divided into three stages. First, the stage we have already reviewed in which it emerged as a legitimate method of social inquiry: this covers the period from 1920 or so until the middle or late 1930s. Few of the studies done during this period make very much explicit mention of the methods used but typically involved the classic field methods of informal interviewing, observation, the collection of personal documents and other documentary sources.[15] Robert Park had been a journalist in the last years of the nineteenth century and saw sociology as concerned just as much with those things of which good newspaper journalists have first-hand knowledge.[16] Overlapping with this and extending well into the post-war period, we have a stage in which there were sustained attempts to develop the method, articulate its applications, its contrasts with other methods and its own justifications more fully. During this period, too, it was detached from the context of social ecology and came to be associated with the approach now known as symbolic interactionism. Though this was a later addition to the method, it is the case that as far as sociology is concerned, participant observation is now closely tied to this conception of sociology. Although the founding principles of the approach were made in the early years of this century, they were developed by Mead and his followers. From the late 1920s onwards, both method and theory coalesced, through the work of Whyte, Hughes and Becker, into a distinctive sociological approach. While a student at Harvard, Whyte conducted what became a seminal study of an Italian community in a slum area of Boston. He later joined the faculty at Chicago and conducted a series of studies of industry.[17] Hughes, also at Chicago, refined participant observation as a method for the study of occupational groups, and sent out a succession of gifted students to study occupations in a like manner. In a series of papers he then tried to codify and unify their findings to draw more general sociological conclusions.[18] Becker, Goffman and others found a whole series of wider applications for the theory and method, and laid the foundations for studies of deviance and other institutions.[19]

While this style of analysis and research continues to be influential, if somewhat peripheral, in social research, there are some grounds for thinking that a third stage in the development of participant observation is being entered into, and shall have more to say about this later in the chapter. For now we want to concentrate on the second stage in which participant observation was most fully developed, and the period in which its uses and methodological implications were carefully set out.

THE RESEARCH PROCESS OF PARTICIPANT OBSERVATION

When it was first deployed in social research, participant observation was primarily seen as one way among others of carrying out social research. Certainly, it was not enmeshed in controversies over quantitative versus qualitative research or particularly associated with a distinctive approach to sociological theorising and research. It was simply one instrument among many others. For many years it was treated thus. Sometimes, for example, it was recommended as a prelude to the use of more formal methods of research. Thus a period of participant observation within a factory, for example, could be useful in helping in the design of questionnaires or interview schedules by sensitizing researchers to the relationships, argot and attitudes that are likely to be found there. However, for the majority of social researchers whose work we shall be reviewing in this chapter, the choice of participant observation as a method was more mandatory, more principled and less instrumental than this. It became, in a word, a theory-specific method. This view is associated with the radical criticism of variable analysis (discussed in previous chapters), especially the interview and the social survey, as failing to meet the standards of what adequate social research methods ought to be.[20] Occasionally, this criticism is also associated with a repudiation of the notion that the social sciences can be scientific in the same manner as the natural sciences. Both these versions reject the quantitative stance of much orthodox social research in favour of a more qualitative and interpretative approach. The contention rests very much on the argument that social life is constructed in and through meanings which cannot be studied in terms which owe more to the requirements of mathematics than to the nature of social phenomena themselves. Not all reject the idea that sociology can be scientific, but instead quarrel with the notion that it can be scientific in the way proposed by positivistic, Lazarsfeldian methods. Sometimes what is proposed in its place is an alternative method of developing social scientific theory in a manner more attuned to the nature of social phenomena.[21] This argument is extensive and subtle at times and (though we shall allude to some of its claims) it is impossible to enter into it fully.

We have made the point that the method of participant observation is now closely associated with a particular theoretical perspective in sociology; a perspective which stresses the interactive, interpretative and negotiated basis of social life, created and sustained by the meanings actors use to make sense of and interpret the world in which they live. There is little sense here of an objective social structure of the kind presupposed by the early surveyors or as articled in many, classic and current, sociological theories, such as those of Durkheim, Marx and, latterly, those of structuralists such as Althusser and, to a degree, Giddens.[22] Instead, the social structure is seen more as a kind of multitude of scenic processes, constantly moving and changing as actors negotiate and renegotiate their courses of action. There is little conception, too, of a society as a macro-structure, more a preference for studying society as the creation of people in the course of constructing interaction together. An essential part of this is being able to see the society from the point of view of the actor concerned since it is this which shapes his or her courses of action.

So there is in all of participant observation research a preference for studying small-scale worlds, small groups of many kinds.[23] It is this coupled with the injunction that the research must be *participant* observation that provides such researchers with the first of their problems: gaining access to the group or setting that is to be the concern of the research. This is a matter of fine judgement. One of the main arguments for participant observation as a method of social research is that it allows for the study of social actors in their natural habitats as opposed to the artificial circumstances of the laboratory or the detached and often remote method of the survey interview. As Burgess put it: 'The objects of social science research, as persons, groups, and institutions, must be studied if at all in the laboratory of community life'.[24] As a result the researcher needs to enter the group or setting in such a way as to disturb as little as possible the lives of those being studied. To enter as a researcher may well generate 'reactive effects' and so contaminate or disturb the naturalness of the action itself. In the case of some groups – exclusive religious cults would be an example – it may be otherwise extremely difficult to enter at all as a fully-fledged researcher and even difficult posing as a devotee, certainly not without considerable thespian talent. However, there may be no role available other than that of researcher because of obvious ethnic differences between researcher and members of the target group. It may be that an 'outsider' role, such as that of researcher, is in fact the appropriate one to adopt. Trice suggests that in cases where two or more groups confront each other, as did affiliates and non-affiliates to Alcoholics Anonymous in a state hospital he was studying, the subjects may invest outsiders with appropriate neutrality enabling them to pursue research goals not only more openly but also with sufficient access to both sides.[25] Vidich goes further, arguing that to the extent to which an observer's data are conditioned by the subjects' responses to the observer's role, a 'stranger' has an important advantage. Researchers can, with justification, maintain an attitude of naïvety and exploit the role to the full. It would be easy for incoming researchers to break taboos, contravene local customs and understandings, inadvertently offend, and so on, and still maintain a tenable position as people who can be excused these things because they are strangers and do not know, yet, what is expected. Such researchers can ask naïve questions in a way that would not be possible of someone presumed to have the familiarity and competence of an accredited member. Fieldworkers can present themselves 'as an interested incompetent who needs toleration and remedial instruction'.[26] On many occasions there is little need for concealment of the research role: individuals often welcome the interest shown by a researcher and respond in much the way that Vidich claims.

The general lesson in this is that there are no hard-and-fast rules dictating what sort of role to adopt, and even less about determining what kind of role will be the most efficacious. What is clear is that access is not simply a matter of presence, but of acceptance, which may take both time and thought. Indeed, the process of gaining access and acceptance can itself be highly informative. In his early, and classic study, Whyte adopted the rather vague role of a writer concerned to write a history of 'Cornerville'. For his purposes this turned out to be an apposite choice: the inhabitants of Cornerville knew something about writers. Though not a regular job in the usual sense, it was respectable, done by educated people, and, moreover, involved unconventional hours. Further, the role gave Whyte a licence to ask questions without being deemed too inquisitive, since it was understood that writers needed to gather material.[27] In other cases, nothing so beautifully ill-defined a role as a writer will do.

An example of just how difficult these kinds of problems can be is provided by a study of the motivations and attitudes of enlisted men which required a researcher to 'enlist' as a basic trainee in order to become a fully-fledged member of the group involved. His identity as a researcher was unknown, even to his commanding officer. Since the observer was to enlist under an assumed name and remain in the group for a long period, an identity had to be constructed for him so that his false identity could be verified as 'true' if necessary. So successful was the coaching he received as a putative member of the adolescent subculture that the recruiting sergeant at the post where he was to enlist recommended that he be rejected because, on all the evidence, he was a juvenile delinquent.[28]

While not all participant observation studies necessitate such extreme identity creations there are numerous examples of the considerable trouble researchers have gone to so that they may 'pass' within the group they are investigating. It is worth noting, however, that Whyte, as have others, found that acceptance within the groups in the district he was researching depended far more on the personal relationships he was able to develop than on any rationale or explanation, spurious or otherwise, of what he was doing. As long as he was able to win the support of key individuals he was fairly confident that he could obtain what he wanted from those he approached.

I soon found that people were developing their own explanation about me: I was writing a book about Cornerville. This might seem entirely too vague an explanation, and yet it sufficed. I found that my acceptance in the district depended on the personal relationships I developed far more than upon any explanation I might give. ... If I was all right, then my project was all right; if I was no good, then no amount of explanation could convince them that the book was a good idea.[29]

It should not be forgotten that fieldworkers, whether concealed participants or not, are fitted into a role by the people they are studying, and there will, inevitably, be variations from field situation to field situation in these identity assignments and no little variation between individuals within the group. Identities, as well as the kind of activity being observed, are likely to affect the access to information and generally play a part in shaping the data the researcher is able to gather. Karp, for example, in a study of the 'public sexual scene' in Times Square in New York tried a number of strategies for initiating interaction and, at times, was perceived as a hustler or a cop. Though his experience paralleled the nervousness shown by frequenters to such places, it failed to result in other than minimal participation.[30] What this also shows is that problems to do with access, along with the importance of developing good personal relationships in the field, can modify the original aims of the study. Liebow, for example, set out to study the child-rearing practices among low-income families and was designated to collect material about young, low-income men to complement interviews with families. He intended to do several small studies but, after 'hanging about' a number of locales, fell in with Tally Jackson, who became sponsor and confidant, and whose circle became the eventual focus of the research.[31] In this case, the redirection of the research produced an impressive contribution to ethnography, and also warns of the need for flexibility and opportunism. Tally Jackson 'opened the gates' for Liebow but, conversely, 'gatekeepers' can also close them.

Four roles open to the participant observer are usually identified.[32] The first, the *complete participant*, is that role in which the researcher becomes a full-fledged member of the group under study, any research purpose being concealed. A major feature of this role is, obviously, the necessity for a great deal of pretence. The second role is that of *participant-as-observer* in which both researcher and subjects are aware of the fact that theirs is a fieldwork relationship. Good examples of this role are the numerous community studies in which the fieldworker develops contacts and enduring relationships with individuals in the community. Since the research purpose is not concealed, it is much easier for the fieldworker to use other techniques of social research, including interviewing, surveys, and so on. *Observer-as-participant* is the third role in which involvement with subjects is deliberately, or for a number of practical reasons, kept to a minimum.[33] Typical of this research role is the 'one visit interview'. Similarly, the fourth role, *complete observer*, requires investigators to insulate themselves from any social contact whatsoever with subjects as one might do in observing behaviour in 'public places'. Our main concern is with the first two mentioned.

Although the choice of participant role can often require delicate judgement, sometimes even courage, matters usually boil down to a careful weighing up of the nature of the group, its accessibility and openness, research exigencies such as time, resources and opportunities, as well as the personal qualities of the researcher.

However, one possibility needs to be anticipated which could, arguably, affect the objectivity of the research, Earlier it was pointed out that one of the major justifications of participant observation as a research strategy was that it facilitated an 'insider's' view of the social world through participation in the naturally occurring organisation of the group of persons being studied. One danger of this is that researchers may become so much participants that they are no longer capable of maintaining the role of researcher and become instead fully-fledged participants; a process aptly, if bluntly, called 'going native'. There is a dual emphasis to the role of participant observer: that adopted to gain entry and acceptance within the group, and that of researcher. At the best of times, these are difficult to balance. If observers err too much on the side of researcher they will run the risk of exposure which, at the very least, could mean ruin of the research and the waste of considerable effort, not to speak of more serious consequences. If the balance tips too far in the other direction the risk is a different one, namely becoming so immersed in the group that it is impossible even to pretend to any detachment or objective observation.

These and similar risks vary according to the role adopted. Since that of 'complete participant' involves the most pretence it would seem to incur the greater risks. Gold states the problem dramatically enough:

The complete participant realizes that he, and he alone, knows that in reality he is other than the person he pretends to be. He must pretend that his real self is represented by the role, or roles, he plays in and out of the ... situation in relationships with people who, to him, are but informants. ... He must bind the mask of pretence to himself or stand the risk of exposure or failure.[34]

Thus, 'complete participants' face two day-to-day problems: first, becoming so self-conscious about not revealing their true identity that their observation is severely handicapped by attempting to give a convincing performance; second, becoming so immersed in the role chosen that the 'native' view is adopted entirely. In the case of the 'participant-as-observer' the risks of immersion are still there but, obviously, since the research role is an open one, the problem of concealment does not arise. But, as Vidich has noted, being both a participant and an observer is 'the strategy of having one's cake and eating it too. Deceiving the society to study it and wooing the society to live in it'.[35] The researcher's position is always ambivalent and remains marginal to the group or organisation being studied. Although, it must be said, that in some respects marginality or at least sufficient distance is just what the fieldworker needs. Clearly, there are important ethical considerations which are relevant here and which intermesh with research requirements. Normally, the rule is to inform subjects of the research, irrespective of whether it is interviewing or ethnographic, sufficient for them to choose to participate in the research contract. However, there may be a number of good reasons why specifying in full what the research is about can seriously inhibit the research itself by unduly influencing the behaviour of the people involved.[36] Once again there are no 'solutions' to this kind of dilemma which, after all, is a feature, to varying degrees, of most social research. It does particularly afflict, however, covert research where the deception is most pronounced. Indeed, it is worth pondering whether covert participation is unavoidable. Not only is it unwise, and not just for ethical reasons, but also it can rebound if the disguise is revealed. Building up trust, negotiating access through the course of the research, trading off gains and losses, weighing up the ethical problems carefully, all are probably better in the long run. In any event, protecting the identity of subjects should always be of paramount concern.[37]

There are a number of strategies that have been used to cope with the often excrutiating ambiguities and divergent loyalties built into the participant observer role. In the study of motivations and attitudes of enlisted men mentioned earlier, the observer was given every opportunity to report back to the research group for debriefing, and to disengage, even if only for a short time, in order to maintain the necessary balance of commitments. Irrespective of the research role adopted the researcher does need to find time for reflection and seclusion in order to write up field-notes. Observers must always remember that there will come a time when they must disengage from the group and report back the findings. Problems of detachment versus involvement will generally become more severe the longer the observer stays within the group unless satisfactory arrangements have been made to sustain or reinforce the research side of the role.

Once entry into the target group has been achieved – and it needs to be pointed out that the activities required to gain entry often tell us something about the nature of the group or the organisation[38] – the observer's next task is to make full use of the role selected in order to gather data relevant to the research purpose. It is at this time that all the personal qualities and skills of watching, listening, questioning, sociability, shrewdness, tactfulness, recollection, and more, come into play to collect the material required.

An essential tool in the fieldworker's craft is a notebook in which everything felt to be relevant is noted down. At first such notes may look little more than random jottings of odd remarks, notes of an unusual occurrence, a pet name, a tentative sociogram of relationships, vague analyses, suggestions, and so on. The main problem in the early stages of the research is deciding what not to record since until a plausible scheme of interpretation has emerged it will be hard to judge the relevance of anything. The temptation to record anything and everything will be hard to resist; a temptation not always helped by tape-recorders where these are usable since such material always has to be transcribed later. Once again Whyte's experience is instructive here. He kept copious notes. Although for much of the time he was hanging around street corners, he would go to his room periodically to write up his observations. Most of his mornings were spent recording what had happened the previous day. In the beginning these notes were kept chronologically, but this soon became unmanageable. His choice then was whether to file his material under topics, such as politics, the family, church and religious affairs, rackets, and so on, or to file according to the group he was with at the time. At this stage it became clear to him that it was the groups who were crucial to his conceptualisation, so he decided to file by this principle. The opportunities and places for note taking will, of course, vary from the setting and role adopted.[39]

This also illustrates an important feature of participant observation, namely the way in which the analysis of data accompanies the process of data collection itself or, as Becker terms it, 'sequentially'.[40] Becker goes on to identify four main stages of analysis in participant observation research: the selection, identification and definition of problems, concepts and indices; the estimation of the distribution of phenomena; the incorporation of the findings into a model of the group, community or organisation under study; and, finally, the presentation of the conclusions and their evidence and proof. It is important to note that the first three of these stages are carried out while fieldwork is in progress and form an integral part of that fieldwork. This pattern of working, though Becker's formulation of it makes it appear rather more ordered and systematic than it is in actuality, is not typical of the other methods of data collection.

During the first stage of identifying problems, concepts and indices, a stage on which much of the remainder depends, the observer looks for concepts that offer the greatest promise in yielding fruitful and interesting findings. Although a researcher may note that X occurred in a certain place at a certain time, this will remain an isolated and uninteresting finding unless it is placed within the some context of interpretation to determine its significance. An observer might notice, for example, that in a work group when a particular foreman appears the workers display an exaggerated involvement in their work tasks, relaxing the moment the foreman goes away. This may suggest something about the nature of the relationship between this foreman and these workers or it might signify something more general to do with the wider context of work within the plant and the kind of supervisory practices in force. By appropriate questioning and continued observation the researcher can begin to develop specific and more firmly drawn ideas about the interaction in the setting.

Initially, then, the observer will use materials mainly to speculate about possibilities and, very important, to direct future observation and inquiry. In terms of the example just used, the observer will need to look for other modes of behaviour which may throw light on the relationship between foremen and workers, and for other kinds of instances which may illuminate the kind of authority relationships that hold between them. Further observations may, of course, force the researcher to discard a number of provisional interpretations. In addition, the researcher can make use of a number of principles, 'rules of thumb' if you like, to evaluate individual items of data. Statements by informants can be judged for their credibility. Has this informant got a particular axe to grind? Does the informant have a reason to lie or otherwise embroider the truth? Did the informant actually witness what is being reported? Was the statement volunteered? Does the pattern of behaviour occur repeatedly? Is it done jokingly, insultingly, or for effect? And so on. Important here, too, is the relationship between observer and informant. If researchers are 'complete participants' they have to evaluate whether the role being played, whatever it might be, affects the behaviour observed or the statements offered. If the researcher is a 'participant-as-observer' then it might be that the observer aspect of the role results in behaviour which would not normally occur. This may or may not matter, and it can work both ways. Subjects may say something or act when alone with the observer in ways which accurately reflect their perspective, but which might be inhibited by the presence of other subjects. However, the contrary to this is also possible, especially when the presence of others may give support to the expression of one's perspective.

None of the above problems has a solution which can be reduced to some technical routine, and it is not always easy to determine whether, in the case of any particular research, they are problems or not: this is a matter of judgement by the observer.

The next stage of research suggested by Becker, one not sharply distinguishable either analytically or practically from the first, is discovering which of the many provisional hypotheses, interim interpretations, problems or ideas are worth pursuing as major elements in the study. In part, this is done by checking if the events or phenomena that prompted the initial hunches are widespread or typical within the group. This will almost certainly require collating various kinds of evidence about the group from many different sources, informants, observations, and so on. Normally because of the practical difficulties inherent in fieldwork, judgements about the frequency or typicality of some event, pattern, behaviour or perspective, will not be quantitative in character. None the less, estimates of likelihood are more than possible.

Becker's final stage of analysis consists of incorporating particular findings into some more general model of the social system of the group or organisation. This amounts to designing a descriptive model which best accounts for the data assembled. The most common kinds of conclusions to emerge at this stage include: statements about the necessary and sufficient conditions for the existence of some phenomenon; statements that some phenomenon is 'basic' to the group or organisation in question, and identification of a situation as an instance of some process designated in sociological theory. Once again, it is important to note that this stage is a major part of the fieldwork. Preliminary models are refined by searching for possible negative cases, and the construction of such models, partial as they may be at times, is an operation very closely connected to the observer's techniques and interests at the time of the fieldwork. Of course, more systematic working-out of the models must await a time when the observer can disengage from the fieldwork. This brings us to Becker's last stage, namely the final analysis and the presentation of results.

This final stage consists of rechecking and refining models as carefully as possible. With the practical difficulties of fieldwork behind them, researchers can look over their material to take account of all the information to assess the accuracy and plausibility of any conclusions. Models can be built more systematically, hypotheses and interpretations subjected to even greater scrutiny and interconnections formed into an overall synthesis.

An important consideration is the presentation of conclusions and evidence either for a research report or some other kind of publication. In contrast to quantitative research, qualitative data and the inferences drawn from them are difficult to present succinctly – a feature which is, by the way, much overrated as a characteristic of quantitative work. The relatively highly systematised methods of quantitative social research, such as the tabular presentation of statistical data, the use of measures of association, correlation and even causal models, permit highly formalised presentations in ways not open to ethnographic reports. Such qualitative material will normally consist of many different kinds of observations that need to be presented in something of their original character to retain their value as data. Yet, a highly conscientious presentation of all the evidence will run the risk of boring readers or bury them in a surfeit of information. Becker's suggested solution to this particular problem is to present conclusions in the form of a natural history 'presenting the evidence as it came to the attention of the observer during the successive stages of his conceptualisation of the problem. ... In this way, evidence is assessed as the substantive analysis is presented'.[41] This, he claims, would give readers the opportunity to make their own judgement as to the adequacy or otherwise of the research and the confidence that can be placed on its conclusions.

Problems of Participant Observation

While passionately defended by its supporters, it should be no surprise to find that observational methods are heavily criticised, especially by those who subscribe to the view that the social sciences should strive to emulate the natural sciences. For these the methods rely far too heavily on techniques which are unsystematic, leave too much to the whims of individual researchers, are not replicable, are far too subjective and generally fail to conform to what is expected of an effective science. However, in many ways quantitative social research is hardly free of its own serious problems; let us look at some of these kinds of criticisms of observational methods a little more closely.

One of the major justifications of participant observation especially, but it is also true of other observational methods, is that it enables a researcher to study a group in its natural setting and, moreover, for far longer and in more depth than is possible with other research strategies. Against this it can be objected that by taking a role within a naturally organised group a researcher may well affect the structure and the character of the interaction being studied. This kind of 'control' or 'reactive' effect has been noted in connection even with more formalised methods, such as the experiment, and is by no means peculiar to observational methods. However, the problem with such effects is when they are unintentional and, thereby, unforeseen and affect the outcomes of the research in unknown ways. Were Whyte's street-corner gangs unaffected by his presence? Is a company of recruits with a disguised officer in their midst the same as a group without such a researcher?

But it is not only the group that has to be worried about in this case. Researchers, too, may be affected by their participation, which may happen in a number of ways. For example, taking a role within a group tends to impose restrictions on a fuller understanding of any situation as it might appear from a differently located role. Further, as Whyte discovered, as a researcher matures into the selected role, perceptions are likely to become more inflexible representing a reduced willingness to entertain alternative hypotheses and schemes of interpretation. Whyte remarks that as he became more a part of the community and his data increased in richness, he found himself tending to 'take for granted the sort of behaviour that is taken for granted by the people I was observing'.[42] The process of 'maturation', to call it that, can also affect subjects. People studied by the participant observer, whatever role is adopted, are of two major types: respondent and informant. Informants, like Doc in Whyte's study, have a special relationship with the researcher; there is normally a bond of trust between them, they give information more freely, explain what is going on, and so on. The informant becomes more like a colleague to the researcher and the relationship can develop into one of special intimacy; however, the respondent does not have this kind of relationship to the researcher. Normally there will be no special trust, no giving of privileged information, questions answered only when asked, and so on. By contrast, the informant acts as an observer for the researcher and as a means of access to the group under investigation. However, it is possible for the informant to develop too deep a commitment to the researcher and the aims of the study and, not to put too pejorative an emphasis upon it, becomes over-enthusiastic in the provision of information.

Once again there are no hard-and-fast rules to counter these and similar objections: as with any research, costs have to be weighed against benefits. Sometimes it is the case that a fieldworker serves as a sounding board for the group, the person whom people talk to because he or she is not an intimate member of the group. Also, the objectives of the research need to be borne in mind in assessing whether or not reliance on a few informants does, in fact, jeopardise the validity of the findings. In a study of air traffic controllers, special involvement with one watch out of the five in the centre facilitated rather than hindered the objective of studying the work and the interaction of controllers around a controlling suite: the objective of the research was not to produce an ethnography of an air traffic control *centre*, but a *segment* of the work of controllers.[43] However, it is not as if those who advocate the method are unaware of such problems, as Becker's recommendations presented earlier show. Indeed, Becker goes further and claims that the participant observer, more than any other type of social researcher, is better placed to appreciate just what these and similar problems involve,

because he operates, when gathering data, in a social context rich in cues and information of all kinds. Because he sees and hears the people he studies in many situations ... he builds an ever growing fund of impressions, many of them at the subliminal level, which give him an extensive base for the interpretation and analytic use of any particular datum. The wealth of information and impressions sensitises him to subtleties ... and forces him to raise continually new and different questions, which he brings to and tries to answer in succeeding observations.[44]

Becker, however, represents a tendency among some supporters of participant observation who claim, in effect, that it is a better method for achieving the goals of a science of social life than other, more quantitative and formal methods. He argues that it is possible to construct and test hypotheses using the method. Indeed, he claims that more than other methods of research it fulfils better the aim of sociology, originally formulated by Weber, of providing explanation at the level of meaning. For many supporters of the method, then, participant observation as a method of data collection was not a crucial option but a necessary part of the development of more adequate sociological theory.

To try and catch the interpretative process by remaining aloof as a so-called 'objective' observer and refusing to take the role of the acting unit is to risk the worst kind of subjectivism – the objective observer is likely to fill in the process of interpretation with his own surmises in place of catching the process as it occurs in the experience of the acting unit which uses it.[45]

It is, none the less, undeniable that a great deal of interpretative work is necessary on the part of the participant observer to bring conclusions out of the materials: work which is not part of any explicitly formalised procedure. Can a highly educated middle-class researcher really empathise and understand aspects of the lives of lower-class people? How far can a young, fresh-faced university-trained sociologist really empathise with drug addicts, hustlers, prostitutes, beggars and panhandlers, and other members of 'deviant subcultures', who seem to form a large proportion of the subject-matter of participant observation? Might not his or her own life experiences cause the researcher to draw inferences from the materials that may be widely at variance with the conceptions held by the subjects themselves?

Schwarz and Schwarz note that a certain amount of

retrospective reworking ... goes on without the observer being aware of it. Rather than finding a simple and direct connection between the occurrence of an event and its representation as data, we discovered that our observation began to expand the longer we thought about it.[46]

But what direction does this 'reworking' take? Is it necessarily a refinement, as Becker would like, of the initial materials and their significance or is it one which owes more to the researcher's own conceptions and preferences?

These kinds of problems, if such they are, can be compounded by the kind of contacts a participant observer is able to make within a group and the relationships allowed to him or her. Clearly, this will be shaped in large part by the researcher's social characteristics and by the norms and expectations of the group under study. An example of this is Gans's *Urban Villagers*.[47] He points out that his observations were limited because of strict segregation between the sexes. At gatherings the men grouped themselves in the living-room while the women stayed in the kitchen; men were distinctly uncomfortable in the presence of women. The overriding feeling was that if a man and a woman are alone sexual contact between them is unavoidable. In light of this state of affairs more of Gans's data were collected from men than from women. In some societies racial and ethnic barriers are difficult to surmount, as are those to do with status and power. It is perhaps for this reason, among others, that participant observation studies of lower-status groups are more frequent than are studies of high-status groups. The powerful are less likely to feel flattered by the attentions of a researcher and, who knows, perhaps also have more to hide. Age, too, can affect the relationships a researcher is able to establish. Lofland suggests that young people may, on the whole, be more acceptable in fieldwork roles. He argues that since the participant observer must always be watching and asking questions, in most settings younger people can more easily be accepted as 'incompetents', as people who do not know all that much and, hence, will not be offended by being told 'obvious' things by members of the group.[48]

Many of the researcher's social characteristics, such as age, sex, social class, ethnicity, and so forth, can crucially affect the relationships that he or she can develop and, in addition, affect the inferences the researcher draws from the materials collected. Even the best fieldworkers are limited in the kinds of relationships they are able to develop, and by their own social characteristics as well as the structure of the setting being studied. Matters such as personal appearance can be highly significant not only in affecting access but also in shaping the relationships that can be entered into.[49] Gender, too, is becoming increasingly recognised as an omni-relevant, but highly variable, factor in establishing fieldwork relationships. In so far as women are stereotypically seen as 'unthreatening' they may gain access to settings and information with some ease.[50] But gender may limit access in all kinds of ways. Ethnicity is another identity that may create all kinds of problems, but not always straightforwardly. White researchers find it difficult to gain access to black ghetto areas in the large American cities, especially if they are American researchers. Hannerz, however, as a Swede felt that his nationality gave him some distance from other, particularly American, whites.[51] One could go on itemising such matters.[52]

We have already referred to the fact that participant observation puts the researcher into a strange setting with all the attendant difficulties this may engender. The research process itself, of necessity, isolates fieldworkers from their more usual social world. A new environment, new situations and new ways of living have to be mastered, and in a way that not only displays that mastery but also retains research objectives. A new social role must be established, one which allows freedom not always open to members of the group, which can, on occasion, provoke resentment. Many researchers report feelings of unease, to put it no stronger than this, about not being fully accepted by their hosts or, perhaps, a feeling of inauthenticity and disloyalty to them. There is the perennial problem of how much to disclose about oneself and about the research, a dilemma particularly acute in the case of covert observation. None the less, although such feelings may pass with experience, and they can often be exaggerated, there is little doubt that the fieldwork role is an ambivalent one. Since the gathering of data is the major aim, personal sentiments must often be suppressed to avoid antagonising important sources of information. As Hammersley points out, the ethnographer cannot choose informants as one might choose friends.[53] But, the general point is that unlike the other methods of social research we have described, there are no clear rules to follow; much advice and wisdom from others who have done such work, but no clear 'textbook' guidelines. Carefully and strictly formulated hypotheses are rarely the inspiration of the work. There is normally no question of selecting samples, no statistical means of testing hypotheses, and so on. What sampling does occur is what can be described as theoretical sampling where the choice of site, of group or of occupation is informed by theoretically driven interests which may be no more, though this is by no means a critically meant comment, than a desire to see if, for example, police work is like its more salient images, or how street corner gangs organise their day-to-day activities.

All of this may well generate anxieties about whether or not the researcher is being sufficiently objective, is gathering the right kind of material, being in a position to witness matters of relevance, being able to determine what is or is not of relevance, and so forth. It may be that in response to such feelings researchers become over-reliant on the first people to come to their assistance and, as a consequence, they exert undue influence on the researcher's perceptions and ability to effect good rapport with other subjects. It is possible that fieldworkers become so intent on developing good relationships that they begin to lose grasp of the fact that the point of the involvement is sociological research. Admittedly, an essential part of the task of participant observation is that researchers 'resocialise' themselves through the experience of research itself. But it can go too far. As Whyte reported:

As I became accepted with the community, I found myself becoming almost a non-observing participant. I got the feel of life in Cornerville, but that meant that I got to take for granted the same things that my Cornerville friends took for granted. I was immersed in it, but I could as yet make little sense of it.[54]

The extreme form of this is 'going native'. While in its extreme form this is, perhaps, rare, and when it does occur of little interest since it is not likely to result in anything for sociological evaluation, it can, none the less, result in analyses which are almost wholly one-sided, even if sympathetic to the subjects studied.[55] This is not a question of deliberate distortion or deception; rather, it is one of natural sympathy which affects the analysis and must, accordingly, be evaluated appropriately.

These points concern the effect the mode of research itself can have on the collection, interpretation and analysis of data produced by the method. Another set of influences is less directly concerned with fieldworkers' perception and more to do with their effect on the group and its patterns of interaction. Fieldwork takes place in a natural setting and it requires no great leap of imagination to suspect that the researcher's presence may well alter in significant ways the situation being studied. As Doc, one of Whyte's informants said: 'You've slowed me up plenty since you've been down here. Now, when I do something, I have to think what Bill Whyte would want to know about it and how I can explain it'.[56] The manifold ways in which such effects can occur are difficult to summarise. However, it is worth noting that 'reactive effects' are not confined to participant observation studies. Laboratory experiments, surveys and interviews are all prone to such effects; one reason why so much effort has been devoted to evaluating or eradicating them. To the extent that nearly all social science data collection techniques involve the creation of, or the participation in, social situations, we would expect such influences to be endemic. The problem is to account for them in order better to judge their effects. As far as participant observation is concerned, Becker for one argues that the method is probably less prone to such unacknowledged influences than are other methods. Prolonged involvement in the scene, careful weighing of informants and information, rechecking, and so on, means that little will be hidden from the observer.[57] Some participant observers, however, regard the researcher's ability to influence the setting as a positive asset. Whyte, for example, helped to organise the gangs to make a protest about the lack of hot water in the district, with some success. However, this does conflict with the standard advice to fieldworkers, which is not to take sides on issues affecting the subjects. The dangers of taking sides are obvious enough: it may cut the researcher off from what could be important aspects of group life, unduly influence a 'natural situation', and so on. Yet, sometimes such intervention can be valuable in testing out ideas. Whyte's action was based on over three years of fieldwork with the gangs, and, it is arguable, helped further by his understanding of the structure, the culture and the political situation of the gangs and their environment.

The general point about all the foregoing is that a researcher cannot avoid having an influence on the setting being studied; one can reasonably surmise that these influences will vary according to setting, type of participant role adopted, length of observation, and so on. However, it is a moot point as to whether any of these factors, and more, do make a systematic difference to the conclusions that might be reached. The important point is that researchers should be able to make informed judgements about how and to what extent such influences affected the data they were able to collect, the inferences that may be made, and, ultimately, the analysis presented. (Aside from these methodological points there are some ethical issues surrounding deliberate intervention which we shall return to towards the end of this chapter.)

Apart from these general complaints about the effect of participant observation itself, there are others which begin to attack the theoretical value of the method. It should be obvious by now that the participant observer does not produce data of the kind generated by the survey and the experiment. Fieldworkers may spend months assessing subjects, talking and listening to them; rarely do they systematically interview randomly chosen large samples. They do not test causal hypotheses of the kind proposed by positivist and variable analytic approaches, and they do not present their materials statistically. Instead, their raw data are likely to consist of detailed field-notes, reports of observations, encounters, happenings, reflections, etc. The question is: what theoretical value do these kinds of data have?

The first point to make is that a participant observation study is not based on systematic sampling procedures. Normally, fieldworkers are able to develop contacts with only a small minority of people in a group or a community or an organisation. Indeed, it is also likely that this small group of people will be unrepresentative in a strict statistical sense of the whole. The nature of the method requires that contacts be made through existing and established networks which may well bypass others. More than this, though, is whether the group studied is typical of other groups. Are Whyte's street corner gangs typical of other urban gangs? Are they a phenomenon of a particular period or phase or urban growth or decline? And so on. The actual group chosen for study depends upon a number of contingencies, especially those to do with ease of access and entry. Often the researcher has little discretion about where the fieldwork can be done, and chance encounters often play an important part. Gans, for example, wanted to study a slum and the way of life of a low-income population.[58] He felt that he should study a white slum because it would be easier for a white researcher to gain access. The one he chose was facilitated by the fact that an already existing research project concerned with redevelopment of the area was willing to offer him a job. However, by the time he entered, redevelopment had caused many of its inhabitants to leave and those that were left were disproportionately older and, for personal and financial reasons, could not move. Accordingly, he ended up studying a single, working-class Italian community at a particular time in its history, and one which had unique and perhaps atypical features. The question is, then, whether his analysis and description of family life in the area can be extended to other low-income areas?

For this sort of reason, many fieldworkers are content to limit the scope of their generalisations and regard their research as exploratory, to be supplemented by further studies on the same or similar themes. It is important to recognise that any piece of research, regardless of its method, has limitations and takes its place within a corpus of other research and a process of sociological evaluation. However, it is worth noting that this problem, if it is a problem, of generalising from a single case is not unique to participant observation studies.[59] Many surveyors, for example, sample particular cities, towns, organisations, factories, etc. But one supposed virtue of quantitative studies compared with qualitative studies like participant observation is the explicit way in which the results can be presented. Earlier we summarised Becker's recommendations on this matter, but there is no doubt that, compared with the social surveyor, more discretion is available to the fieldworker. Fieldworkers are not bound by strict rules of statistical inference or evidence in the same way. Moreover, since field data come from many different situations in many different forms rather than as explicitly measured variables, it is much more difficult for the observer to give a systematic account of how such-and-such a conclusion is reached or warranted. As Becker admits, it would be ridiculous to present all the descriptive material necessary for readers to make their own assessment of the data and any inferences drawn from it. He notes that

Participant observation ... has not done well with this problem, and the full weight of evidence for conclusions and the processes by which they were reached are usually not presented, so that the reader finds it difficult to make his own assessment of them and must rely on his faith in the researcher.[60]

We have already seen how Becker recommends problems such as these be overcome. None the less, for many the reports of participant observation studies remain little better than good journalism, or worse, or anecdotal accounts of social life, usually of the seamier side. In other words, they are not scientific in the way required. However, for others all these criticisms are beside the point. Such criticisms, for example, would have a point if ethnographic studies had the same objective as those using the methods of variable analysis. Although we shall develop this point later, it is worth noting that very often the aim of participant observation studies is more descriptive than explanatory, or at least not explanatory in the sense in which variable analysis understands this. More often than not the aim of such studies can be reasonably glossed as 'describing a slice of social life' or 'describing aspects of the social organisation of an occupational group/community/ group, or whatever'; this is as important an endeavour to social research as are other approaches. After all, much of science is as concerned with the basic description of things as it is with theoretical explanation.

The extent to which the results of participant observation should be regarded as merely descriptive or 'good journalism' can, of course, be exaggerated. It can be argued that the point of observational studies is to obtain detailed accounts of particular social processes by which events or outcomes can be explained. Most observational studies feature incidents or events, recorded in some detail, and are featured because of the way in which they sum up or symbolise the social situations described and the processes and mechanisms involved in them. Because the events and processes are described as part of a set of meaningful social relationships, there is an obvious sense in which ethnographic accounts are more than descriptive. They suggest that because individuals share a given repertoire of meanings, or common culture, and are involved in a particular set of circumstances, or set of social relationships, the effect on their behaviour is profoundly formative. There is, too, a way in which this kind of understanding can be used to suggest more general explanations. The similarities between the processes revealed by fieldwork in various situations suggest that these may be 'exemplary' of processes general in social life.[61]

PARTICIPANT OBSERVATION AND SYMBOLIC INTERACTIONISM

Perhaps no other sociological theory is more closely associated with a particular research method than symbolic interactionism is with participant observation, even though it had little to do with the origins of the method itself. Indeed, the elements that we tend to regard as distinctively belonging to the symbolic interactionist approach were assembled rather late in the day. Moreover, there is little doubt that both the theory and the method are rather peripheral to mainstream sociology. As far as the method is concerned this is not so surprising given the immense demands it makes, personal and intellectual, on the fieldworker. As far as the symbolic interactionist approach is concerned, this grows out of a special conception of sociological knowledge and, inevitably, of the nature of society and social life. For symbolic interactionists the current technological and quantitative emphasis of most of sociological method has usurped the proper concerns of the discipline, namely the nature of human society. They stress, too, that 'the activity of research is itself a proper object of sociological inquiry. Research is not taken to be a disembodied agent of pure logic, but a social encounter'.[62]

Symbolic interactionists reject efforts to create a science of sociology through formal, deductive, causal and quantitative models of inquiry. Indeed, they would argue that the method of participant observation itself is ineffable – beyond formal instruction and elucidation. Sociological knowledge and understanding cannot be acquired through methodological formulae but must be the result of being in the world: knowledge is the result of praxis. Efforts to reduce methodology to a routine technology by defining concepts precisely, rigorously and, if possible, quantitatively, merely serve to distort the social world in fundamental ways. Any hypotheses should be developed out of ethnographic work and not before. Knowledge should be an emergent property of inquiry not predetermined by abstract and socially unengaged intellectualising. Concepts should merely sensitize sociologists, not blind them to the reality in which they are to become involved. Understanding should flow from an 'on-going exploration of society, it cannot be engendered by fixed schemes and carefully manufactured hypotheses'.[63]

Fairly obviously presupposed here is a very different conception of knowledge compared with the variable analysis and the previous methods we have discussed. To put it simply, they presuppose that relatively precise and rigorous general theories could be developed to explain a durable social world. The way to attain this knowledge is by the application of proper methodological principles aimed at providing objective, detached, rigorously formulated facts or data. In an important way, and this constitutes one of the major criticisms made by the interactionists against such methodologies, it is not necessary for the researcher to experience directly in any way the world being investigated. Research is an anonymous enterprise; a matter of method rather than people. For the symbolic interactionist authentic knowledge is furnished by immediate experience, not by the application of a scientific method. Put this way, participant observation affords the symbolic interactionists with the only method of grasping social reality, a method, moreover, which cannot be reduced or communicated by way of a programme or set of formulaic techniques.

At this point we begin to confront some of the theoretical presuppositions of symbolic interactionism which are built into the method of participant observation. The vision of social reality incorporated in the previous methods we have discussed, namely the survey and interviewing, implies that it can be known only through the use of particular rationally developed methodologies which enable the user to 'discover' or 'unearth' facts about the social world in the form of data. Social reality is not obvious to either the lay person or to the social scientists. Indeed, social reality as it appears to the 'unscientific observer' may not furnish unaided knowledge of the real social processes at work. Observation of surface appearances cannot yield scientific knowledge of social reality. Thus, Marxism, structural-functionalism, conflict theory, psychoanalysis, structuralism, and many more, presuppose or postulate underlying, deeper processes at work beneath the phenomenal world of appearances which must be uncovered through rigorous methodological and theoretical work. On the other hand, participant observation and symbolic interactionism attend to the visible social world in which 'interaction is defined as an order which is *sui generis*, not simply as the vehicle for the manifestation by the sovereign and deep structures of society'.[64] Moreover, any attempt to study interaction with so-called 'scientific methods' merely serves to distort this phenomenal social world. The observable is social reality: it lies nowhere else. To quote Rock: 'Interactionism espouses participant observation because it is based on an epistemology that describes immediate experience as an irreducible reality'.[65]

This can be seen in the flavour of participant observation reports which often consist of long quotations from members of the group being studied, are full of intimate and minute details, replete with the language and argot of those under investigation, contain little in the way of abstracted reflection, theory, or statistically based arguments. Instead (in the best of them) the reader is given an overwhelming impression of access to the meaningful life of those studied: an insight into a microcosm organised and shaped by those who live within it. There is a stress on the immediate, the particular, and the unique. Of course, crucial in all of this are the observers themselves, who select, interpret, and present the world they have studied for our perusal. But, if we remind ourselves of the non-routine character of fieldwork, it appears that observers have a great deal to do with the production of the picture of the reality being investigated. It is intimately their picture and no one else's. Knowledge of social life has to be knowledge grounded in direct experience of that life. This is one reason why fieldwork, unlike the other methods we have discussed, cannot be programmed. A full grasp of social reality can arise only from engaging in the social life itself. If this were not the case, sociology could rely on reason and observation alone; participant observation would be unnecessary.

Yet there is a crucial paradox in all this. If direct experience is necessary and, by implication, prestructured research distorts social reality, what status, then, can be accorded the fieldworker's own analysis? If, on the other hand, fieldwork is the only way to grasp social reality, what commonly accepted and grounded principles can we use to evaluate this grasp? It is these and similar questions which make the issue of 'going native' an ironic one for, in an important sense, 'going native' would seem to be the only available public evidence that the fieldworker has successfully completed his or her research. As Vidich remarks:

If the participant observer seeks genuine experiences, unqualifiedly immersing and committing himself in the group he is studying, it may become impossible for him to objectify his own experiences for research purposes. ... Anthropologists who have 'gone native' are cases in point; some of them stop publishing entirely.[66]

And yet, in some formulations of symbolic interactionism, 'going native' would seem to be an achievement, at least in the sense that the observer has become fully socialised and enculturated into the group being studied: the observer has fully grasped the life being investigated by becoming a member, and is no longer a 'stranger' or an 'incompetent'. It is for reasons such as these that a number of sociologists charge participant observation with not only being unscientific but also, worse, being unsociological. It also gives some understanding of the very real ambiguities which are built into the participant observer role. We spoke earlier in this chapter of the stratagems used to reinforce the research side of the role and the anxieties fieldworkers often report about their efforts. Marginality has to be a way of life for the fieldworker. As Hughes observes:

The unending dialectic between the role of members (participant) and stranger (observer and reporter) is essential to the very concept of fieldwork, and this all participant-observers have in common: they must develop a dialectic relationship between being researchers and being participants.[67]

Here we have another paradox: participant observation becomes impossible if there is a full commitment to the participant role or to the observation role. Indeed, it can be argued that a tension between the two is crucial. Without marginality the world being observed would not become strange and interesting; it would cease or fail to be rendered problematic. Yet, this may well isolate the researcher from the sociological domain by inferring connections, themes, and so forth, without adequate warrant – from a sociological point of view.

We have already discussed some of the strategies often employed to cope with this marginality, but one more comment is worth making. In some cases, marginality may be built into the situation being researched. Much of participant observation is used to study various deviant groups of which few, if any, sociological researchers have any prior experience. This may have the effect noted by Rock:

The juxtaposition of familiarity with unfamiliarity may furnish a proper combination of phenomenological distance with interpretability. Deviant worlds are rarely so isolated that there is no common symbolic currency between them and the outside. They provide significant refractions of meaning which are both strange and intelligible. The courting of deviancy by many interactionists may lie in that unusually provocative quality of the rule-breaking episode.[68]

Whatever the truth or merits of these points of view, there is no doubt that participant observation does represent a very different tradition of sociological inquiry and approach to data collection than either the survey or the interview. Its reliance on sociological knowledge interpreted as intimate experience of the social world especially, marks it off from these other methods. Data, if this is quite the correct term, emerge as a result of the fieldworker's engagement with social life. Moreover, such data are not so much the product of an accredited method which can be taught to other practitioners, used again and again, but the result of the interpersonal and face-to-face encounters that researchers have with their subjects. There is little sense, too, of knowledge produced in this way as being cumulative. The social world revealed through participant observation is a world of shifting microcosms, constantly built and reassembled and only occasionally glimpsed through the efforts of fieldworkers. Society can only be shown, and not understood through abstract, reifying and rationally conceived principles.

CONCLUSION

There is little doubt that the theoretical tradition now closely associated with participant observation methods in sociology is very different from that represented by Lazarsfeld's variable analysis. There is no doubt, too, that this can be presented as a major divide within the discipline. On the one hand, there are qualitative methods and, on the other, there are quantitative and never the twain shall meet since both are regarded as fundamentally antithetical to each other. There is, again no doubt, some truth in this. Many of the arguments for participant observation studies are arguments *against* the effort to quantify social phenomena, as are many of the arguments for quantitative studies arguments *against* qualitative research. More than this, however, it is the case that in significant respects there are issues here to do with the nature of sociology itself and how it should proceed with its inquiries. A discussion of some of these will have to wait until the concluding chapter. However, it is also important to stress that ethnographic methods do not necessarily have to be associated with symbolic interactionism. They are also used, and becoming more widely so, in a variety of theoretical perspectives, and largely on instrumental grounds as the appropriate method for the research task in hand.

For now we want to make one or two points of a more general kind about participant observation as a method of data collection. The first has to do with what is often seen as the restrictive scope of such studies in that they are often small-scale, case studies of a group, a type of social role, an organisation, or whatever. The problem with such studies is that it is difficult to generalise from them to other groups, social roles or organisations. This is an important matter and one that needs to be considered very carefully. But, as is not uncommon in methodological dispute in sociology, the issues here are clouded. There is, for example, a confusion between empirical generalisations and theoretical generalisations.[69] Variable analysis sought the latter through the former, but for the reasons we discussed in Chapter 3, this does not look to be a promising route.

More important, however, is the presumption underlying such criticism that the only worthwhile objective of social research is statistical generalisation of the kind sought by variable analysis and surveys. Sometimes researchers want to investigate some group or organisation or process in detail just to see what it is like: just as an anatomist might wish to see how a particular organism works, so a social researcher might wish to see how a group or an organisation works.[70] This was certainly the impulse behind many of the early Chicago studies. Such inquiries can be of immense research benefit: this is particularly true where very little is known about some phenomenon.

This last point has relevance for the kind of criticisms made by such as Blumer against variable analysis and, more recently, developed by Garfinkel, Sacks and other ethnomethodologists.[71] In general, the argument is that the kinds of measurement procedures developed within variable analysis are essentially stipulative in that they make presumptions about the mathematical properties of social phenomena, hence the kind of measurement systems that are appropriate to them, in advance of studies of such phenomena. In other words, most measurement efforts in social research, so the argument goes, are premature since we do not know sufficient about social phenomena to be able to determine what kind of mathematics, what kind of measurement, will reflect their properties. It is important to note that the objection here is not against quantification *per se*, but against inappropriate quantification. That is, it is not an argument about principle, about qualitative research versus quantitative research, but about the status and effectiveness of current measurement systems. This apart, what is argued for is a recognition that social research is as much in need of good descriptive work as it is in need of research which seeks to determine explanatory variables. So, by offering patiently assembled analyses of small, naturally occurring settings, ethnographic research can be seen as seeking to provide knowledge of how the experts in social life, that is ordinary members of society, construct their social lives as recognisable lives for them.

In this respect, observational methods come into their own. One of the common complaints levelled against macro studies is that they present us with a general picture of society and its workings, often itself derived from correlations between grossly defined variables. By their nature, such methods average out the fine variations that can be found. So, from the point of view of developing and refining macro theories ethnographic methods have an important role to play. This is one way of looking at Whyte's study of his street corner gang, as a corrective to the dominant picture of inner city areas as disorganised social wastelands. What Whyte's work showed was that this image was a major oversimplification. As Hammersley and Atkinson point out, ethnographic methods can play an important role in developing and testing macro theories.[72] But, theory development relying upon ethnographic and qualitative studies is not limited to supplementing macro interests. They can result in major redirections of theoretical interests. A classic case of this is the work stemming from Durkheim's original study of suicide. One of the interests his study encouraged was the use of official statistics, and later, survey statistics, for examining the causes of, for example, crime and delinquency. However, what studies of coroners, police officers, lawyers, etc., many of them ethnographic, have shown is that 'rate producing processes' are the result of organisational personnel engaged in official decision-making dealing, day-to-day, with 'crime and criminality'. In doing so they make use of their own common-sense knowledge of social structures and individuals to produce the instances of deviant behaviour. This kind of inquiry goes beyond a criticism of the validity of official statistics and represents a whole new area of sociological interest in how members, using their common-sense knowledge, categorise and organise social activities.[73]

In addition, and cross-cutting the macro–micro distinction, is a more specific theoretical interest involving observational methods, namely that between substantive and formal theories.[74] The macro–micro distinction concerns the variation in the scope of the cases investigated from society down to the more local forms of social organisation. What the formal–substantive distinction points to is altogether different. For example, Whyte was keen to study a street corner gang and paints a life-like portrait of such a gang and what it means to the participants in the gang. Such a substantive interest is to be contrasted with, say, the interest shown in patterns of deference within different kinds of groups. Both theoretical interests can be exploited ethnographically, and both are equally legitimate interests for social research to exploit, though the direction of the actual research is clearly going to be influenced by them. Of course, the formal–substantive distinction is not a hard-and-fast one and many studies do one through the other. Ethnomethodological studies, for example, display a formal interest in social activities using substantive material drawn from naturally occurring settings. Thus, its methodological stance is concerned to describe 'members' methods' for producing the scenes and activities of everyday life as they are ordinarily experienced insisting that the scenes and activities of daily life be understood as the accomplishment of the parties to them.[75]

NOTES

1. See, for example, D. Silverman, *Qualitative Methodology and Sociology*, Aldershot, Gower, 1985.
2. H.S. Becker and B. Geer, 'Participant observation and interviewing: a comparison', in W.J. Filstead (ed.) *Qualitative Methodology*, Chicago, Markham, 1970, p. 133. This volume, though now long in the tooth, contains valuable material on participant observation.
3. T.S. Simey and M.B. Simey, *Charles Booth: Social Scientist*, New York, Oxford University Press, 1960. See also G. Easthope, *A History of Social Research Methods*, London, Longman, 1974, p. 59.

4. As, for example, in the encyclopaedic work of Sir James Frazer whose *Golden Bough*, abridged edn, London, Macmillan, 1957, was first published in 1890 and extended to twelve volumes of collected reportage by 1915.

5. B. Malinowski, *Argonaughts of the Western Pacific*, London, Routledge & Kegan Paul, 1922. Though his posthumously published, *A Diary in the Strict Sense of the Term*, New York, Harcourt, Brace & World, 1967 demolished many of the myths of anthropological fieldwork.

6. See J. Ditton, *Part-time Crime*, London, Macmillan, 1977, an ethnographic study of bread delivery men and bakery workers. There have also been numerous studies of industrial workers using this method.

7. See, for example, A.L. Epstein, *The Craft of Social Anthropology*, London, Tavistock, 1967.

8. See R.E.L. Faris, *Chicago Sociology, 1920–32*, Chicago, University of Chicago Press, 1967, and M. Bulmer, *The Chicago School of Sociology: Institutionalisation, Diversity and the Rise of Sociological Research*, Chicago, University of Chicago Press, 1984.

9. See H.P. Becker and H.E. Barnes, *Social Thought from Lore to Science, Vol. 2*, New York, Dover, 1952; L. Bramson, *The Political Context of Sociology*, Princeton, Princeton University Press, 1961. See also Bulmer, *op.cit.*

10. Sumner's most celebrated work is his *Folkways*, New York, Mentor Books, 1960. For an informative discussion of Spencer's influence on Sumner see H.E. Barnes, 'W.G. Sumner: Spencerianism in American press', in Barnes (ed.) *Introduction to the History of Sociology*, Chicago, University of Chicago Press, 1948.

11. C.W. Mills, 'The professional ideology of the social pathologists', *American Journal of Sociology*, 49, 1943, pp. 165–180.

12. P. Rock, *The Making of Symbolic Interactionism*, London, Macmillan, 1979, p. 92.

13. N. Anderson, *The Hobo*, 2nd edn, Chicago, University of Chicago Press, 1961; F.M. Thrasher, *The Gang*, Chicago, University of Chicago Press, 1963; P.G. Cressey, *The Taxi Dance Hall*, Chicago, University of Chicago Press, 1932; E.C. Lindman, *Social Discovery*, New York, Republic, 1924.

14. E.W. Burgess, 'Research in urban society: a long view', in E.W. Burgess and D.J. Bogue (eds) *Contributions to Urban Sociology*, Chicago, University of Chicago Press, 1964, p. 4. See also Bulmer, *op.cit.*, especially ch. 6.

15. As Bulmer, *op.cit.*, p. 90, points out, there was a lack of self-consciousness about method in sociology at this time. Not only were there few textbooks on methods, but also such statements were not as required as they are today.

16. Park said, 'Sociology deals with just those aspects of social life which ordinarily find their most obvious expression in the news and in historical and human documents generally'. Quoted in Bulmer, *ibid.*, p. 91.
17. W.F. Whyte, *Street Corner Society*, 2nd edn, Chicago, University of Chicago Press, 1955.
18. E.C. Hughes, *Men and their Work*, New York, Free Press, 1958.
19. Of the many seminal works of these scholars that could be mentioned, H.S. Becker, *Outsiders*, New York, Collier-Macmillan, 1963 and E. Goffman, *Asylums*, Harmondsworth, Penguin, 1963, are worth looking at. It should be pointed out that Goffman's work is distinctive in that although borrowing from symbolic interactionism, it owes as much to Durkheim.
20. See H. Blumer, 'What is wrong with social theory?', *American Sociological Review*, 19, 1954, pp. 3–10. and his 'Sociological analysis and the variable', *American Sociological Review*, 21, 1956, pp. 683–90.
21. See, for example, B. Glaser and A. Strauss, *The Discovery of Grounded Theory*, Chicago, Aldine, 1967.
22. For an illuminating discussion of the concept of social structure from an ethnomethodological viewpoint which is also of more general interest, see J. Coulter, 'Remarks on the conceptualisation of social structure', *Philosophy of Social Science*, 12, 1982, pp. 33–46.
23. See M. Hammersley and P. Atkinson, *Ethnography: Principles in Practice*, London, Tavistock, 1983, for a review of many ethnographic studies and some methodological issues.
24. E.W. Burgess, 'Basic social data', in T.V. Smith and L.D. White (eds) *Chicago: An Experiment in Social Science Research*, Chicago, University of Chicago Press, 1929, p. 47. Quoted in Bulmer, *op.cit.*
25. H.M. Trice, 'The "Outsider's" role in field study', in Filstead (ed.) *op.cit.*
26. A. Vidich, 'Participant observation and the collection and interpretation of data', *American Journal of Sociology*, 60, 1955, pp. 354–60. See also A. Schutz, 'The stranger: an essay in social psychology', in his *Collected Papers, Vol. II*, The Hague, Nijhoff, 1964. See also R.B. Klatch, 'The methodological problems of studying a politically resistant community', in R. Burgess (ed.) *Studies in Qualitative Sociology, Vol. 1*, Greenwich, Con., JAI Press, 1988, pp. 73–88.
27. Whyte, *op.cit.*
28. M.A. Sullivan *et al.*, 'Participant observation as employed in the study of a military training programme', in Filstead (ed.) *op.cit.* See also J. Hockey, *Squaddies Portrait of a Subculture*, Exeter, Exeter University Press, 1986.

29. Whyte, *op.cit.*, p. 300.
30. D.A. Karp, 'Observing behaviour in public places: problems and strategies', in W.B. Shaffir, R.A. Stebbing and A. Turowetz, (eds) *Fieldwork Experience: Qualitative Approaches to Social Research*, New York, St Martin's Press, 1980. In other contexts, loitering can be a more than useful approach. See, in same volume, W.G. West, 'Access to adolescent deviants and deviance'.
31. E. Liebow, *Tally's Corner*, London, Routledge & Kegan Paul, 1967.
32. R.L. Gold, 'Roles in sociological field observations', in Filstead (ed.) *op.cit.* Also B. Junker, *Field Work*, Chicago, University of Chicago Press, 1960, and Hammersley and Atkinson, *op.cit.*, p. 93.
33. In some circumstances full participation is impossible. In some work research, for example, a lack of the requisite skill could well inhibit full participation. None the less, valuable results can still be obtained. See, for example, S. Ackroyd and P. Crowdy, 'Can culture be managed? Handling "raw" material', *Personnel Review*, 19, 1990, pp. 3–13.
34. *ibid.*
35. Vidich, *op.cit.* See also S. Holdaway, 'An inside job: a case study of covert research on the police', in M. Bulmer (ed.) *Social Research Ethics: An Examination of the Merits of Covert Participant Observation*, London, Macmillan, 1982.
36. See, for example, L. Festinger, H.W. Riecken and S. Schacter, *When Prophecy Fails*, London, Harper & Row, 1964, in which covert observers joined a religious cult as believers in the prophecy that the world was due to end, but that its members would be rescued on a given date. Presenting themselves as believers actually enhanced the morale of this small group, though it is doubtful if the research would have been allowed if the observers had made their intentions clear.
37. In this connection fieldwork studying the very powerful is extremely rare. Douglas, in his *Investigative Social Research: Individual and Team Research*, Beverly Hills, Sage, 1976, claims that in such cases 'suspicion should be the guiding principle.' See also J. Cassell, 'The relationship of observer to observed when studying up', in R. Burgess (ed.) *op.cit.*, pp. 89–108.
38. And this may well be something surprising. For example, what are often regarded as 'closed' organisations can often be receptive to fieldworkers. See Hockey, *op.cit.*
39. See Hammersley and Atkinson, *op.cit.*, ch. 7, for a full discussion of note-taking and recording data.
40. H.S. Becker, 'Problems of inference and proof in participant observation', *American Sociological Review*, 23, 1958, pp. 682–90.

41. *ibid*. The research examples Becker uses in this article are taken from his study, *Boys in White*, Chicago, University of Chicago Press, 1961.

42. W.F. Whyte, 'Observational field-work methods', in M. Jahoda, M. Deutsch and S.W. Cook, (eds) *Research Methods in Social Relations*, vol. 2, New York, Dryden, 1951, pp. 510–11.

43. See J.A. Hughes, D.Z. Shapiro, W.W. Sharrock and R.J. Anderson, *The Automation of Air Traffic Control*, ESRC/SERC Report, Department of Sociology, Lancaster University.

44. Becker and Geer, *op.cit.*, p. 141.

45. H.S. Becker, 'Interpretative sociology and constructive typology' in G. Gurvitch and W.E. Moore (eds) *Twentieth Century Sociology*, New York, Philosophical Library, 1945.

46. M. Schwarz and C. Schwarz, 'Problems in participant observation', *American Journal of Sociology*, 60, 1955, p. 345.

47. H. Gans, *Urban Villagers*, Glencoe, Free Press, 1962.

48. J. Lofland, *Analysing Social Settings*, Belmont, Calif., Wadsworth, 1971.

49. See Liebow, *op.cit.* P. Atkinson, *The Clinical Experience*, Farnborough, Gower, 1981, reports how a haircut and a suit eased some of the anxieties of an 'influential gatekeeper' about providing access to a medical school.

50. See, for example, H. Roberts (ed.) *Doing Feminist Research*, London, Routledge & Kegan Paul, 1981; L. Lofland, 'The "thereness" of women: a selective review of urban sociology', in M. Millman and R.M. Kanter (eds) *Another Voice: Feminist Perspectives on Social Life and Social Science*, New York, Anchor Books, 1975.

51. U. Hannerz, *Soulside*, New York, Columbia University Press, 1969.

52. See Hammersley and Atkinson, *op.cit.*, for a review.

53. M. Hammersley, 'The researcher exposed: a natural history', in R.G. Burgess (ed.), *The Research Process in Educational Settings*, Lewes, Falmer.

54. Whyte, *Street Corner Society*, *op.cit.*, p. 301.

55. An extreme example is that described by Tobias Schneebaum, a painter, in his book, *Keep the River on Your Right*, New York, Grove Press, 1969. The author claims to have absorbed the 'stone age' culture of a Peruvian jungle tribe almost completely.

56. Whyte, *Street Corner Society, op.cit.*, p. 301.

57. H.S. Becker, 'Field work evidence', in his *Sociological Work: Method and Substance*, Chicago, Aldine, 1970.

58. Gans, *op.cit.*

59. See J. Platt, 'What case studies can do?', in Burgess (ed.), *op.cit.*, pp. 1–23.

60. Becker, 'Problems of inference', *op.cit.*

61. Certainly, social theorists have no difficulty in using fieldwork studies in this fashion. To this end, Glaser and Strauss offer an inductive approach to theory building based on fieldwork studies.

62. Rock, *op.cit.*, p. 182.

63. *ibid.*, p. 183.

64. *ibid.*, p. 186.

65. *ibid.*, p. 187.

66. Vidich, *op.cit.*, p. 357. Also, K. Lang and G. Lang, 'Decisions for Christ: Billy Graham in New York City', in M. Stein *et al.* (eds) *Identity and Anxiety*, Glencoe, Free Press, 1960; Rock, *op.cit.* pp. 200–1.

67. E.C. Hughes, 'Introduction: the place of field work in social science', in B. Turner (ed.) *Fieldwork: An Introduction to the Social Sciences*, Chicago, University of Chicago Press, 1960, p. xi.

68. Rock, *op.cit.*, p. 212. Interestingly, while symbolic interactionism has produced few studies of the 'familiar', to put it this way, ethnomethodology takes as one of its methodological tasks that of rendering the familiar and the ordinary 'strange' in order to made it 'visible' for investigation. See H. Garfinkel, *Studies in Ethnomethodology*, Englewood Cliffs, Prentice-Hall, 1967.

69. See J.A. Hughes, *The Philosophy of Social Research*, 2nd edn, London, Longman, 1990, for a discussion of some of these issues.

70. Incidentally, and relevant to the issue of generalisation, anatomists do not normally sample the specimens they study. Often one or two examples suffice to enable them to say in great detail how the organisms work or are structured, enabling them to generalise to other organisms of the same type.

71. See, for example, Garfinkel, *op.cit.*, and R.J. Anderson and W.W. Sharrock, *The Ethnomethodologists*, London, Tavistock, 1986.

72. Hammersley and Atkinson, *op.cit.*, p. 205.

73. This is a long and detailed debate but see P. Eglin, 'The meaning and use of official statistics in the explanation of deviance', in R.J. Anderson, J.A. Hughes and W.W. Sharrock, (eds) *Classic Disputes in Sociology*, London, Allen & Unwin, 1987, pp. 184–212. Also A.V. Cicourel, *The Social Organisation of Juvenile Justice*, New York, Wiley, 1968; J.M. Atkinson, *Discovering Suicide: Studies in the Social Organisation of Sudden Death*, London, Macmillan, 1978.

74. See Glaser and Strauss, *op.cit.*

75. See, for example, Anderson and Sharrock, *op.cit.*

CHAPTER 7

Recent developments in the context of data collection

If we had concluded the discussion of research methods at the end of Chapter 6, the reader would be quite justified in drawing the conclusion that the main trend in research methods has been the gradual development of survey methods on the one hand and observational techniques on the other. Our presentation has placed considerable stress on the way that the main examples of research methods we have considered have been progressively developed and improved, a thesis advanced as much by implication as by direct advocacy. Thus, the first type of social survey to be produced, which we labelled the factual survey and which had the relatively simple aim of obtaining factual information about the whole population, was followed by social-psychological and the explanatory surveys which have, from the point of view of sociological knowledge, rather more sophisticated objectives in mind. Although we ourselves have made some critical remarks about these newer uses of the survey, there is little doubt that in social research it is the predominant and pre-eminent instrument of data collection.

Much of the material in this book describes the intellectual and practical processes that have been necessary to the development of empirical social science along the particular lines it has taken. The steps we have described in Chapter 3, in which the idea of the social variable was clarified and the production of the first scales exemplifying the idea were devised, were necessary preliminaries to the new uses of survey methods described in Chapter 4. The social-psychological survey would not have been possible until the semantic differentiation scale was invented. Similarly, what we have called the explanatory survey also depended to some extent on scaling techniques but, as important, also on the practical adaptation of the logic of experimental design to the interpretation of survey materials using inductive statistics. As we have argued in Chapter 5, the requirements of scaling also produced significant adaptations within interviewing. One of the points we want to emphasise, is that modern surveys have required a good deal of intellectual and practical work to be brought to their present form.

For much of the recent history of sociology, the development and refinement of particular methods was the main trend in methodology. For long periods of the post-war history of the discipline, social investigation was undertaken without very serious consideration being given to the justification of the methods used. H.W. Smith, in a widely used text on social research, has observed that:

Much research has employed particular methods out of methodological parochialism or ethnocentrism. Methodologists often push pet methods because they are the only ones they are familiar with.[1]

For our part this is perhaps unduly cynical even though it has to be admitted that the question of which method to use is not always considered thoroughly enough. But, in addition, it also has to be recognised that the close association that some methods have with some approaches means that, in these cases, the choice of method is never merely just a choice of technique: such a choice is to buy into a nest of theoretical commitments that, in sociology at least, are regarded as crucial for the fundamental character of the discipline itself. Such reasons may be arguable (as we have shown) but are certainly not without some justification. However, realism does suggest that methodological choices were and are often conventional. Sociologists work within specific traditions of thought and research; these traditions make habitual recourse to particular methods over others. However, because of this kind of inertia, it is appropriate to question the methodological choices that are made.

It is also the case that conventional methodology, and particularly the survey, has come under serious critical scrutiny in recent years, and for this reason we need to examine the basis of choices made about method more scrupulously and carefully. Indeed because there has been a great deal of controversy and argument in methodology in recent years, so disrupting the stable continuities in the development of methodology described in earlier chapters have been disrupted. Researchers have been questioning the validity of orthodox methods on a variety of grounds, and this has been associated with a good deal of willingness to use new methods of research and new research procedures. From a period in which the main trend in methodology has been the steady development of a small number of selected methods, there has been increasing innovation and the proliferation of new methods and new ideas concerning their rationale. Some commentators have gone so far as to suggest that orthodox methods or at least thinking about research in orthodox methodological ways, are more of a hindrance than a help to scientific advance.[2]

While it is difficult to generalise about a subject that is so rich and diverse as sociology and which has such a rapidly growing number of areas of use and application, it does seem clear that only some areas of the subject have been content to continue to employ and develop the old methods. By contrast, in some areas of social science today there has been almost complete disappearance of the notion that research should follow set rules or procedures and the use of survey methods, in particular, has been set aside in favour of other methods of data collection. There has been an interest in seeking new forms of data, generating more data from the same data sets or situations, for combining different kinds of data that relate to the same problem or situation, for re-using existing data generated for other purposes and for accumulating the results of many studies. To the proponents of these changes, these innovations are evidence for a new openness and flexibility in research. It can be argued that there is a need to make sociology applicable to research problems otherwise not studied or not studied very adequately.

In this chapter we have two broad objectives. One is to consider recent criticisms of the orthodox methods we have discussed. Such criticisms have been mainly directed at the survey, but they have extended to affect empirical research more generally. The other is to offer some account of the main innovations in methodology: to consider what the main suggestions about new methods of data collection have been in recent years, the main reasons for their adoption as well as offering some sort of preliminary evaluation of them. It will be argued that the way to interpret criticisms is not to reject orthodox methods out of hand but to see them as one method of data collection that is economical and useful in particular circumstances. The problem with many of the earlier views on method is that there was an inappropriate optimism and over-advertising about the effectiveness of particular conventional modes of data collection. But, as with theory, one of the more important things to find out about a method is its limitations.

THE CRITIQUE OF ORTHODOX SURVEY METHODS

One of the most interesting developments in methodology in the sixties and seventies has been the critique of the dominant orthodoxy in research methods, which is attitude surveying. Cicourel is commonly credited with initiating serious criticism of the dominant orthodoxy in methodology.[3] His criticisms were taken up and combined with a number of other ideas, ideas from philosophy as well as from sociology, to constitute a powerful and general criticism of orthodox sociology.[4] This is a matter of more than passing interest because, as we and a variety of other writers have suggested, post-war sociology was dominated by a particular approach to the subject: a combination (as we discussed in Chapter 4) of functionalistic theory and the widespread use of what we have called the explanatory survey. Rightly or wrongly, sociologists had come to see the construction of data from surveys as uniquely appropriate to the development of knowledge of social organisation. Whatever we may think of this with the benefit of hindsight, the fact remains that, for many sociologists, the use of the survey was highly appropriate for the systematic development of social knowledge.

Criticism of the exclusive use of surveys in methodology was often part of a more general critical attitude toward social science. A common thread in much critical writing was an objection to the treatment of social phenomena by orthodox sociology as if they were like the subject matter of the physical sciences; that is existing independently of the observer as real objects. The explanatory survey was held to be guilty of this because it assumed that the data derived from surveys would yield data which, when handled and deployed appropriately, would demonstrate causal connections between things and events. The use of theory and method in this way – which was widely held to imitate the physical sciences in its insistence on appeals to the facts and emphasis on establishing causal relations – was labelled 'positivism'.[5]

However, these controversies have forced some close attention to the procedures actually involved in data collection using surveys and have drawn attention to the complicated and rather unsociological nature of some of the presumptions of the methods. Once close and critical examination of the way data are constructed by the survey method was undertaken, many of its assumptions were exposed as less than satisfactory. One area that has come in for sustained examination and criticism is the way in which data derived from responses to attitude questionnaires. So many uses of the explanatory survey depend on collecting responses to attitude questions in order to produce descriptions of what social groups and collectivities believe. The problems with such assumptions turn out to be many, and though some are quite subtle, there can be no doubting their importance. It is not simply that respondents might not be willing to tell the truth in answer to questions, though a great number of the recommendations about how the public should be encountered in interviews (some of which we discussed in Chapter 5) are aimed at improving the prospects of obtaining truthful answers, or the removal of obvious reasons for being devious or deceitful.

There are in fact very much more serious objections to the idea that attitudes can be a reliable source of data. One of the most basic arises from the perception that there may not be a true real value of an attitude on many questions, either because it is not a subject that the group concerned has thought much about, or because attitudes are inherently variable in response to external pressures. If this is the case there may not be a precise 'score' for an attitude that can be ascertained for any individual; for that reason there are problems about using a summary of the attitudes of a group as a reliable indication of the attitudes of the group. A whole series of points could be made here.[6]

Let us illustrate some of these points by the following example. A fairly well-known story concerns one respondent's answer to a question along the following lines: 'Do you have a different attitude to homosexuals and heterosexuals?' To which came the answer: 'What do I care, they are all perverts!' This might be regarded as a failure to produce the presumed correct datum, that this respondent does regard homosexuals and heterosexuals differently. If this is inferred then the problem is that the question is insensitively worded; it uses long words when short ones would be better. On the other hand it can be argued that there is a more basic problem here which is that the views of most respondents are actually quite complicated, and so long as we use our own understanding to frame questions, we run the risk of distorting the thinking of others. Unless questioning is part of a dialogue aimed at finding out what the other person has in mind, responses will be distortive. It is likely, for example, that although people do express extreme attitudes to categories like 'homosexual' in some situations, they treat actual homosexuals they know – to whom they may be related or know well – no differently from other friends or acquaintances. If this is the case, the inference that this respondent does regard homosexuals differently may not be the correct datum at all: the answer may be no more than a statement that the respondent knows that there are such things as differences of sexual proclivity and knows that they are commonly thought about as being perverted; that is all. The correct datum may be negative. However, what the respondent actually believes about homosexuals may not be available or fixed. In that case the correct datum is, it all depends! Just conceivably, the answer might be a joke at the expense of the researcher, indicating a refusal to take the interview seriously. Hence, it can be argued convincingly that unless we let clients speak for themselves, and go to considerable lengths when doing so, we will always distort the way they actually think. By the use of questionnaires in particular, we may be foisting on respondents attitudes on subjects about which they have very little concern, or tying their answers to specific alternatives on subjects where their opinions are very subtle indeed.

Attitudes are inherently variable and, in collecting them, all that may be carefully garnered is what the respondent was willing to say to an interviewer at a particular time and place, not something of enduring or general significance. Moreover, once the collective dimension is introduced, in that individual attitudes have to be aggregated so that they represent the views of groups, there are many additional complications. The assumption that one respondent's views should be assumed to count the same as any other seems to be particularly dubious for many purposes; it is, after all, usually true that some individuals will be far more influential than others in determining the collective view. Yet, by adding the views of respondents together, as is invariably done in the presentation of data, this possibility is obscured. What this reveals then is a preference among researchers for regarding the opinions of respondents as equal, with the clear implication that a democracy of one person one contribution to the collective view is appropriate. In fact, however, the relationship of attitudes and actual behaviour is very indistinct, the more so with collectivities than individuals.

All of the points of criticism so far discussed relate to a connection between attitude data and the social world it is purported to describe. What critics have opened up for consideration is the question of how attitude data produced by surveys with structured interviews might relate to the social world respondents actually inhabit. There are many reasons for doubting whether that relationship can reasonably be assumed to be straightforward. Because they had a perception of this, the very first surveyors felt that it simply would not be safe to ask questions which do not have an unambiguously factual answer. However, as we have suggested, this injunction has long since been dropped; the problems arising from doing so have, relatively recently, been more fully exposed. Hence, the question of the status and meaning of reported attitudes is not something we can continue to overlook.

There are two points to be emphasised. First, it is necessary for social researchers to take appropriate precautions as far as is possible to ensure that their data is reliable. Second, since there is not really any way of resolving problems entirely, it is also wise to regard survey data as indicative rather than definitive evidence. Regarding the first point, it is possible to check the responses of respondents by the use of different questions on the same topic, to ask open-ended questions as well as fixed answer questions, in short to probe and test the validity of the answers being given. It is always valuable to pilot a questionnaire and to consider the responses given reflectively. It will also be valuable to look for other sources of knowledge about the aspect of social life under investigation (a point to which we shall return later in this chapter). Suffice it to say there are reasons that derive from the critique of the attitude survey that incline researchers these days to seek to supplement survey data with other kinds of data.

In his helpful discussion of the survey method, Bateson suggests that there are four connected aspects to the process of data construction.[7] These are the social world about which knowledge is sought; the respondents from whom data are actually collected; the researchers themselves and, finally, the clients or audiences to which researchers report. In any research process, researchers seek to construct data from respondents about the social world and to constitute it as information for the consumption of their clients or audiences. The appeal of the survey was originally the way in which it could, very economically, provide some information about large sections of the social world. Sampling was the way in which small-scale studies could obtain representative data. What we have to acknowledge today is that a relatively small shift in the kinds of data sought – from common-sense facts to attitudes – together with a substantial improvement in our capacity to make inferences from data have fundamentally transformed the exercise of surveying. The sophistication of techniques of inference from data have vastly outgrown the qualities and attributes of the data themselves. In many ways, modern statistical analysis is over-engineered in terms of the data it works on. The result has been to make advanced survey methods vulnerable to criticism not least to those who argue that the method obscures the nature of social life itself.

In his own discussion of the survey method, Bateson suggests that the most important aspect of the process of construction of survey data is the relationship between the researcher and the respondent. He puts forward a variety of propositions about how to improve the quality of data elicited from respondents in their encounters with researchers. If the way respondents respond to interviews is better understood, he reasons, so the quality of data will be dramatically improved. Thus, he argues that the interview is an appropriate site for the involvement of applied psychologists who will be able to develop an understanding of the conditions under which more reliable data will be forthcoming from the respondent. He also suggests that the academic community must be actively involved in appraising the quality of survey research, so the adequacy of survey research can be improved by criticism. The idea seems to be that if claims are made about the nature of the social world which are particularly poorly founded in terms of the data used, then the academic community can and should reject the finding. These suggestions are logical, but whether they will be tried and made to work seems quite doubtful. More likely expedients are the suggestions that have been already made about the checking of the repondents' answers and the use of probing and open-ended techniques. For certain research purposes, more use could be made of multiple questions and scaling. Attention could also be validly paid to question weighting and scaling in the aggregation of attitude data. However, such a proposal assumes that the academic community of social research is agreed about what needs to be done. It is far from clear whether this is so.

While many expedients will no doubt be found for attempting to improve the quality of survey data by, for example, close examination of the encounters between the interviewer and the interviewee, the main point to make is that it is now very clear that the problems of survey data cannot be resolved only by attention to improvements of technique. Analyses like Bateson's reveal very clearly how profoundly social the process of survey research – indeed, by extension, any empirical research – actually is. It is this that needs to be understood more fully. In the case of the survey, the question of the relationship between what the respondent is willing to say in an interview and what actually happens in the world has been shown to be something that cannot be assumed. This is perhaps the most important area of problems for the survey method, by the side of which the distortions and biases introduced by the interview encounter and the selections made in reporting research to audiences pale into relative insignificance. However, an appropriate conclusion is that research methods are becoming a lively area of interest for social scientists again as they were in earlier decades of the twentieth century.

SOME LIMITS OF CRITICISM

Although the criticisms of survey methods are serious and have led to far-reaching reappraisal of the technique, it has not been discarded. The survey healthily survives in a great number of specialist applications (some of which we shall describe in this chapter). In the 1990s, however, there is much more awareness of the limitations necessarily involved in making inferences from survey data especially when it is primarily based on attitudes.

However, arguably the survey does have some strengths which make it indispensable in dealing with certain kinds of research problems. It is a method which allows some data to be fairly easily collected from large and diverse populations. It would be very difficult indeed to research some topics if the only option available was direct observation. This approach was tried in some interesting social research, known as Mass Observation, in the 1930s and 1940s before the advent of the computer.[8] The method relied upon data collectors gathering all kinds of information about the lives of the people in their localities. Although by the standards of the 1990s the material was unsystematically gathered, it did produce much interesting and valuable material. The technique, however, used up vast amounts of time and personnel: in the 1990s such large-scale observation studies would be far too costly to contemplate. Where very little is known about a topic, yet it is something that is familiar to the target population, then a well-designed survey can be very helpful in getting some sort of view about the beliefs, attitudes and values of people on that subject. It is extremely economical of effort if intelligent use is made of stratification and sampling. (We have seen something of the potential scale of economies when quota sampling was discussed in Chapter 4.)

Another of the valuable things that a survey can do is to produce findings that challenge common-sense assumptions about what is the case. In this respect modern surveys can still play a similar role as the early poverty surveys. We know that there are problems with the findings of surveys, but there are also problems with common-sense assumptions about what is the case. Just as there were prevailing beliefs about poverty at the turn of the twentieth century when serious social surveying was first undertaken, so there will be prevailing views about most subjects that can be researched including (we might add) current levels of poverty. These views may be taken as being true, but the factual underpinning for the belief is not very secure. Thus, a marketing manager may have no doubt which products will sell, or a politician may think the mood of the voters is clear, but it is very common for marketing managers and politicians to look at the available research data just the same. They know they could be disastrously wrong. In a similar way social research often throws up surprises, and while the results may not cause people to change their minds dramatically, it can challenge assumptions, initiate debate, stimulate new research efforts and so on.[9]

Although there may be problems with the construction of survey data as offering significant information about society, they might still be regarded as better founded and more accurate and reliable than existing knowledge. Indeed, on some topics very little may be known. Alternatively, and perhaps more commonly, people may assume they know what is the case when they do not. Indeed, it is obviously a possibility that received wisdom on many topics may well be not very well-founded at all. The point being made here is that all knowledge, even the common-sense kind, has to be put together in some way. Everyday understanding may also be regarded as being constructed and will, in some ways, feature supporting evidence. With common-sense or everyday knowledge there may be only very inadequate empirical support for what is firmly believed and staunchly advocated. Looked at in this way, social survey data do not have to be without problems to be useful. We just have to have as much respect for propositions based on them as we do for common-sense assumptions and everyday beliefs. If survey data lead us to question our beliefs and to question why we think as we do, they will be playing a useful role. And, again by way of a reminder, no research is ever definitive but ought to provoke further questioning and research.

Of course, if we are going to study things we will have to make methodological choices. Basically there will have to be a selection from the universe of potential observations and choices will also have to be made about how to handle and use what has been selected. Because they involve selections and choices, methods will leave things out and emphasise certain advantages at the expense of others. For the early factual survey, for example, selections were made on the basis of representativeness and the achievement of this was not without its costs. There is also the problem of the validity of the data. By way of contrast, direct observational methods solve the problem of validity in a very different way. We have much more confidence that an observational study of a group is securely based, other things being equal, than a survey, no matter how detailed the questionnaire. But this security is also not without its costs, one of the more important being lack of confidence in the typicality of what happens in the group. This contrast is sometimes expressed by saying that there is a fundamental methodological dilemma: either you are sure that your data are true, but you are not sure how general they are (observation); or you are sure that your data are general, but you are not sure how true they are (surveys).

Finally, if it is true that there are no perfect methods, that all methods involve some compromises, it might be argued that it is an advantage to have some clear perception of what the limitations of a particular method actually are. With this carefully noted, we have the possibility of making a decision whether the disadvantages of a particular method outweigh the costs, of attempting to reduce or correct the known problems or in some way compensating for perceived limitations. Methods never dictate the terms of their employment. Choices about method ultimately have to rest on general beliefs about what the purpose of research is. To some extent therefore, there is a choice whether we use particular strategies of data collection or not.

THE EMERGENCE OF MULTI-METHOD RESEARCH STRATEGY

There were a few sociologists who recognised from an early date that excessive specialisation in methodology would have costs as well as benefits, and costs which are likely to outweigh the benefits. As early as the 1950s some writers suggested that the tendency to develop specialised methods of data collection would result in narrowness of vision and perhaps also limited understanding.[10] However, very few were to foresee the extent of the danger: that the development of specialised methods might set in motion a social process with results very much to the detriment of the discipline. Thus, it can be argued that the adoption of the explanatory survey produced a cadre of statistically trained experts in methodology: a group which virtually monopolised methodological expertise, encouraged the use of advanced methods by ordinary practitioners without proper understanding, and restricted innovation and even debate over methodological issues. The end result was an alienation of social scientists from their subject matter.[11]

In a celebrated book published as long ago as 1959, C. Wright Mills criticised this tendency towards over-specialisation in sociology. He saw this as part of a more general process of professionalisation in social science in which the discipline was losing all critical purchase on the major events of the day. He was particularly scathing about those sociologists who focused their attention on the detailed statistical analysis of data collected by surveys. This he labelled 'abstracted empiricism', not meaning to criticise the use of quantitative data, but that their refined methods had caused researchers to lose track of what the data might mean.[12] As we have argued throughout this book, observed events are without intrinsic meaning; it is the ideas and interpretations that we bring to them that give them significance as useful or important information. Wright Mills was making, in a very general way, the point that too much concentration on technique without appropriate ideas and theories will lead to a deficient understanding.

As a remedy, Mills proposed the use of different methods to study the same subject. He argued that complicated social processes – and especially those that are significant enough to affect large sections of society – will require the examination of all available data. Without this inclusive approach to data, Mills argues, significant changes in the world will simply be missed or not be adequately understood. Indeed, in his own work, Mills collected a variety of data about his chosen topics.[13] Social scientists who write about methods are not usually so forthright as Mills, but many of them have, subsequently, recognised the problems of over-specialisation. Some have argued along similar lines and have attempted to defend what they have taken to be his central idea; that is, that different approaches to the same subject can add to understanding. More data can lead to a fuller appreciation of complex topics. A favoured procedure along these lines is called 'triangulation'.[14]

The notion of triangulation is a metaphor drawn from surveying or navigation. If you want to fix the position of a point on a building site or the position of a ship at sea precisely, it is necessary to locate it in relation to two other points of known position. Thus, the compass bearing of a location beacon from a ship gives some idea of its location, but the bearing of a ship to two beacons fixes the position of the ship precisely. If the bearings of the beacons are drawn on a navigation chart, the ship is located at the point of intersection between the bearings. The principle involved is that the location of a third unknown point can be uniquely fixed in relation to two known points – hence triangulation. The general idea being promoted with the triangulation metaphor is that the best way to develop knowledge of a subject is to study it from a number of points of view. As Denzin expresses it,

no single method is free from flaws – no single method will adequately handle all the problems of causal analysis – and that no single method will yield all the data necessary for a theory's test. Consequently, the researcher must combine his methods in a process termed triangulation; that is, empirical events must be examined from the vantage provided by as many methods as possible.[15]

The advantages claimed for triangulation are that it encourages a more systematic continuity of both theory and research. By combining multiple observers, data sources, theories and methods, social researchers can overcome the bias that is regarded as inevitable in single-method, single-observer, single-theory studies. However, despite the fact that triangulation is widely recommended as a sensible research strategy, it has to be said that much of this is lip-service rather than effective practice if only for the simple reason that such a method is likely to prove expensive. Another reason, not always given sufficient weight, has to do with the close affinity methods often have to particular sociological approaches and their conception of the social world. It is not simply that the survey and participant observation, say, collect different kinds of data, but what these data signify, what they mean and what phenomena they portray, have a great deal to do with their respective theoretical contexts; contexts which are incompatible and even incommensurate. The metaphor of triangulation is a beguiling one, but cannot be pushed too far. Locating position using multiple bearings from known points is clearly a powerful and immensely useful technique in surveying and navigation for fixing the true position of some point. But this is possible only by reference to a known grid system: the task of triangulation is to determine a point *within* a system of conventional grid lines described in terms of a mathematical notation which provides the measurement. However, in social research we do not have either the equivalent of the grid lines or an appropriate metric to describe the location of any findings; we do not have the equivalent of a known grid system on which to map our position.

There are at least two ways in which the idea of triangulation can be understood. One is to see it as a strategy which is intended to reveal the one true picture of whatever it is the research is about. This interpretation would be to take the metaphor very seriously indeed. It would also need to assume that the qualities of methods are relatively fixed and stable, whereas as we have tried to demonstrate, this is far from the case. Certainly, to the extent to which the triangulation model of research assumes a causalist and empiricist view of the point of social research, namely that such research is concerned to discover relationships between variables in order to test theories, then it would also need to assume that the 'flaws' and the 'strengths' of methods do balance out. This is the rationale behind the call for more data, more situations and different methods, in order better to uncover what the 'true' picture is. However, it is not clear that the so-called 'flaws' and 'strengths' of methods are always to be understood in this way. For one example, though it is claimed that the survey is best suited for studying relatively stable patterns of interaction over a large scale and ethnographic methods more appropriate for revealing the dynamics of small-scale interaction, it is not clear that the theories in which the two methods are often embedded imply quite the same conception of social structure.[16] While the survey is predicated on the idea of stable patterns of interaction, ethnographic methods, or at least some of their theoretical justifications, make no such presumption. The general point is that in social research we do not have any stable grid system within which we can locate the bearings of triangulated studies. Triangulation, however, assumes there are criteria upon which all agree and which can be used to decide between alternative theories, methods and inconsistent findings. If a survey should provide one set of results, participant observation another and experiments still another, how are we to decide which result to accept?[17] Resolution to this kind of problem can be achieved only if parties to the disagreement agree on the same domain assumptions and beliefs regarding the nature of the problem and its place within the discipline's theoretical alternatives. Ultimately, it is likely that disagreement must prevail. Indeed, it is in regard to such a problem that Cicourel uses the term 'indefinite triangulation' on the grounds that in social research there is no final grid and no final set of answers.[18]

Nevertheless, in the 1980s there has been a generally increased scepticism about the idea that certain sorts of data can give privileged access to social reality. Indeed in some areas of social science there has been almost complete rejection of conventional methods and even of the idea that research should use any set procedures. The emphasis today is on flexibility and inventiveness, and it is common to emphasise the need to build up a picture from diverse sources.[19] There has been the tendency for more sources of data to be sought, to look for new and innovative ways of generating data from everyday situations and to combine the use of different sources of data. Social scientists have recommended the use of other people's data – with suitable precautions,[20] the use of historical and archive material,[21] the development of indirect and unobtrusive measures of behaviour,[22] as well as persisting with the production and use of conventional sociological modes of data construction and use. Methods formerly treated as discrete are now thought suitable to be used in conjunction. All this has been, in part, motivated by recognition of the limitations of conventional methods.

Few of these writers on methodology suggest that the collection of diverse forms of data is all that one needs to do to produce good research. The basic problem is that data do not simply exist, but have to be constructed. For this reason the use of multiple forms of data is not straightforward; discrepant and contradictory findings are more than possible. The reasons for this are very often complex and intimately related to the whole business of research itself. Thus, contradictory findings may be due to the use of different methods, different theories, different samples, and so on, as to the fact that the world is different, to put it this way. The prescription that we should amass as much data as possible from as many points of view as possible is not so simple to put into practice yet is, it can be argued, precisely what should be done in order to test and examine our theories, our methods and our knowledge as effectively as we can. Far from triangulation being a 'new' approach to research, it is the very stuff of the arguments within disciplines.

THE PROLIFERATION OF DATA AND OPPORTUNITIES FOR STUDY

So far we have considered developments in data collection in the context of social science itself. We have considered the development of broader research strategies and a more catholic approach to data almost exclusively in terms of the needs and requirements of social science itself without much reference to factors external to it. While the move away from reliance on specialised methods and the development of mixed methods of data collection are related to the way sociology has itself changed, the discipline cannot be isolated from the wider social context. Changes in society have also had an impact on data collection practices. What we have observed in the move away from exclusive reliance on specialised methods in the social sciences has been greatly facilitated by changes in the world at large.

One of the most obvious developments in the post-war period – which has had a substantial impact – is the proliferation of data and of sources of data. From being one of the only sources of social data, the social sciences have become only one among many. From being a relatively scarce resource in the recent past, data about people and data that have some sort of relevance to the understanding of social life, have become very much more prevalent. Both these changes can be seen to be related to the introduction and subsequent mass availability of computer technology. There are many instances we should perhaps cite. Organisations, for example, now have the capacity for the collection, storage and manipulation of large amounts of data. This has allowed an interest in social data to be tacked on to systems originally designed for other things. Management information systems now quite often include such data. For example, the personnel records of firms are likely to include the results of personality and aptitude tests, the records of counselling programmes and staff development exercises, as well as the more usual records of overtime, absenteeism and so on. There are many examples these days of firms and public sector organisations – particularly very large ones – using social survey techniques to find out the knowledge and interest of employees in particular topics, of monitoring their knowledge of particular new policies, or of simply measuring their morale. In short, many of the techniques, and, sometimes, the objectives of social science have been taken over and institutionalised by other organisations and the capacity to do this has been made possible by the development of social science knowledge and new information technology.

Perhaps the most important example to discuss here is the vastly expanded capacity of the state to collect and handle social data, and the increased involvement of the state in its various branches with social science. We have alluded to such developments in earlier chapters. In Chapter 4, for example, we discussed the way in which social surveys, aimed at finding out facts about the population, were pioneered outside the state but gradually incorporated by it. Thus the state has simply taken over what have been historically the most significant forms of social research, and made them part of the vast range of social and other data about the population which it routinely collects. For much of the twentieth century the ministries of state have been among the main producers of social data. Government departments routinely produce facts and figures on such things as income levels, patterns of consumption by households, employment and production figures and so on. No private foundation and certainly no university can compete with the government in these areas. In a way this should not be a surprise because the origin of our science of inductive numbers – statistics – lies in the propensity of the state to collect facts and figures about its populations. So far as the origin of the word was concerned, statistics in the beginning meant state-istics.[23]

It is sometimes argued that, in the process of incorporation by the state and other organisations, quantitative social research has lost a good deal of its critical edge. Survey research could no longer have such an impact on government thinking by revealing new facts, because the facts are known, and in considerable detail. If the agenda for social research was to get something done about poverty by revealing the extent of low incomes, then new research strategies would have to be devised. The need to pioneer new definitions of poverty and new lines of research into inequality has preoccupied large numbers of social scientists since the Second World War. The strategy has shifted from revealing facts and expecting them to speak for themselves to arguing about the data that ought to be collected and arguing about the interpretation of the data that are available. Hence the incorporation of one form of social research by the state has simply changed the kinds of research that are commonly regarded as critical, rather than taken away the critical role from policy-related research. Universities and, typically, specialist research institutes within them, now undertake a great deal of policy evaluation research, in which they undertake to assess critically the effects of policies or specific innovations in order to help the political processes of policy-making and the administrative process of planning. Although it can be argued that much of this research is evaluative, it is evaluative only within certain obvious limits and assumptions. Let us briefly consider some examples.

One example worth considering is some extended research looking at the educational effects of different kinds of schooling undertaken by social scientists at Lancaster University in the 1970s.[24] The design of this research was complicated, but, roughly speaking, a large number of schools were rated according to their internal organisation and styles of teaching. Then, information about examination results and other measures of performance by the schools were also collected. The statistical associations between kinds of internal organisation and educational success were then used to see whether particular kinds of organisation delivered examination success more consistently. Although not dependent on attitude data the research did depend for its conclusions on the use of sampling and the inferential use of statistics. The way the study was set up was to produce findings that were both politically relevant and policy related. Different political parties have views about appropriate forms of schooling; the state (either at local or central level) did not have sufficient data or the expertise to decide for itself. The research provoked considerable debate, but had no very enduring effect on educational policy.

Another example is research sponsored by the Department of Health and conducted by a team from the University of Newcastle upon Tyne.[25] In this research the effectiveness of different kinds of residential care for elderly patients was assessed. In this study it proved possible, because of the co-operation of the consultants involved and the availability of significant resources, to allocate patients to different kinds of residential establishment on a random basis. Hence a very much closer approximation to experimental design was possible. In fact, allocation of patients to different kinds of institutions was 'double blind', meaning that not only were the patients themselves allocated to different kinds of institutions on a random basis, the personnel looking after the patients and assessing their progress had no connection with the allocation process or access to data until the research was complete. This sort of design, which excludes participants from involvement in the design and conduct of the research, is used to rule out as far as possible extremely subtle effects on the research results known as 'experimenter' effects. Experimenter effects arise where experimental subjects respond to the fact that they are being subjected to special attention by being studied, rather than the curative effect of the treatment itself.

These are two examples of very conventional research designs being used to evaluate policy. There are, however, also examples of much more radical departures from orthodoxy in use. An increasing number of organisations – in both the public and private sectors – have been using a very unconventional new kind of research design called action research.[26] Action research does not involve standing outside the situation under study and carefully collecting data about it, and hoping not to affect it too much. On the contrary, action research starts from the assumption that the goal of the work is to change the organisation in which it takes place. Action research teams aim to obtain the active co-operation of the participants in an organisation in a programme of change, and thus aim actively to persuade people to diagnose their situation, to plan a sequence of necessary changes and to carry them through. In this case the researchers see themselves as facilitating the process of social change in an organisation, and the point of the research is to see how far effective change in the organisation of work-groups can be induced. Data collection does feature in such research, because change in behaviour is monitored and assessed by reference to key indicators.

These examples suggest that the proliferation of opportunities for research, and the widespread availability of data, have not in themselves been enough to disrupt the pattern of specialisation in the development of research methods described in this book and criticised by C. Wright Mills. The deep involvement of social science research with the state is perhaps the single most important aspect of the complicated division of labour that has grown up between social science and other institutions. What the above examples may be taken to illustrate is a process in which the state and other institutions take over some of the data collection practices originated by the univerities, leaving them to develop new research techniques and to colonise new areas of work. What is interesting is the way they do this.

Whole areas of social research originally pioneered in the universities – marketing and political research are interesting examples – have been taken over by commercial agencies and developed on a commercial basis. But this does not mean that these areas of study have been lost by the universities. Studies of voting behaviour (technically known as psephology) are an interesting case in point. We have already alluded to the way in which early commercial attempts to predict the outcome of American presidential elections by surveys failed and suggested that this led to innovations in economical techniques for collecting data about voting intentions as a basis for predicting the outcome of elections. American universities, in fact, played an important role in the production of more adequate methods of attitude measurement and of sampling in the 1930s and 1940s. The development of viable quota sampling – the basis of almost all commercial voting studies – was also dependent on the activity of the state in collecting the information necessary for the accurate estimation of population characteristics.

The incorporation of social science by the state and commerce, then, has had a number of important effects. The first point to make is that there is no evidence of a decline in the scale of operations of sociology and applied social science. However, what we do see is the displacement of academic social science from some fields of activity as these activities are incorporated by the state and other institutions. At the same time, however, social science actually adopts other roles which are, quite often, more closely related to the work and needs of institutions. The emergence of clientelistic relations with the state and commerce is very common. In the examples of research cited above, it is clear that, whatever the different details of the design of research, all the examples are of work that is highly adapted to the needs of the organisations studied or those of their political controllers. Thus there is a good deal of evidence of a growing relationship of mutual dependence between social science and other institutions. On this view, far from being broadly based, critical and independent as Wright Mills suggested it should be, much social science is narrow, specialised and highly receptive to the clienteles it habitually serves.

CONCLUSION

There are, of course, various interpretations of what is happening. One reading of recent developments is that the main drift of social research is to perpetuate tendencies towards specialisation in methodology. On such an account one of the main functions of social research is to serve the needs of particular institutions, especially those of the various arms of the state. Despite the conviction of some writers on methodology about the need for broader based studies which might retain some significant critical stance, research has become more narrowly defined and accepting of the perspectives and priorities of the institutions it now serves. The emergence of a number of social science specialisms, in such areas as education, health, management, various branches of policy and organisation studies, is evidence of this.

An alternative view is to suggest that the above account is far too simple a conception of the way in which sociology and social research are produced and consumed. Indeed, it can be argued that social science can never be subservient to the interests of client groups for a variety of reasons. One is that although such groups may sponsor research, they cannot control findings or the uses subsequently made of them. The best they can do is ignore findings they do not like. While critics such as Wright Mills would argue that specialised methods will always lead to a narrow focus which is always controllable, against this is the argument that focused research often leads to a sharpened perception of the limitations of knowledge and, as a result, a search for broader and wider ranging inquiries. The process of assessing research does not stop with the publication of the results. Publication makes it available to academics and practitioners, among others, to scrutinise and to use, argue over, debate with, criticise, build upon, and so on. The conclusions of one study are often put together with those of another; interpretations from one area of work are connected with the findings of another. Periodically, textbooks are written in which the results of accumulated knowledge are assessed and made available to new scholars and new researchers. As Popper emphasised, no one can predict the growth of knowledge or control its use once it is made public.[27] Furthermore, and a point not sufficiently realised within a culture which emphasises the expert, the specialist and scientific knowledge, *at best* knowledge can only be the best we know at the time. Although physicists may feel that they are near to unlocking the ultimate secrets of the universe – if only they had another multi-billion dollar machine – some scepticism should be attached to such claims. However, while such claims may have a ring of plausibility in respect of contemporary physics, they can have no such plausibility in respect of social science. Despite two centuries of economic science we still have inflation, recessions, over-production, and more; despite centuries of politics and, latterly, political science, we still have intense conflicts; despite many years of social welfare we still have poverty, child abuse, hunger and deprivation, and more. Thus, our social scientific knowledge from this perspective leaves much to be desired.[28] However, this is not an argument against social science but a reminder about how much we need yet to know.

Our main point is that other social researchers will use, debate with and argue over the results of research in addition to those who commissioned it. It is important to recognise that the exchange of knowledge works the other way round as well. Although researchers often develop specialised expertise in particular areas of institutional life, this does not mean that they have no interest in other domains. Just because there is a division of labour between theorists and researchers, this does not mean that they do not share ideas.[29] Indeed, it is a particularly myopic view of a discipline which sees it as overly compartmentalised such that there is no interchange between specialist researchers, theorists and methodologists. Such interchanges can be a matter of degree and vary over time, but they are rarely totally insulated one from the other.

Finally, in recent years there has been a greater appreciation of the interest and importance of method as something that can contribute to the growth of knowledge and so realign methodology with the mainstream of the subject. Since the early 1980s there has also been a notable improvement in the understanding of the social role of research. From being widely disregarded as a field of peripheral concern, there are strong intimations of the beginnings of a sociology of methodology which, potentially, could serve to transform the sociological enterprise from the inside out.

NOTES

1. H.W. Smith, *Strategies of Social Research*, London, Prentice-Hall, 1975, p. 272.
2. See, for example, P. Feyerabend, *Against Method: Outline of an Anarchist Theory of Knowledge*, London, Verso, 1975; G. Morgan (ed.) *Beyond Method: Strategies for Social Research*, London, Sage, 1983.
3. A.V. Cicourel, *Method and Measurement in Sociology*, New York, Free Press, 1964.
4. See, for example, D.L. Phillips, *Abandoning Method*, San Francisco, Jossey-Bass, 1973. Earlier Winch, in a philosophical critique, presented a very different conception of social science. See his *Idea of a Social Science and its Relation to Philosophy*, London, Routledge & Kegan Paul, 1958.
5. This is not the place to deal in detail with the question of how far quantitative methods are indicative of positivism in social science. The issues are handled in a number of books. See, for example, M. Shipman, *The Limitations of Social Research*, 2nd edn, London, Longman, 1981; C. Marsh, *Survey Method*, London, Allen & Unwin, 1982. A more philosophical treatment of the topic is to be found in J.A. Hughes, *The Philosophy of Social Research*, 2nd edn, London, Longman, 1990.
6. See D. Silverman, *Qualitative Methodology and Sociology*, Aldershot, Gower, 1985.
7. N. Bateson, *Data Construction in Social Surveys*, London, Allen & Unwin, 1984; p. 15.
8. For an account of Mass Observation see J. Madge, *The Tools of Social Science*, London, Longman, 1953.
9. Some commentators on social science think that the main role social science should play is to challenge received opinion and provoke more informed debate.
10. See, for example; E.G. Boring, 'The role of theory in experimental psychology', *American Journal of Psychology*, 66, 1953, pp. 169–84; D.T. Campbell and D. Fiske, 'Convergent and discriminant validation by the multi-trait, multi-method matrix', *Psychological Bulletin*, 56, 1959, pp. 81–105. Similar warnings are also sounded today, see J. Martin, 'Breaking up the mono-method monopolies', in J. Hassard and D. Pym (eds) *Theory and Philosophy of Organisations*, London, Routledge, 1990.
11. E. Gellner, 'Alchemists and sociology', *Inquiry*, 2, 1959, pp. 126–35.
12. Mills was a colleague of P.F. Lazarfeld's at Columbia and many felt that his attack was a thinly disguised and unjustified onslaught on Lazarsfeld. See I.L. Horowitz, *C. Wright Mills: An American Utopian*, New York, Free Press, 1983.

13. See, for example, C.W. Mills, *White Collar: The American Middle Classes*, New York, Oxford University Press, 1951; *The Power Elite*, New York, Oxford University Press, 1956.

14. See N. Denzin, *The Research Act*, Chicago, Aldine, 1970; Smith, *op.cit.*

15. N. Denzin (ed.) *Sociological Methods: A Sourcebook*, London, Butterworth, 1970, p. 3.

16. See J. Coulter, 'Remarks on the conceptualization of social structure', *Philosophy of Social Science*, 12, 1982, pp. 33–46.

17. D.L. Phillips, *Abandoning Method*, San Francisco, Jossey-Bass, 1973, p. 91.

18. A.V. Cicourel, *Method and Measurement in Sociology*, New York, Free Press, 1964.

19. M. Bulmer (ed.) *Sociological Research Methods*, London, Macmillan, 1977; R. Burgess, *Field Research and Field Manual*, London, Allen & Unwin, 1982, and *In the Field: An Introduction to Field Research*, London, Allen & Unwin, 1984; A. Bryman, *Quality and Quantity in Social Research*, London, Unwin Hyman, 1988; J. Scott, *A Matter of Record: Documentary Sources in Social Research*, Cambridge, Polity, 1990.

20. B. Hindess, *The Use of Official Statistics in Sociology*, London, Macmillan, 1973, and his *Philosophy and Methodology in the Social Sciences, Brighton*, Harvester, 1977; M. Bulmer, 'Why don't sociologists make more use of official statistics?', *Sociology*, 14, 1980, pp. 511–13.

21. D. Dunkerley, 'Historical methods and organisational analysis', in A. Bryman (ed.) *Doing Research in Organisations*, London, Routledge, 1988; Scott, *op.cit.,* 1990.

22. E.J. Webb, D.T. Campbell, R.D. Schwartz and L. Sechrest, *Unobtrusive Measures,* Chicago, Rand McNally, 1966.

23. See J. Irvine, I. Miles and J. Evans, *Demystifying Social Statistics*, London, Pluto Press, 1979.

24. N. Bennett, *Teaching Styles and Pupil Progress*, London, Open Books, 1976.

25. J. Bond, D.A. Atkinson, B.A. Gregson and D.I. Newell, 'Pragmatic and experimental trials in the evaluation of experimental National Health nursing homes', *Age and Ageing*, 18, 1989, pp. 85–93; J. Bond, 'Evaluation for innovation in continuing care of very frail elderly people', *Ageing and Society*, 9, 1989, pp. 347–81.

26. See, for example, W. Pasmore and F. Friedlander, 'An action-research programme for increasing employee involvement in problem solving', *Administrative Science Quarterly*, 27, 1982, pp. 343–62; C. Argyeris, *Action Science: Concepts, Methods. Skills*, New York, Jossey-Bass, 1986; W.F. Whyte, *Action Research: Learning from the Field*, London, Sage, 1988.

27. See K. Popper, *Objective Knowledge: An Evolutionary Approach*, London, Oxford University Press, 1972; and Hughes, *op.cit.,* for a review of Popper's ideas.
28. See C. Lindblom, *Inquiry and Change*, New York, Yale University Press, 1990.
29. For example, M. Mann, *The Sources of Social Power*, Cambridge, Cambridge University Press, 1986, primarily a theoretical contribution to historical sociology, notes 'we select our data, see whether they confirm or reject our theoretical hunches, refine the latter, collect more data, and continue zigzagging across between theory and data until we have established a plausible account of how this society in this time and place "works"', p. 7.

CHAPTER 8

Concluding remarks

In this book we have reviewed some of the major methods of data collection currently used in social research. There are others which we have not dealt with, perhaps the most serious omission being those dealing with historical materials, but hopefully we have conveyed a sense of the importance of method, even if the nature of this importance is highly debatable. Throughout what we have tried to stress is the theoretical importance of method, for a number of reasons. First, data are collected in order to bear upon theoretical questions: this is perhaps the most widespread view. Second, methods of data collection instantiate theories of their own which serve both as legitimators of the method and as justifications for the method doing the job it is intended for: these we referred to as instrumental theories. Third, attention to these instrumental theories is crucial since they make presumptions and stipulations about the nature of social life itself; that is, as befits instruments of social research, they have themselves to rely upon a conception of the social. In this respect, of course, methods of social research are no different from those of natural science which similarly must incorporate conceptions of the natural world in order that it can be appropriately investigated.

One consequence of tying methods of social research closely to theory in this way means that methods cannot be cavalierly treated as atheoretical tools which serve their purposes as and when required. Methods, their significance, their effectiveness, and more, are responsive to theoretical shifts and changes and, in some cases, as their theories are proved wrong, displaced altogether. This latter fate is, of course, rare. This is one reason why it is difficult to present a collection of definitive conclusions about methods of data collection. Another is that we seem to be entering a phase whereby the relatively secure and well-trodden divisions and themes are beginning to erode. If this is correct, then it is a neat paradox. As recent studies in the history of social research and of some of the institutions which pioneered it, such as the Chicago School, are showing, the evolution of social research method is much less coherent a progression than was commonly thought.[1] Indeed, the rise and then entrenchment of what we referred to as the 'tool box' view of method had much to do with the professionally inspired efforts to portray and present sociology and social research as a respectable scientific discipline that could take its share of public acclaim and funds. This movement began immediately prior to the Second World War in the United States and spread to other countries, particularly Britain, soon after. Despite some reluctance on the part of recent governments in the United Kingdom to accord sociology the status given to economics or to psychology, the techniques of social research whose development and legitimation, if not always their birth, owed much to sociology are firmly in place if awaiting their fuller incorporation into a professionalised discipline.

In most industrialised and industrialising countries the demands for social research of all kinds from organisations of all kinds has proceeded apace. The image of the social scientist has changed, too. Comte described the sociologist – far too extravagantly – as philosopher-kings or secular priests exercising their quasi-religious authority over the newly emergent industrial order. With Durkheim, however, the motif changes from the sacerdotal authority of the social scientist to that of the professional, the independent expert having specialised knowledge.[2]

The idea of the independent professional, though it would be wrong to hold Durkheim responsible, has become an important one in the development of the social sciences.[3] We have noted that in Britain the substantial incorporation of social research, if not social science, into the bureaucratic structures of the state was achieved relatively early, and only subsequently have social scientists emphasised the independence required by professional status. In the United States, the process was the reverse of this, with the emphasis on professionalism preceding the full incorporation of social science into the political and bureaucratic order. But whatever the precise details of the process, it is the claim to specialised, esoteric knowledge which is the hallmark of professionalisation, and social research expertise is part of this. So much so that training and experience in social research methods are becoming increasingly mandatory elements in a social science education, particularly in sociology.

Another important theme in the development of social research, and one which is often forgotten these days, is the impulse for social change and reform. This was apparent in the work of Comte and remained a major concern of sociology for long after. The origins of a number of research methods, particularly but not only the survey, grew out of nineteenth-century reformist movements both in the United States and in Britain. Durkheim and Weber shared, in different ways, this desire to understand the forces which shaped human social fate so that they could be better controlled and used for a greater benefit. Marx, of course, though revolutionary rather than reformist, sought to develop a scientific method to explain and change the self-destructive capacity of capitalism. Many of the early American sociologists were unashamedly reformist in orientation. However, it was with the professionalisation and institutionalisation of social science, that far greater emphasis was placed on the science aspect than on the practical or the applied. Even Weber, who was involved in live political issues in Germany, stressed the importance of value neutrality on the part of the social scientist *qua* scientist rather than the direct engagement of reformist zeal.

So, we begin to see the slow, gradual and often unclear distinction emerging between social *science* and practical, directed change. In all of this it was the development of methods of social research which played a key role in buttressing the professional claims of social science. But not these alone. The idea of a social *science* not only required properly scientific methods, but also required theory to give the methods a scientific point. Thus, whereas Booth and Rowntree, for example, were motivated by deeply felt concerns about the appalling living conditions of a large proportion of their fellow citizens, their aims were relatively modest: to gather the facts about a social problem so that others might be persuaded to do something about it. They were little interested in theory as we know it, and did not provide much of a model for the professional social scientist who is master of an esoteric body of knowledge. In this particular respect it was the sociologists at Chicago just after the First World War who might have provided an appropriate role model. They were learned in philosophy as well as in the social science of their time, had a definite point of view, committed to change and reform, and access to research funding. Following in this particular tradition of social research was, however, a long and arduous apprenticeship; it did not result in the kind of codified and cumulative knowledge which could form the basis of social engineering.[4]

There were other attempts, especially in the United States, in the 1920s and 1930s to try to apply scientific ideas to problems of social organisation. Psychologists, sociologists and anthropologists interested in industrial organisations undertook research on a consultancy basis with the aim of engineering changes in work and management. Much of Lazarsfeld's own research was funded on a consultancy basis for private commerical bodies. Such efforts were occasionally marked by extravagant claims about the efficacy of such endeavours, Elton Mayo, for example, claiming that if social scientific knowledge had kept pace with material technology, then war could be prevented, but the experience was a formative one.[5]

However, the professional model was not one that suited everyone. Its first blooming in the post-Second World War years as sociological functionalism took over as the theoretical orthodoxy, along with the substantial development of the survey and statistical methods, did not escape criticism. Symbolic interactionism maintained a guerrilla action and in Britain and Europe the strong academic rather than professional model retained, and still does, a considerable degree of tenacity.

Marxism has always been strong in Europe and a resurgence of this intellectual tradition in the late 1960s, and continuing for many years after, sustained a strong posture of critical theorising directed at the very institutions from which a professional social science might expect encouragement.

What became more apparent in the 1980s (in some quarters at least) was that the efforts to professionalise social research, and with it sociology, were not building upon scientific achievement so much as a hope. The eclecticism of method that was typical of the early social researchers had a point in the context of a discipline such as sociology which was trying to find its empirical feet and which, as a result, lacked any agreed upon theoretical framework, a body of agreed and cumulative knowledge and agreed upon methodological principles. In such a situation, the use of a variety of research methods is as reasonable an option as opting for one supposedly definitive approach. With hindsight, it is perhaps clearer that the rise, not to say the imposition, of variable analysis as the orthodox method and the orthodox way of thinking about social research and its problems was, at best, premature. Not only has it failed to contribute to a social science which could begin to rival the mature natural sciences, such as physics, but also even by lesser standards it seems not to have lived up to its early enthusiastic promises.

Much of this disquiet, though not as yet widely appreciated it has to be admitted, is due to antagonisms not only from different sociological persuasions, but also from well-qualified exponents of the highly mathematically and statistically sophisticated arts of modern variable analysis. In brief, their complaints are not the kind made by Blumer and other symbolic interactionists, or particularly by ethnomethodologists such as Cicourel, but are to do with the failure of the methods to meet their own standards. The methods, no matter how statistically sophisticated, cannot produce even fairly firmly established empirical generalisations and, if Lieberson is right, may even produce wrong answers. There have, of course, been various diagnoses of the problems here, including the old myths about the inevitable infusion of values into social research, the immaturity of the social sciences and the complexity of its subject matter.[6] Blalock, for example, argues that more attention should be devoted to the 'measurement problem', which he sees in Lazarsfeldian terms of devising 'auxiliary measurement theories' to bridge the gap between theoretical concepts and data.[7] Lieberson's position almost boils down to the need to begin anew in ways that recognise that the social world is exactly that, social, and that current statistical modelling cannot deal with the complex problems this poses. 'Selectivity', as he calls it, operates, variably and complicatedly, in all areas of social life and until these can be described satisfactorily there would seem little point in going on in current ways.

Of course, such complaints are mainly levelled against the data analysis techniques associated with variable analysis, but many of the problems identified have their source in data collection itself. As any statistician knows, the results of their mathematical manipulations are only as good as the data fed into them. Poor data cannot be repaired by even the most sophisticated of quantitative tools. The familiar adage of computing – 'garbage in, garbage out' – applies just as much to the analysis of social research data as it does to the material for computer processing. But in the case of data collection we are not simply talking about inadvertent mistakes in coding, errors in calculation, failures to sample adequately, or the sudden floor-opening shock of not having asked a crucial question in the interviews, but about the instrumental presuppositions and structures of inference that underpin the methods.

One of the main purposes throughout the discussion has been to emphasise not only the theoretical relevance of data collection methods, even when the research objective could be described as collecting the 'facts', but also the way in which theoretical considerations are integral to the methods themselves; an argument which leads us not only to question the 'tool box' conception but also to accuse it of myopia at best, and at worst, a wilful turning away from the vitally important problems not just of methods and social research but of the social sciences themselves. Unlike the more mature natural sciences, sociology and (we would add) most of the other human sciences, including economics and psychology, lack that necessary agreement about the fundamentals of approach. The question, for example, of whether sociology is a science remains a contentious issue, which is still reflected in so many of its debates about, to list but a few, quantitative versus qualitative research, the nature of theorising, structuralist versus action perspectives, and so on. These debates are not simply about which is a better explanation of some phenomenon, but about how the discipline should proceed, what its phenomena are, its methods, and so on. Indeed, many of the empirical studies in sociology are not only about gathering data, facts if you like, relevant to some theory, but are also about instantiating some conception of the sociological project. There is, as yet, no approach-neutral way of carrying out empirical studies and about which there would be widespread agreement that this is the method or the data to acquire. Debate about studies can never confine itself to the facts and the methodology of the study but would, in short order, spread itself much wider until issues about fundamentals are reached. This is, perhaps, one reason why what passes for theoretical work in sociology tries to work toward some synthesis of the available approaches by way of exegesis of and critical commentary upon classic texts.

However, none of the foregoing should be read as a complaint against sociology and social research or, least of all, an ackowledgement of its ultimate pointlessness and failure. If we do have a complaint it is that for too long, in its urge to become scientific, sociology, and again much of social research, has diverted itself by trying to emulate what it saw as the methods of the natural sciences. That the version of natural science was largely drawn from the philosophy of science simply served to compound misunderstanding. Similarly, efforts to professionalise social science by securing some orthodoxy of theory and methods forgot that the fundamentals of a discipline are not to be had by wishing them in place, but are hard-won achievements of thought and investigation.[8] Sociology and social research, in their urge to take a short-cut to scientific respectability, ignored the fact that the maturity of the natural sciences was something that they themselves achieved over many long years by conducting inquiries into those aspects of the world that were their special interest. They did not try to emulate some model of science but developed their ways and means in the course of investigating the world.

Of course, the above remarks are a slight misrepresentation of the development of methods of social research in that many of those responsible did just that: investigated the world and devised methods of data collection and analysis as they needed them. We are thinking of the early days of Chicago, the early surveys of Booth and Rowntree, the industry of Lazarsfeld and his colleagues, and more. But, despite this qualification, since then there has been a prolonged period, in sociology at any rate, in which an orthodoxy of method asserted itself, in which there was a clear hierarchy of method from the 'scientifically respectable' techniques of survey and variable analysis, with its hypothesis testing and quantification, to the less scientifically credentialled methods of fieldwork and observation. And this was strongly paralleled by an orthodoxy of sociological approaches from the structuralist/objective theories down to the action/subjective perspectives.

There is some evidence that this hegemonic ordering is breaking down and in a healthy fashion. It is not that sociology or social research has at last found the direction it needs to go, on the contrary. If anything it owes much to the recognition that the orthodoxy was simply unjustifiable as an orthodoxy, and, as a consequence, a realisation that there is a great deal wrong, as well as a great deal right, with all of the methods of social research. What there is not is a clear superiority of one over the others. It is possible that we might be entering a period not dissimilar to the early days of social research, when there was not only an eclecticism about methods, but also a lively debate about them relating such issues to the nature of the disciplines themselves.

Of course, the question arises as to how and about what this debate should be? What we have suggested in this book is that methods cannot be considered as atheoretical tools since they embody theories, often implicitly, about the nature of the social actor and the relationships s/he has with others. Many of the 'instrumental pre-suppositions' are profoundly social in their reference. Even the apparently non-sociological principles of random sampling, when used in much of social research, have implications about the way in which sampling units, usually individuals, are related. They have relevance for, in short, theories of social relationships and how these, in the context of some social research investigation using them, are to be constituted and reflected as the phenomena for study. It is more than possible to argue that the survey is predicated on a rather different image of society and the social actor to that presumed in participant observation. One could go so far as to say that each not only produces different types of data, but also addresses different sociological phenomena. If this is correct, it means that we cannot, in principle, compare the data produced by different methods and effectively choose *on the basis of the data* between the theories the data are claimed to support.[9]

This looks to be an intractable problem, not least because it is not clear what kind of problem it is. Does it require more sophisticated methods? Or better theories? Or a mixture of both? And if so, how are we to find them? The answer to all of these and similar questions is that there is no short answer: no one thing that we need to find which will suddenly solve all our problems. There is really no option but to follow the example of the natural sciences, not by slavishly adopting some putative version of its method, but by trying to work the problems through on a piecemeal basis. Sociology and social research are replete with grand recommendations about how to solve the problems; few of them are little better, at best, than good sense, and many more a great deal worse than that.

It is possible to suggest a number of ways in which we might proceed, none of them in any absolute sense any better than any other in terms of their future promise. To a large degree it has been social science's addiction to promissary notes that has resulted in the measure of disappointment that its achievements are not more than they are.

The first is, as far as empirical research is concerned, to worry less about 'being scientific' and more about the quality of the studies. In other words, to dispense with the presumption that some kinds of data are intrinsically more scientific, more objective, 'harder', rigorous, than are other kinds. This remark is clearly directed at the kind of presumption that is often offered on behalf of the survey and, implicitly if not explicitly, against ethnographic methods. We need to be careful what we are saying here, the more so since there are a number of complicated issues involved which are beyond the remit of this book.[10] Our plea is not about dispensing with standards and imagining that social research can, henceforth, be an exercise in unrestrained imagination. What we are saying is that 'objectivity' is not served by the slavish emulation of some putative scientific standards derived from philosophical versions of the supposed scientific method.

There is, we want to say, too often a confusion between 'objectivity' as a moral quality and 'objectivity' as a feature of data. The former refers to things like the scrupulousness with which the study was done, the care with which the evidence, the data, was weighed, the rigour with which the argument was conducted, the detachment with which the conclusion was formed, and so on. The latter, and more contentiously, embodies a claim about the nature of data such that quantified data are *by their nature* more objective than impressionistic or, better, qualitative data.[11] It is a conception that is to be found in Marxist claims about the ontological primacy of the material world, for example, and as it is in Durkheim's conceptions of 'social facts' as 'thing-like'. It is also to be found in Lazarsfeld's original formulations of variable analysis and its structuring format for data. This is not to say that these examples, and the others that could have been offered, incorporate the idea in the same way. Durkheim was no Marxist materialist and nor was Lazarsfeld. Nor is our point an objection to Marx's materialism, or to Durkheim's 'associational realism', to realism itself, or to Lazarsfeld's variables. It is to the conflation, especially when done surreptitiously, of the two senses of 'objectivity'. There can be no intrinsic virtue to quantification done badly, or to materialist studies which fail to stick to their precepts, and so on. A lack of objectivity in the use of data is a reason for criticism whatever the claims made about the nature of the data.

Moreover, to regard theories such as those of Marx and Durkheim, and the methodological principles of Lazarsfeld, to continue with our examples, as making ontological claims is unhelpful, to say the least. Admittedly, both Marx and Durkheim, and they are not alone in this by any means, did feel it necessary to ground their theories and substantial studies in philosophical claims, but there is no necessary reason why we have to follow their example. The theories of physics, the classic yardstick of what a scientific theory should look like, make no ontological claims. They do not, it is true, talk about mind, about feelings, about attitudes, about ideologies, about all kinds of things that we might regard as 'subjective', but their silence on these matters is not a reason for thinking that they do not exist. Physics' silence on these has to do with its *interests as a discipline* not to some metaphysical claims about materialism. The nature of matter is the limit of physics' domain of interest. Its lack of interest in other things is not, therefore, a reason for supposing that all human life should be fundamentally construed as material in its nature. One can, of course, be a sociological materialist but one does not need the mandate of physics, or of science for that matter, to be so.

We have spent some time dealing with this issue because it is one which, in various guises, has ramifications for conceptions of methods.

Much of the concern about methods of social research has too often become embroiled in the metaphysics of science to no great purpose. We would regard 'objectivity' in the former of the senses we identified as by far the more important quality to encourage since it directs attention not to ontological issues but to considerations of how well studies are done. In short, it directs attention to the research itself.

The second proposal we have to make follows in close order from the first. In dispensing with the idea that there are intrinsic and canonical virtues to some kinds of data over others, and by implication to those methods which produce those data, we are also making the life of social research more difficult. What is implied is that there are no distinctive and specifically social data: and this is exactly what we do mean to imply. What turns materials into data, is (as we said from the beginning) the frameworks brought to that material. Once again, this is a difficult idea to grasp, partly because of its obviousness, and partly because it seemingly flouts common sense. Surely, we might say, there are a great many things in the world which are intrinsically social, such as friendships, families, groups of various kinds, cities, towns, and so on. Most of human life as we know it is social and, surely, this is entirely correct. What makes them intrinsically social is that we, as social beings, reproduce and sustain society through our activities.[12] But, and this is to unravel the paradox noted earlier, the social in this sense is not the data of social science; it is more the material out of which such data are constructed. The social world of common sense (to call it that) is the referent of the social sciences as constituted through their respective domains, and what it is about that world that ends up as data has much to do with disciplinary frameworks. Thus, cities can be seen through the eyes of the economist just as much as those of the sociologist and just as much as through those of political science and history. Such disciplines will not always, or even very often, look at cities in the same way, with the same problems in mind for the gaze of all disciplines is selective and organised around their own specific interests. Data belong to disciplines; their theories and what material is embraced by them has to do with their problems and the structures of inference linking materials to theories.

Third, what has just been said leads up to the suggestion that social research should give more attention to the structures of inference that effect the link between data, theories and eventually the world that is their referent. This is not to say that the point of such inferential structures is to reproduce the world of common sense, though some might have this as their aim, but rather to offer demonstrations of how features of the common sense world of social life can be seen *as data relevant to some theory or some problem*. It is to effect a demonstration that, say, absence from work is an indicator of alienation or that an 'agree' response to a questionnaire item is indicative of a particular attitude dimension, or that observed patterns of interaction reflect an organisation of friendship within a work group. Of course (as we have seen) such demonstrations may not prove successful, either in the short or the long term, and are never immune from criticism; but this is what one would expect from any discipline, including natural science. Certainly, what we would be averse to is, and this harks back to the sentiments expressed in our first proposal, taking on trust the notion that because data are quantified, therefore their inferential structure is the more rigorous, the less open to criticism. Once again, this is not an objection to measurement and quantification *per se*, or to the use of statistical methods; it is to the presumption of superiority of these over other inferential structures for dealing with data. As many critics from all sides have pointed out, there is a great deal wrong with current practices and ignoring this does not solve them.[13] Cicourel's remarks, for example, on current practices of measurement in social research stress that they are *ad hoc*, stipulative, and pay little or no attention to the properties of the phenomena they are supposed to measure. They represent, in short, measurement by fiat not measurement as is normally understood in the mature sciences. There is an important dispute about measurement in social research which is neither pointless nor malevolent, but is about trying to be clear about what the problems are and how they may be tackled.[14] The point about more attention being given to inferential structures of data is not, of course, limited to measurement and quantification; it applies to all data uses.

Fourth (to stress a point made earlier in this conclusion) problems of method are not intended as a recommendation that we do no further research until they are resolved. On the contrary, they can be resolved only through studies, by trying things out, thinking about them, opening them to critical examination, and so on. It is also to recognise a number of other things, too. For one, still worth a reminder, that any one empirical study, or theoretical one for that matter, makes a variable contribution to an ongoing debate that is disciplinary life. How and in what ways is not easily foreseen. No doubt we would all like to produce the study that will make a massive difference to social research but this is not likely to happen because we wish it. This belongs to the judgement of history. For another, it is to recognise that the inferential structures of data incorporate, reflect and make use of what we called 'instrumental theories'; that is, theories which are every bit as deserving of the label 'substantive' as the kinds of theories data are presumed to illuminate or even test.

As we have been trying to show throughout, methods of social research are embedded in a social context: a banal remark that needs further explication. One feature it points to is the fact that the very possibility of social research depends upon characteristics of the society itself. The very existence of the institution of social research, as an activity, a career, a contribution to social issues and problems, as an education, and more, reflects not only the importance attached to knowledge for its own sake but also the value placed on the need for scientific knowledge about society and its workings. Of course, the respective importance attached to the different social sciences is variable. Economics is, by far, the most applied of the social sciences, with some branches of psychology running it a close second. Although some social sciences do have a more direct input into policy and applications, either singly or by contributing to fields such as educational research or social administration or business studies, all make a contribution to the wider sense of what society is like. Without the widespread acceptance of social research, many of the social encounters upon which methods of data collection depend would be impossible. Being interviewed, being observed, allowing a researcher into one's home, looking through the records of a firm, and so on, all critically depend upon a generalised trust in the need for research and in the probity, responsibility and professionalism of researchers. Without such a normative framework, social research itself would be very hard indeed.

Methods are social in another sense, and this has to do with the 'instrumental theories' and the 'inferential structures' embodied in them. Measurement in natural science is a species of engineering. A measuring instrument incorporates principles derived from theoretical science relating them to the observational domain. This is the justification for measurement.[15] Although we have said in our earlier discussion on this that social measurement is based on a misunderstanding of measurement in natural science, nevertheless, and to widen the point, methods of data collection are in an important way a form of social engineering. True, we may know little about the theories and laws they instantiate, they, none the less, deploy social competences and skills that enable us to constitute not only research encounters but also those of ordinary life. The principles of interviewing, for example, are predicated upon conceptions of how social relationships work, as do the principles and methods of questionnaire construction depend upon conceptions of language use and meaning. Gaining access to a group and sustaining the interpersonal relations throughout the fieldwork depend upon knowledge of how to play roles, the etiquette of managing personal encounters, and so forth. Data collection is, through and through, not simply an aseptic collection of techniques; it is informative about social life itself.

NOTES

1. See, for example, M. Bulmer, *The Chicago School of Sociology: Institutionalisation, Diversity and the Rise of Social Research*, Chicago, University of Chicago Press, 1984; S. Turner and J. Turner, *The Impossible Science: An Institutional Analysis of American Sociology*, Newbury Park, Sage, 1990.
2. See S. Lukes, *Emile Durkheim*, Harmondsworth, Penguin, 1973. It is interesting to note that although Durkheim was a professor working within the French state educational system, a system he did much to develop and promote, he chose to emphasise the element of independence so important to the rhetoric of professionals.
3. See Turner and Turner, *op.cit.*, for a discussion of this in the United States.
4. It is doubtful if it was intended to.
5. E. Mayo, *Social Problems of Industrial Civilization*, London, Routledge & Kegan Paul, 1949, p. 21. See also J.H. Smith, 'Elton Mayo revisited', *British Journal of Sociology*, 12, pp. 236–248, 1974.
6. We say myths because they belong to a familiar list of excuses which, on examination, are not sustainable, partly because they arise from presumptions about how the social sciences can be scientific. The complexity argument, for example, misses the point that one of the great achievements of the natural sciences was to simplify their problems so that they could begin to deal with the complex natural world. There is clearly much more that could be said on this but is beyond the scope of this book.
7. See, for example, H. Blalock, *Basic Dilemmas in the Social Sciences*, Beverly Hills, Sage, 1984.
8. See, on this, Turner and Turner, *op.cit.* who provide an account of the ways in which American sociology tried to professionalise itself after the Second World War.
9. There are other grounds for choosing theories, of course, including personal preference.
10. See J.A. Hughes, *The Philosophy of Social Research*, 2nd and rev. edn, London, Longman, 1990, for a review of some of the more philosophical ones.
11. Of course we do not mean to imply that qualitative data are impressionistic.
12. We do not *intentionally* reproduce society. We go to work, get married, get divorced, rear families, become unemployed, grow up, etc., etc., and in doing all of these kinds of things in association with others we produce society as we know it. This is only the beginning for sociology and the social sciences, of course. The rest of it is to produce theoretical accounts of these

processes from the varied disciplinary perspectives.

13. Not unless one adopts the Charlie Brown dictum that no problem is too big to run away from.
14. See R. Pawson, *A Measure for Measures: A Manifesto for Empirical Sociology*, London, Routledge & Kegan Paul, 1989, for such a contribution.
15. Pawson, *op.cit.,* pp. 106–7.

INDEX